Toronto Medieval Texts and Translations

VIKING POEMS ON WAR AND PEACE:
A STUDY IN SKALDIC NARRATIVE

The Old Norse and Icelandic poets have left us vivid accounts of conflict and peace-making in the Viking Age. Russell G. Poole's editorial and critical analysis reveals much about the texts themselves, the events that they describe, and the culture from which they come.

Poole attempts to put right many misunderstandings about the integrity of the texts and their narrative technique. From a historical perspective, he weighs the poems' authenticity as contemporary documents which provide evidence bearing upon the reconstruction of Viking Age battles, peace negotiations, and other events.

He traces the social roles played by violence in medieval Scandinavian society, and explores the many functions of the poet within that society. Arguing that these texts exhibit a mind-style vastly different from our present 'individualism,' Poole suggests that the mind-set of the medieval Scandinavian could be termed 'non-individualist.'

The poems discussed are the 'Darraðarljóð,' where the speakers are Valkyries; 'Liðsmannaflokkr,' a rank-and-file warrior's description of Canute the Great's siege of London in 1016; 'Torf-Einarr's Revenge'; 'Egill's Duel with Ljótr,' five verses from the classic *Egils saga Skallagrimssonar*; 'A Battle on the Heath,' marking the culmination of a famous feud described in a very early Icelandic saga, the *Heiðarvíga saga*; and two extracts from the poem *Sexstefja*, one describing Haraldr of Norway's great fleet and victory over Sveinn of Denmark, and the other the peace settlement between these two kings.

The texts are presented in association with translations and commentaries as a resource not merely for medieval Scandinavian studies but also for the increasingly interwoven specialisms of literary theory and anthropology.

RUSSELL G. POOLE is Senior Lecturer in English at Massey University, New Zealand.

R.G. POOLE

Viking Poems on War and Peace
A Study in Skaldic Narrative

UNIVERSITY OF TORONTO PRESS
Toronto Buffalo London

© University of Toronto Press 1991
Toronto Buffalo London
Printed in Canada

ISBN 0-8020-5867-1 (cloth)
ISBN 0-8020-6789-1 (paper)

Printed on acid-free paper

Canadian Cataloguing in Publication Data

Poole, Russell Gilbert
  Viking poems on war and peace

  (Toronto medieval texts and translations; 8)
  Includes bibliographical references and index.
  ISBN 0-8020-5867-1 (bound) ISBN 0-8020-6789-1 (pbk.)

  1. Scalds and scaldic poetry. 2. Old Norse poetry –
  History and criticism. I. Title. II. Series.

  PT7172.P66 1991   839'.61'008023   C91-094196-3

Publication of this book has been made possible by a grant from the Publications Committee, Massey University, Palmerston North, New Zealand.

Contents

PREFACE vii
ACKNOWLEDGMENTS xiii
ABBREVIATIONS xv

Introduction 1
Lausavísur and Other Verses 3
Excursus: The Present Historic Tense in Poetry 24

The Poems 57
Þjóðólfr Arnórsson: The Battle of the River Nissa (from *Sexstefja*) 59
'Friðgerðarflokkr': The Peace Negotiations between Haraldr and Sveinn 73
'Liðsmannaflokkr': The Campaigns of Knútr and Þorkell in England 86
'Darraðarljóð': A Viking Victory over the Irish 116

Three Reconstructed Poems 157
'Torf-Einarr's Revenge' 161
'Egill's Duel with Ljótr' 173
Eiríkr Viðsjá: A Battle on the Heath 182

Conclusions 195

BIBLIOGRAPHY 199
INDEX 211

Preface

The poetry to be presented in this book comes down to us in our sources as the work of Scandinavians or Icelanders living between the ninth and eleventh centuries. Some of it originated at home in Scandinavia or Iceland, some of it in the British Isles. Although most of this corpus appears to be authentic, a part of it may be the work of later poets, attributed to the heroes of the Viking past as an imaginative realization of what they might have said or thought.

My particular concern in this book is with a set of poems that trace the progress of hostilities or (exceptionally) peace making. I shall argue that they constitute a special genre. They tell their story in a highly distinctive fashion: in narrow compass (five to thirteen stanzas, approximately), with use of apostrophe, dramatic monologue, and the present historic tense. Their narrative technique is characterized not by smoothness or linearity but by abruptness and jaggedness.

Skaldic narrative of the kind I shall be discussing offends against the canons of narrativity that most readers hold to be self-evident. These canons, having reached their full rigour in the classic nineteenth-century novel, with the work of Henry James as their logical extreme, are now a staple feature of mass-cultural genres (Jameson 1981). Formative here is an individualist ethos, which, where narrative technique is concerned, demands consistency with the perspective of one psyche, whether that of the protagonist, the narrator, or the reader.

In the interests it is pursuing, then, my book takes its cue from the recent critical and scholarly interest in 'anti-narrativity' (Mitchell 1981). Its focus is in one vital respect distinct from anti-narrativity, however. We are not here dealing with the fragmented narration that one associates with the fragmentation of the modern individual consciousness.

My focus is rather the fragmentation that a modern reader will discern in the poetics of traditional societies. This type of fragmentation is apparent rather than real, in that it has become discernible only with the advent of a fully modern individualism. What I shall be describing is a narrative mode that is in part non-individualist – in other words, one that is lacking the focus and consistency characteristic of individualist writing, in virtue of the fact that the modern psychological subject had not yet become fully established.

Of course there have always been deviant forms of narrativity, even when the narrative unities were *de rigueur* with most writers. One thinks, for example, of Emily Brontë's *Wuthering Heights* or Charles Dickens' *Bleak House,* not to mention Lawrence Sterne's *Tristram Shandy.* But such bold experiments with chronological sequence or point of view, or both, are not generally felt to constitute the mainstream of narrative discourse. As a result, when criticism focuses itself on medieval texts (*Beowulf* would serve as an example) any major deviance from linear narrativity is quite commonly felt to provide grounds for scepticism regarding the manuscript text. This is very distinctly a problem with the genre to be analysed here, and has been so ever since the Middle Ages. In much twelfth- and thirteenth-century saga compilation and composition, interpretation was, as we shall see, already conducted in accordance with an individualizing and personalizing notion of the poetic text.

To establish and exemplify the genre I am referring to, I have chosen seven poems. Of these, one is in a relatively simple 'eddaic' stanza form. The other six are 'skaldic,' as that word is applied in modern scholarship, meaning that in addition to the rules of 'eddaic' poetry a strict count of syllables and an elaborate system of line-internal rhyming and consonance had to be observed.

Probably the most familiar of the seven poems is the one in 'eddaic' form, 'Darraðarljóð.' Here the Valkyries of Norse myth are imagined as weavers. The poem is their work-song, and their work (imaged as weaving) is winning a victory over the Irish for a young Viking king. The sustained use of weaving terminology makes this the most extraordinary example of poetic invention in the genre. Elsewhere the speaking voice is not of such a strongly characterized sort. In 'Liðsmannaflokkr' we hear a Viking warrior-skald describing the campaign that has brought Canute the Great to power in England. In this 'soldier's tale' we can detect a certain political shrewdness; the setting is London, immediately after the end of the wars, and the claims of Canute's chief ally are not to be ignored. In the extract from *Sexstefja,* we have our one example of a safely attributable poem; the author is Þjóðólfr Arnórsson, a skald in the entourage of Haraldr harðráði (the Norwegian king whose advance to military fame began in the Varangian Guard but who was doomed to ultimate defeat in England in the year of the Battle of Hastings). The speaker recreates the scene as the king's great fleet is launched and goes on to recount its victory over Sveinn of Denmark. The 'Friðgerðarflokkr' is my one example of a poem where peace is made. Following closely upon the events told in the previous poem, it describes the negotiation of a treaty by the kings of Norway and Denmark. Here the speaker places himself among those who congratulate the peacemakers, pouring scorn upon the promoters of hostility and showing a certain suspicion of the kings themselves.

Each of these first four poems appears more or less as a unity in our sources, although editorial and critical doubt has in some cases been cast upon this unity. The three poems that follow are, by contrast, not presented as unitary works in our sources and so represent my reconstruction. I offer these reconstructions with some confidence because the narrative technique and other genre characteristics are closely similar to those of the four poems presented previously.

One of these reconstructed poems is a dramatic monologue in which Torf-Einarr, the earl of Orkney, is shown avenging his father's death. In another, the celebrated skald Egill Skalla-Grímsson becomes the victor in single combat against a berserk warrior from Sweden. Here the heroism is tinged with comic exaggeration. Finally, a poem ascribed, perhaps correctly, to Eiríkr viðsjá describes the culmination of one of the most famous of Icelandic feuds.

I provide a text, translation, and discussion of each of these seven poems. My texts are based on the transcriptions and apparatus in the A volumes of Finnur Jónsson's *Den norsk-islandske skjaldedigtning*, to which references have been provided (abbreviated to *Skj* A). In editing and interpreting these texts I have taken account of Finnur Jónsson's B volumes, together with all other modern editorial discussions known to me. Where my edited text is derived from a single particular modern edition a reference to this edition is also provided.

The topic of the relationship between poems and prose is taken up for systematic discussion in the introduction. My main concern here is with comments or narratives in the prose that purport to show how a poem or individual stanza came to be uttered. Although sometimes the prose embodies independent and even reliable-seeming traditions, I shall argue that sometimes too it is founded purely upon inferences from statements in the poetry. Often the inferences depend on a mode of interpretation that attaches undue importance to the circumstances in which the speakers represent themselves as speaking. For example, if the poem described events in the present tense, the prose story would show the poet composing as the events dealt with in the poem took place. This is, as I shall show, one type of interpretation that has lingered on into the twentieth century. In the second chapter, an excursus on the present historic tense, I argue that this interpretation, though prevalent, is unwarranted. The present tense can be shown to belong quite idiomatically in poetry composed retrospectively. The usage is in some respects parallel to the present historic usage found so profusely in Old Icelandic prose works. Being distinguished, as I have noted, by the frequent occurrence of present-tense verbs, the poetic genre isolated in this book has been especially vulnerable to misinterpretation, to the point where its very existence has become obscured.

My exposition of these topics, some of which are of course controversial, is necessarily attended by the use of technical terminology. Fortunately, both skaldic poetry and its technical terms are now more accessible to an English-speaking audience than formerly, thanks to the appearance of two introductory works, *Scaldic Poetry*, by E.O.G. Turville-Petre (1976), and *Old Norse Court Poetry: The Dróttkvætt Stanza*, by Roberta Frank (1978). Both these books provide strangers to skaldic poetry with a detailed account of the rules and aesthetic and with a carefully annotated short anthology. In addition, Frank briefly discusses the various editions, readers, and anthologies available for those who have a command of German or the modern Scandinavian languages (ibid 212–13). Here I assume an acquaintance on the reader's part with the Frank and Turville-Petre introductions; some references to their definitions and explanations have been provided. I have cited all Old Norse texts in a normalized form. For the prose I follow the practice of the *Íslenzk Fornrit* series (íf in text), for skaldic poetry Finnur Jónsson's *Den norsk-islandske skjaldedigtning*, for *rímur* his *Ordbog til de ... Rímur*, and for eddaic poetry the Neckel-Kuhn edition. Names of medieval Scandinavian men and women are given in their Old Norse form. Verse is sometimes silently repunctuated so as to clarify the word order and clause structure. In quoting from *Encomium Emmæ* and *English Historical Documents* I have used the translations supplied by the editors of those works. Other translations are my own, unless otherwise indicated: they are intended to bring out the literal meaning of the words, as far as possible, and make no pretence to literary merit. Full references to works cited in the text are supplied in the bibliography.

To reach a satisfactory sequence in the discussion of the seven major works has proved difficult. The first four poems, 'Liðsmannaflokkr' and 'Darraðarljóð' in particular, pose such complex problems that I was tempted to postpone their discussion until the end of the book, out of consideration for readers who are relatively new to skaldic poetry and to the kings' sagas. The interrelationship between the various compilations in which the verses are preserved is notoriously intricate and has accordingly been the subject of intricate debate. This has inevitably involved me in what may seem a disproportionately extensive analysis of the sources. Readers who are relatively new to skaldic poetry may prefer to skip the sections of each chapter that deal with the sources, concentrating at first on the more literary part of the discussion. They might also prefer to postpone their reading of the excursus on the present tense in poetry, where the evidence and argument are also necessarily rather complicated.

Acknowledgments

The origins of this book go back some twenty years, and in the intervening period I have incurred debts of gratitude to many people. Some of the material revised for inclusion here originally formed part of my University of Toronto doctoral thesis: this project benefited greatly from the advice and encouragement of my supervisor, Roberta Frank, along with John Leyerle, Brian Merrilees, Harold Roe, and other University of Toronto faculty, in particular the late Denton Fox. Other scholars who have provided assistance at various stages of my research are Frederick Amory, Theodore Andersson, Hans Bekker-Nielsen, Paul Bibire, Carol Clover, Ursula Dronke, David Dumville, Bjarne Fidjestøl, Peter Foote, Kari Gade, Philip Grierson, Ludvig Holm-Olsen, Shaun Hughes, Ann Johnston, Jónas Kristjánsson, Simon Keynes, John Lindow, Bill Manhire, Oliver Padel, Raymond Page, Richard Perkins, Margaret Clunies Ross, Forrest Scott, Sverrir Tómasson, Maureen Thomas, John Townsend, John Tucker, and Vésteinn Ólason. The readers for the University of Toronto Press made valuable suggestions, many of which I have used. Additionally, the staff of the Press have gone to great pains to save me from bibliographic blunders and stylistic infelicities. I am grateful to all the above-named, and must stress that any errors or misjudgments that may be found in this book are of my making, not theirs. My edition of 'Liðsmannaflokkr' and my discussion of *Sexstefja* and *Háttatal* have previously been published in *Speculum* and *JEGP* respectively: I am grateful to the editors of these journals for permission to use these materials here. My colleagues in the English Department at Massey University undertook some of my teaching during my periods of study leave. The president and fellows of Clare Hall, University of Cambridge, granted me membership of the college during the 1983-4 academic year. I am especially indebted to the Publications Fund of Massey University, without whose generosity the book could not have been published. Financial support for earlier stages of the project was provided by the Commonwealth Scholarships scheme, the Government of the Province of Ontario, the Canada Council, and the Killam Foundation. Finally, I owe thanks to Fiona Farrell and Susannah and Ursula Poole for indulging my attempts to survey Ultima Thule from the distant perspective of Terra Australis Incognita.

Abbreviations

AM	*Arnamagnæana*
ANF	*Arkiv för nordisk filologi*
ÅNOH	*Aarbøger for nordisk Oldkyndighed og Historie*
APS	*Acta philologica Scandinavica*
BiblAM	*Bibliotheca Arnamagnæana*
EdAM	*Editiones Arnamagnæanae*
EHD	*English Historical Documents*
ÍF	*Íslenzk fornrit*
JEGP	*Journal of English and Germanic Philology*
KLNM	*Kulturhistorisk leksikon for nordisk middelalder*
Med Scan	*Mediaeval Scandinavia*
MM	*Maal og Minne*
Neophil	*Neophilologus*
NF	*Nordisk filologi*
(N)HT	*(Norsk) Historisk Tidskrift*
Proc Battle	*Proceedings of the Battle Conference on Anglo-Norman Studies*
SBVS	*Saga-Book of the Viking Society for Northern Research*
Skj	*Den norsk-islandske skjaldedigtning*
SS	*Scandinavian Studies*
SSÍ	*Safn til sögu Íslands*
SUGNL	[Skrifter udgivet af] *Samfund til udgivelse af gammel nordisk litteratur*
Vid Skr	*Videnskapsselskapets Skrifter.* II. *Historisk filosofisk Klasse*
ZDA	*Zeitschrift für deutsches Altertum und deutsche Literatur*

INTRODUCTION

Lausavísur and Other Verses

When we attempt to study the longer poem in Old Norse, 'longer' meaning anything over five or six stanzas, we are not well served by the surviving evidence. Astonishingly few poems of any extent survive, either complete or nearly complete. Many apparent examples in the standard edition, Finnur Jónsson's *Den norsk-islandske skjaldedigtning*, are in reality a set of fragments, painstakingly but sometimes very misleadingly reassembled into a semi-coherent poem. If they ever existed, medieval anthologies of poetry in the more elaborate metres and stanza forms have not come down to us. Especially in the period before 1000 the very few longer poems that survive in substantial portions are difficult and uncertain in their interpretation. Because of the paucity and obscurity of the evidence, theories about the structure, style, narrative technique, or other aesthetic aspects of the longer skaldic poem are very insecurely based.

This means that in considering any sort of skaldic poem, whether short or long, we must have constant recourse to our only significant class of source material – those medieval Icelandic and Norwegian prose works whose text includes poetic quotations. The quotations found there are of two sorts. Some verses are presented as brief spontaneous improvisations, made up by a personage within the story in response to a particular event. Other verses are presented not as self-contained improvisations but as excerpts from more extended poems. I shall refer to the former as *lausavísur* and to the latter as 'excerpted verses.'

A simple example of a *lausavísa* is the twelfth stanza in *Egils saga*. While on a Viking expedition Egill and his brother Þórólfr learn that they are within convenient reach of Lund, a prosperous market town. They debate whether to raid it. Þórólfr is in favour, but their followers

4   Introduction

are divided. When Egill is asked for his opinion he answers in a verse
(ÍF 2:119):

> Upp skulum órum sverðum,
> ulfs tannlituðr, glitra;
> eigum dáð at drýgja
> í dalmiskunn fiska:
> leiti upp til Lundar
> lýða hverr sem bráðast;
> gerum þar fyr setr sólar
> seið ófagran vigra.
> (Skj A 50 v 6)

> Let us brandish our swords, warrior, so that they glitter in the
> air; this summer we have exploits to perform. Let every one of
> us make his way to Lund forthwith; let us fight a battle there
> before sunset.

This verse settles the question, and preparations for the raid begin.

On the face of it, Egill's *lausavísa* is delivered to satisfy the requirements of a particular real-life situation. Þórólfr and the others have not been able to reach a decision: Egill supplies it with his verse. So far as we are told, he does not have to express himself in prose on the topic. The *lausavísa* therefore has a function in determining the course of events and is essential to the narrative. Furthermore, when Egill speaks, his utterance is not some general panegyric on fighting and the Viking life, capable of being used in a dozen different situations: the specific mention of Lund implies that the verse is new-minted in response to the demands of the here and now.

This functional use of *lausavísur* is common in the sagas. In *Gísla saga* there is a scene where the hero, supposing himself alone, recites aloud a verse that reveals that he has killed a man. He makes no other admission of guilt, but the verse is overheard and the ultimate outcome is Gísli's death.

Where a *lausavísa* does not initiate new action it represents at the least a comment on an actual situation or person with which the speaker is faced. The sagas seldom show *lausavísur* as a mere sport or diversion among the characters, composed on irrelevant or imaginary subjects. Verses are sometimes attributed to characters in situations so pressing or adverse that narrative plausibility inevitably is compromised. The final *lausavísur* ascribed to Þormóðr Kolbrúnarskáld are a well-known example. He leaves the battlefield at Stiklastaðir after his lord, Óláfr Haraldsson, has fallen and, fatally wounded, seeks out a place where wounds are being dressed. Having spoken the *lausavísur* in reply to questions from a woman who attends him, he dies, leaving the last word of the last verse to be filled in by Haraldr harðráði (ÍF 6:269–76).

The treatment of the other category, the excerpted verse, is different. Describing the exploits of Haraldr harðráði in another sphere, as captain of the Varangian Guard, Snorri states that he fought eighteen major battles while in the service of the emperor. This comment is followed by the words 'svá segir Þjóðólfr' / 'so says Þjóðólfr,' introducing a skaldic stanza (ÍF 28:82–3):

> Þjóð veit, at hefr háðar
> hvargrimmliga rimmur –
> rofizk hafa opt fyr jǫfri –
> átján Haraldr – sáttir:
> hǫss arnar rauttu hvassar,
> hróðigr konungr, blóði –
> ímr gat krǫs, hvar's kómuð –
> klœr, áðr hingat fœrir.
>
> (Skj A 370 v 7)

The people know that Haraldr has fought eighteen exceedingly fierce battles; the peace has often been broken by the king: honoured prince, you reddened the grey eagle's sharp claws in blood before you returned here; the wolf received food wherever you went.

Here, as is typical of such verses, the situation in which the poet composed is immaterial and not mentioned. Accordingly, whereas a *lausavísa* is normally prefaced by a formula of the type 'þá kvað X' / 'then X said,' an excerpted verse is normally preceded by 'svá segir X,' as above, or 'þess getr X' / 'X mentions this,' or variants on these formulas. Sometimes the name of the poem from which the excerpts come is also stated: in discussing Hákon jarl's vengeance for his father's death, for instance, Snorri expressly names two poems that contribute to his evidence, Eyvindr skáldaspillir's 'Háleygjatal' and Einarr skálaglamm's 'Vellekla' (ÍF 26:207–8). But verse citations usually do not carry any reference to the poem in which they originated, and occasionally even the author's name is omitted, as in the formula 'ok var þetta kveðit' 'and this was said.' Although the circumstances in which certain longer poems were composed and delivered are occasionally described, the poem itself is seldom quoted *in extenso*, uninterrupted by prose narrative. In historiography it was not so much the complete poem as the constituent stanzas that were valued and used, either as source material or as corroboration for evidence from other sources. Typically, the stanzas being cited are distributed singly or in groups of two throughout the prose narrative. Even in the *Edda* and the other poetic treatises, which constitute the other main source for poetic quotations and which treat the method and aesthetic of skaldic poetry, complete poems are seldom included or mentioned by title. Citations there tend to be even briefer, at half a stanza, than in the histories.

This habit of brevity among the historians and poetic theorists makes the task of reconstructing poems from the extant fragments a difficult one. Often there is little evidence available to establish which stanzas should be included in a particular poem and which order they should be arranged in. The arrangements in Finnur Jónsson's standard edition largely depend on research summarized by him in *Edda Snorra Sturlusonar* III (1880–7), and are perpetuated unaltered by E.A. Kock in his 'revised' edition of 1946, published posthumously. For the genre of praise poetry, Bjarne Fidjestøl's monograph of 1982 offers a very useful critical re-examination of the evidence.

The particular problem that concerns me here is that *lausavísur* are not always easily distinguished from excerpted verses, and vice versa. As to internal evidence, one might expect the *lausavísa* to be obviously more self-sufficient or improvisatory or informal. Yet, in spite of the very rigorous formal demands posed by most types of skaldic metre and stanza form and diction, we cannot distinguish in any general way between improvised, occasional verses on the one hand and the constituent stanzas of longer, more formal poems on the other hand by using such technical criteria. Nor do theme and genre help greatly. Either form, for example, can convey praise, satire, lamentation, and love, at least so far as the available evidence allows us to judge. Hints of the poet's situation, for instance an address to a listener, are found in the longer poems as well as in *lausavísur*.

As to the external evidence, the prefatory formulas 'þá kvað' and 'svá kvað,' along with their variants, do not offer a hard and fast distinction. Some verses are purportedly both *lausavísa* and excerpt because the poem from which they come is a loose assemblage of verses, supposedly individually improvised to meet various situations, Sigvatr's 'Austrfararvísur' being a well-known example. Also, the adverbs 'þá' and 'svá' are from time to time omitted, leaving one unsure whether the verse to follow is a *lausavísa* or an excerpt.

Occasionally we can see how the process of pruning and abridging the prose narrative, carried on by a succession of redactors, can result in this ambiguity. When in *Heimskringla* Snorri uses a stanza from the *Sendibítr*, ascribed to Jórunn skáldmær, he introduces it with a careful mention of the name of the poem and of its supposed author (ÍF 26:142). The status of his source as a longer poem is shown by mention, without quotation, of 'nǫkkur ørendi' / 'some verses.' In *Flateyjarbók*, on the other hand, this information is reduced to the bare statement 'orti Jórunn skáldmær vísu þessa' / 'Jórunn skáldmær composed this verse' (I 1860:45), leaving open the possibility that it was a *lausavísa*.

The *Saga Óláfs konungs hins helga* contains an account of Sigvatr's 'Nesjavísur' that notes the name of the poet and his poem, its form (a *flokkr*: see Turville-Petre 1976:xxxix), and the time of composition (1941ed I:91-2). Although only one stanza is quoted then and there, the redactor plainly knew more. By contrast, the copyist of the *Bæjarbók* text jettisons this information and prefaces the verse with the words 'hann kvað þetta' / 'he said this,' which leave the status of the verse unclear.

Arnórr's 'Magnússdrápa' (*dróttkvætt*) 9 undergoes similar treatment. In *Heimskringla* Snorri prefaces it with 'þessa getr Arnórr jarlaskáld' / 'Arnórr jarlaskáld mentions this' (ÍF 28:46). In *Hulda/Hrokkinskinna*, two redactions that in part depend on *Heimskringla*, the verse is used twice. On the second occasion the preface is similar to Snorri's (*Fms* 6:75). On the first occasion the meaning is less clear: 'þarum er þetta kveðit' / 'about that, this was said' (ibid 55). The author's name is left unstated, though it could be inferred from a paragraph earlier, where a stanza by Arnórr is cited. The preface in *Flateyjarbók* increases the ambiguity: 'skáldit kvað vísu' / 'the poet spoke a verse' (III 1868:275). Here again, in the absence of other recensions we should be unable to decide whether the verse was a *lausavísa* or not.

The possibility of confusion between the 'þá' and 'svá' types of preface is shown by the history of an anonymous verse about Óláfr kyrri. In *Ágrip* (1929ed:43) and *Morkinskinna* (1932ed:292) it is prefaced 'sem skáldit segir' / 'as the poet says.' In *Heimskringla*, a somewhat later compilation that draws on *Morkinskinna*, the preface is 'því var þetta kveðit' / 'for that reason this was said' (ÍF 28:201). In *Hulda/Hrokkinskinna* the verse acquires its time reference: 'þá var þetta kveðit' / 'then this was said' (*Fms* 6:437). Inaccurate copying may have been the problem here.

Excerpted verses and *lausavísur* could therefore become confused through scribal error and editorial abridgment, and the numbers of ostensible *lausavísur* in the sagas were probably swelled in this way. But in some cases where excerpted verses are mistakenly treated as *lausavísur* the cause seems to be not inadvertence or indifference but artistic convention: I shall discuss six examples in detail now.

One of the most famous and well-preserved of skaldic poems is the 'Bersǫglisvísur,' where Sigvatr offers his sovereign some plain-speaking advice. Snorri's *Heimskringla* and separate *Óláfs saga helga* each have nine stanzas, *Hulda/Hrokkinskinna* have thirteen, and *Flateyjarbók* (representing a lost portion of *Morkinskinna*) has sixteen, out of the total of eighteen stanzas that have customarily been assigned to the poem (on the status of the final stanzas see Louis-Jensen 1977:83–4). Presumably the high intrinsic interest of the poet's advice to the youthful Magnús guaranteed the work immunity from drastic abridgment. Among the various historical compilations *Ágrip* is exceptional in including only one verse (v 12) and in treating this verse as a *lausavísa*. The author notes the initial harshness of the young king's rule and goes on to describe an assembly at Niðaróss where the men of Trondelag, upbraided by Magnús,

> stungu allir nefi í skinnfeld ok veittu allir þǫgn, en engi andsvǫr. Stóð upp þá maðr, Atli at nafni, ok mælti eigi fleiri orð en þessur: 'Svá skorpnar skór at fœti mér, at ek má eigi ór stað komask', en Sigvatr kvað þar þegar vísu þessa:
> Hætt es, þat's allir ætlask –
> áðr skal við því ráða –
> hárir menn, es heyrik,
> hót, skjǫldungi at móti:
> greypt es, þat's hǫfðum hneppta
> heldr ok niðr í feldi –
> slegit hefr þǫgn á þegna –
> þingmenn nǫsum stinga.
> (*Skj* A 254–5 V 12)
>
> Ok raufsk þing þat með [þeima] hætti, at konungr bað alla menn finnask þar um morgininn. Ok fannsk þá í hans orðum, at guð hafði skipt skapi hans, ok var þá freka snúin til miskunnar, hét ǫllum mǫnnum gæzku ok efndi, sem hann hét eða betr,

ok ǫðlaðisk honum af því vinsæld mikil ok nafn þat, at hann
var kallaðr Magnús góði.

(*Ágrip* 1929ed:34–5; text of verse
from ÍF 28:30)

[they] all buried their faces in their cloaks and kept silence,
offering no reply. Then a man by the name of Atli arose and
said just these few words: 'My shoes have shrunk on my feet so
much that I cannot leave my place.' And there at once Sigvatr
recited this verse: 'Menacing is that threat that, as I hear, all the
old men are placing themselves in opposition to the king; this
must be seen to beforehand: it is a sign of danger when the men
at the assembly droop their heads markedly and bury their
noses in the depths of their cloaks; silence has seized the thanes.'
And the assembly broke up in this fashion, that the king
instructed all the men to be there the next morning. And then
it was clear in his words that God had changed his tempera-
ment, and harshness was then transformed into mercy; he prom-
ised benevolence to all men, and kept – or more than kept –
that promise. From that he earned great popularity and the
name Magnús the good.

All other texts that contain verse 12 are agreed that it originated as
part of 'Bersǫglisvísur'; a separate improvisation is neither mentioned
nor implied. The circumstances of composition are described quite differ-
ently, as can be seen from *Heimskringla*, which is typical of the majority
tradition. Here we learn that after his return to Norway Magnús pun-
ished men who fought against his father at Stiklastaðir with confiscation
and exile. Amid complaints from the 'bœndr' / 'free farmers' that Magnús
was breaking the laws of Hákon inn góði, the men of Sogn prepared to
oppose him in battle. Twelve of Magnús' most loyal supporters resolved
that Sigvatr as their spokesman must tell the king of the unrest. He
composed a poem of advice, the 'Bersǫglisvísur', which reached the
king's ears and produced the desired change of heart (ÍF 28:25–31).

Now according to Snorri (ibid 26) the 'Bersǫglisvísur' are a *flokkr*, a
term that could sometimes be applied to a loosely assembled collection
of verses composed on diverse occasions. It is therefore thinkable, as
Alfred Vestlund tentatively suggested, that verse 12 was originally
improvised on a separate occasion and only later added to the other

stanzas to form the sequence as we know it today (1929:290). The difficulty in this view, which Vestlund himself rejects, is that the *lausavísa* in *Ágrip* and the *flokkr* in the other histories have the same plot function in the story of Magnús: each brings about his transformation from a tyrant to a good king. The two versions are clearly variant tellings of the same historical event and ought not to be conflated. Scholars have been unanimous in rejecting the *Ágrip* version (1929ed:35).

Ágrip was probably composed in the last decade of the twelfth century. Its Norwegian redactor wrote somewhere in Trøndelag and drew upon oral traditions current in Trøndelag as well as upon written sources (Indrebø 1922:59–60, Torfinn Tobiassen, KLNM '*Ágrip*'). The present episode in *Ágrip* has a Trøndelag setting and Siegfried Beyschlag regards it as one among a number of 'epic expansions' grafted on to the normally concise source from oral tradition (1950:348). The place-name Niðaróss, used of a settlement that came into existence only in 1172, is to Beyschlag a further indication that the episode is an addition. Characteristically, the episode is introduced by a brief statement that could stand alone without the assembly scene (*Ágrip* 1929ed:34).

Ágrip ranks as one of the oldest, if not *the* oldest, specimens of vernacular historiography in Scandinavia. Fidjestøl has suggested that the *Ágrip* compiler may have been the first to incorporate skaldic verses into a written narrative, perhaps under the influence of the quotations of Latin poetry in Theodoricus' *Historia de antiquitate regum norvagiensium* (1982:20–1). The *Ágrip* compiler is not always accurate in his use of skaldic verse, and it seems likely to me that his handling of the stanza from 'Bersǫglisvísur' reflects the conventions of oral narrative.

The detail in the stanza of the men at the assembly burying their faces (literally noses) in their cloaks is a vivid one. Vestlund described it as 'realistic' and argued that it must spring from personal observation on Sigvatr's part (1929:290). Finnur Jónsson saw it rather as 'symbolic' (*Ágrip* 1929ed:34), and this seems the more reasonable view: the act is a ritualized piece of 'body language,' expressive of anger, alienation, or shame, and Sigvatr's description is closely paralleled in a *lausavísa* in *Egils saga* (ÍF 2:148). Sigvatr need not have had a particular event in mind in composing the stanza. The account of the behaviour of the men at the assembly in *Ágrip* is obviously dependent on the verse (1929ed:34) and represents an explanatory narrative that at some point in oral tradition attached itself to the verse. The story seems to be based on the fallacious assumption that the poet's vivid and emblematic detail could derive only from personal observation of a specific actual event.

A poet called Oddr Kíkinaskáld is credited with three verses on Magnús. The first of them deals with the king's battle against the Wends at Århus, while the other two speak of the grief felt by poet and nation alike after Magnús' death. The handling of these latter two verses in the various prose compilations has some peculiarities that are discussed by Bjarne Fidjestøl (1982:132–3):

> Felldu menn, þá's mildan –
> mǫrg tǫr – í grǫf bǫru –
> þung byrðr vas sú – þengil –
> þeim es hann gaf seima:
> deildisk hugr, svát heldu
> húskarlar grams varla –
> siklings þjóð en síðan
> sat opt hnipin – vatni.
>
> (Skj A 355 v 2; Skj B 327; ÍF 28:106)

Men shed many tears when they bore the generous king to the grave; that was a heavy burden to those whom he had given gold. The minds of the king's retainers were distraught, so that they could scarcely hold back their tears, and afterwards the king's people were often downcast.

> Mák, síz Magnúss ævi
> móðfíkins þraut góða –
> Odd hafa stríð of staddan –
> stillis, harða illa:
> hvarfak hvers manns þurfi,
> harmr strangr fær mér angrat,
> þjóð es at dǫgling dauðan
> dǫpr; því fǫrum vér aprir.
>
> (Skj A 355; B 327–8)

I have fared ill since the life of Magnús the good, the brave king, ended; sorrows have stricken Oddr. I roam about, a petitioner to every man, a cruel bereavement distresses me, the people are grieving for their dead king: that is why we go around dolefully.

In *Flateyjarbók* (III 1868:334), representing *Morkinskinna*, which has a lacuna here, these two verses are quoted in uninterrupted succession, without intervening prose commentary and with the use of the 'svá segir' type of preface. This preface is also found in *Heimskringla* where, however, only the first verse appears. *Hulda/Hrokkinskinna* differ, in that a prose passage is inserted between the two verses (*Fms* 6:236-7):

> Einn dag gekk Oddr skáld úti í hryggum hug; hann var spurðr, hversu hann mætti. Oddr svarar ok kvað ...

> One day Oddr skáld went out in a sorrowful mood; he was asked how he was doing. Oddr answers and said ...

The effect is to turn the second verse into a *lausavísa*, and it is so treated by Finnur Jónsson in *Skj* A 355. But *Hulda/Hrokkinskinna* ultimately derive from *Morkinskinna*, and the treatment of the second verse as Oddr's purely personal reaction is clearly secondary, since in both verses the reaction of the people as a whole is mentioned. We might conjecture that the compiler of *Hulda/Hrokkinskinna* felt that the poet's talk of his personal reaction and emotions ought to be motivated in some way. As Fidjestøl points out, the little scene described in the prose insert looks like an inference from the verse, whose wording it closely follows.

When we look closely at the phonological and lexical features of these two verses we notice that they have a good deal in common, namely alliteration on 'm' and 'h,' together with clauses of similar content (with the word 'þjóð as grammatical subject) in lines 7 and 8. Such resemblances can be assumed to arise from a convention of parallelism: I shall have occasion to mention this and kindred devices frequently later in this book.

Three verses ascribed to Eyvindr skáldaspillir describe the effects of a disastrous famine that many blamed on the misrule of the Christian 'sons of Gunnhildr' over Norway:

12 Snýr á Svǫlnis vǫru –
    svá hǫfum inn sem Finnar
    birkihind of bundit
    brums – at miðju sumri.
                          (*Skj* A 74 v 12; Turville-Petre 1976:44)

> At midsummer snow falls on the ground: thus, like the Finns, we have tethered our goats indoors.

13 Lǫtum langra nóta
  lǫgsóta verfótum
  at spáþernum sporna
  sporðfjǫðruðum norðan –
  vita, ef akrmurur jǫkla,
  ǫl-Gerðr, falar verði,
  ítr, þær's upp of róta
  unnsvín, vinum mínum.

   (Skj A 74 v 13; ÍF 26:223)

Let us row our boat down south to the herrings, fair lady, to see if those which we catch can be sold to my friends.

14 Fengum feldarstinga
  fjǫrð ok galt við hjǫrðu,
  þann's álhimins útan
  oss lendingar sendu:
  mest selda ek mínar
  við mæǫrum sævar –
  hallærit veldr hvǫru –
  hlaupsíldr Egils gaupna.

   (Skj A 74 v 14; ÍF 26:223–4; but cf Frank 1978:115–16)

Last year I received a cloak pin, which the Icelanders sent me, and I used it to buy livestock. I gave away my arrows, chiefly for herrings. Both these things are a result of the famine.

In *Fagrskinna* these verses seem to be used as sources for an account of the famine: verse 12 is quoted in the text. The reference to the failure of the herring catch may be drawn from verses 13 and 14, the latter of which blames Eyvindr's extreme exertions to obtain herrings on the famine. These latter two verses do not, however, appear in the text:

> ... ok gerði hallæri mikit um þeira daga, fyrir því at af tók síldfiski ok allt sjófang; korn spilltisk. Þetta kendi landsfolkit guða sinna reiði ok því er konungarnir létu spilla blótstǫðum þeira. Eyvindr skáldaspillir sagði svá [v 12]. Á þvílíku mátti marka hversu þung ǫld er þá var, er svá mikill snjór var um mitt sumar, at allt búit var inni haft at fóstri. (1902–3ed:53)

14 Introduction

> ... and in their days a great famine occurred, because the herring catch and sea fishing in general failed; the corn was ruined. The people attributed it to the anger of their gods and to the fact that the kings had caused their places of sacrifice to be destroyed. Eyvindr skáldaspillir spoke thus [v 12]. From this can be seen how grim a time it was then, with so much snow at midsummer that all the livestock was kept feeding indoors.

The implication of the prose is that famine gripped the whole of Norway. The redactor goes on to describe the avarice and miserliness of Queen Gunnhildr's sons, quoting two further verses by Eyvindr: for their text see ÍF 26:201 and for discussion Frank 1978:82–4.

Snorri takes verses 12, 13, and 14 closely together and seems, unlike *Fagrskinna*, to associate them not with Norway in general but with Hálogaland, where Eyvindr was living, in particular. He also makes the content of verse 12 more personal to Eyvindr by adding a scene that purports to show how the poet was provoked into composing the verse (ÍF 26:221):

> ... snjár lá þá á ǫllu landi at miðju sumri ok bú allt inn bundit. Svá kvað Eyvindr skáldaspillir – hann kom út, ok dreif mjǫk [v 12].

> ... snow then lay over the whole land at midsummer and the livestock was all tethered indoors. So said Eyvindr skáldaspillir – he stepped out and it was snowing heavily [v 12].

Discussing this passage, Magnus Olsen argued that Snorri had no information beyond what could be learnt from *Fagrskinna* and simply inferred an occasion of composition from the verse. The specific references to Hálogaland in *Heimskringla* are, in Magnus Olsen's opinion, Snorri's inference from the words 'Finnar' / 'Finns' (ie Lapps) and 'norðan' in verses 12 and 13 respectively (1945:177–8).

After verse 12 Snorri makes no further reference to the famine but focuses still more exclusively on Eyvindr's personal privation. The story of the grotesquely heavy cloak pin, sent to the poet in gratitude by the people of Iceland and used by him to buy either livestock (following Snorri) or herrings (following Finnur Jónsson in *Skj* B 65), is told very briefly, presumably as a mere paraphrase of verse 14. Snorri goes on to tell that in spring Eyvindr sights a shoal of herrings and rows out in pursuit: verse 13 is then quoted, with the prefatory formula 'hann kvað' / 'he said.' Snorri continues by explaining that because Eyvindr had expended all his liquid assets buying livestock he was obliged to barter arrows for herrings: verse 14 is quoted, again with the preface 'hann kvað.' This time there is no attempt to locate the verse within a scene. The vagueness of the occasion for verse 14, the use of the imprecise 'hann kvað' expression, the apparent lack of any source other than the verses themselves, and the different treatment of verse 12 in *Fagrskinna* combine to suggest that Snorri had no basis beyond inference for presenting these verses as *lausavísur*.

Internal evidence also suggests that these verses are excerpts from a single poem. In it Eyvindr, like Oddr Kíkinaskáld, would probably have dwelt on his personal hardships as representing those experienced by the nation in general: his complaint about the effect of the famine on his livelihood would function as a satire against the misrule of the *Gunnhildarsynir*. The verses recount a series of cases where nature or custom are disrupted: snow falls at the wrong time of the year, Norwegians must resort to Lappish methods of husbandry, and Eyvindr must forfeit his hunting equipment to obtain fish. The verses are also stylistically distinctive and homogeneous. In nearly all the kennings there are complicated and playful allusions to various types of subsistence – hunting, fishing, gathering, and husbandry. In verse 12 the kenning for 'goat,' 'brums birkihind' / 'the gnawing hind of the bud,' contains the word 'hind' / 'deer': thus the base-word of the kenning denotes a hunted animal, while the referent of the kenning is a domesticated animal. The Norwegians, unlike the nomad Lapps, did not keep herds of deer but hunted them. In verse 14 there may be two kennings for 'herring' where this effect is obtained. In the first, uncertain example, 'fjǫrð-hjǫrðu' / 'herds of the fiord,' the kenning as a whole suggests fishing while the base-word ('herds') suggests husbandry. In the second, 'mæǫrum sævar' / 'thin arrows of the sea,' the base-word ('arrows') suggests hunting, through its characteristic weapon. The reverse pattern is found in the kenning for 'arrows' in verse 14, 'hlaupsíldr Egils gaupna' / 'the tumbling herrings of Egill's palms,' Egill being a legendary archer. In the second half of verse 13 the kennings as whole connote fishing while the base-words, along with the verb, denote pastured livestock, and so husbandry: 'unnsvín ' / 'pigs of the wave' (ie 'ships') 'róta' / 'root up' 'akrmurur jǫkla' / 'the goose-grass of the field of ice-floes' (ie 'herrings'). In the same verse a further kenning for 'herrings' is 'langra nóta sporð-fjǫðruðum spáþernum' / 'the tell-tale [?] terns, with fish-tails for feathers, of long nets'; evidently terns were valued, at least in Iceland, for their eggs (John Bernström KLNM 'måsfåglar'), so that possibly some idea of gathering is implied here. This very distinctive and unusual kind of verbal play is maintained consistently through the three verses and might have served a rhetorical purpose in a satire that dramatized the failure of various types of subsistence.

Hemings þáttr, as preserved in *Hauksbók*, contains an episode where three verses are recited by a troll woman as the Norwegian ships, manned by Haraldr harðráði's invasion force, lie off the English coast at Scarborough (*Hemings þáttr* 1962ed:44–6). The Norwegians see the woman riding through the air on a wolf, carrying in her lap a trough filled with blood and men's limbs. In her verses she prophesies defeat and death for the Norwegian king:

1 Víst es, at allvaldr austan
  eggjask vestr at leggja
  mót við marga knútu –
  minn snúðr es þat – prúða:
  kná valþiðurr velja –
  veit œrna sér beitu –
  steik af stillis haukum
  stafns: fylgik því jafnan.
       (*Skj* A 430 v 8; *Skj* B 400: ÍF 28:176)

It is certain that the king from the east is being incited westwards to an encounter with many splendid bones [ie he will be buried there]: that is to my advantage. The carrion bird will choose its meat from the king's ships; it knows the provisions for it are plentiful: I always play my part in that.

2 Stór taka fjǫll at falla,
  ferr sótt of kyn dróttar,
  eyðisk friðr, en fœðisk
  fjandhugr meðal landa:
  vesa munk yðr sem ǫðrum
  angrljóðasǫm þjóðum –
  ylgr nemr suðr at svelga
  sveita – urðr of heitin.
       (*Skj* A 430 v 9; B 400)

The great mountains begin to fall; pestilence rages among mankind; the peace is broken and enmity is nourished between nations: with you, as with other peoples, I shall be called Fate, full of grieving songs; in the south the wolf starts drinking blood.

3 Skóð lætr skína rauðan
skjǫld, es dregr at hjaldri;
brúðr sér Aurnis jóða
ófǫr konungs gǫrva:
sviptir sveiflannkjapta
svanni holdi manna;
ulfs munn litar innan
óðlót kona blóði.
 (Skj A 430 v 10; ÍF 28:177; cf Skj B 400)

The evil creature makes the red shield shine now the battle draws near; the troll woman sees disaster in store for the king; she rends men's flesh with darting jaws; the frenzied woman daubs the wolf's mouth with blood.

Only *Hemings þáttr* contains all three verses and incorporates them within a single scene. *Morkinskinna*, *Heimskringla*, and *Hulda/Hrokkinskinna* have verses 1 and 3 in separate scenes; *Fagrskinna* has only verse 3. *Hemings þáttr*, though not itself an early source, has in various ways the simplest and most coherent account. Although verse 2 is found only in the *þáttr*, in the opinion of Gillian Fellows Jensen it seems as old and genuine as the other two and is more likely to have been found by the author of the *þáttr* in a lost source than to have been composed especially for the *þáttr* (1962ed: cxxxix).

In the other texts the woman's 'ljóð' / 'song,' as the *þáttr* calls it, is used in a confusing variety of ways, perhaps indicating elaborations in oral tradition. In *Morkinskinna* the setting is England, or at least some port between Orkney and England: a woman comes down to the cliffs and speaks verse 3; she then disappears, but next evening what is thought to be a different woman appears and recites verse 1, before also disappearing (1932ed:266–7). In *Fagrskinna* Haraldr has just set sail for Orkney from Norway when a man on board his ship dreams that he sees a gigantic woman riding a wolf and carrying a red shield: she recites verse 3 (1902–3ed:283). Snorri's account in *Heimskringla*, closely followed in *Hulda/Hrokkinskinna*, contains further variations and elaborations (ÍF 28:176-7); *Fms* 6:403-4). As Haraldr's fleet lies off the coast of Norway, preparing for the voyage to Orkney, Gyrðr, a man on the king's ship, dreams that he sees a gigantic troll woman standing with a sword in one hand and a trough in the other and an eagle or a raven perching on the prow of every ship in the fleet. The woman recites verse 1. Snorri's words in *Heimskringla*, 'honum þótti fugl sitja á hverjum skipstafni' / 'it seemed to him that a bird sat on the prow of every ship,' could derive from a literal-minded reading of the verse, where the kenning for 'ships' is 'haukum stafns' / 'hawks of the prow.' On a ship near the king's a man named Þórðr dreams that the fleet has already reached England and is met by an English army. Both sides raise many standards and prepare for battle. In front of the English army rides a great troll woman on a wolf, which she feeds on corpses. This part of Snorri's description is plainly an inference from the verse:

ok hafði vargrinn manns hræ í munni, ok fell blóð um kjaptana, en er hann hafði þann etit, þá kastaði hon ǫðrum í munn honum ... (ÍF 28:177)

and the wolf had the corpse of a man in his mouth, and blood fell around his jaws, and when he had eaten that one she flung another into his mouth ...

Then the woman recites verse 3 and the chapter comes to an end.

Progressively in these prose histories, if we assume that the *þáttr* is closest to the original version, we see the *ljóð* or vatication being fragmented into *lausavísur*, with a multiplication and constant elaboration of scenes and characters. To this extent, the same process is operating as with the poems of Sigvatr, Oddr Kíkinaskáld, and Eyvindr skáldaspillir. But there is also an important difference. Whereas Sigvatr, Oddr, and Eyvindr were doubtless real persons and are plausibly ascribed the verses in question, the present story of a troll woman who recites verses is obviously fictive. The true author of the poem is unknown, and the speaker within the poem is treated as the author.

A clear instance of this tendency to collapse the distinction between speaker and poet is seen in the prose that accompanies the poem 'Krákumál.' Its speaker is the ninth-century Viking Ragnarr loðbrók. The language of the poem is however much later, showing loss of 'h' before 'l' and 'r.' The diction includes various Christian allusions that are unlikely to stem from the historical Ragnarr: 'ægis asni' / 'ass of the sea,' ie 'ship'; 'strenglágar pálmr' / 'palm of the notch [?] of the bow-string,' ie 'arrow'; and 'odda messa' / 'mass of spear-points,' ie 'battle' (de Vries II 1967:39–41; M. Olsen [1933] 1938:234, 240). On the other hand, the author of 'Krákumál' does attempt to simulate an archaic metre and rhyme-scheme (Kuhn 1937:52).

In one recension of the saga of Ragnarr loðbrók, contained in the manuscript Ny kgl saml 1824b, 4to, the poem follows the saga but each is a separate entity. In another, contained in AM 147, 4to, 'Krákumál' is fully integrated into the narrative, being spoken by Ragnarr as he stands waiting for death in King Ella's snake-pit. In the poem he surveys his past life and exploits. The work may well have been accepted as genuine by the audience of the saga. We see from *Skáldatal* that by the twelfth or thirteenth century Ragnarr was regarded as among the oldest of the skalds (*Edda Snorra Sturlusonar* III 1880–7:259). In the section of *Háttatal* devoted to archaic metres and rhyme-schemes, Snorri supplies a stanza of a type that he says Ragnarr himself used (*Snorra Edda* 1931ed:238 v 54). Of the other 'forn skáld' / 'early skalds' whom he mentions here, two seem really to have lived and composed poetry (Bragi and Egill), one is now wholly unknown (Fleinn), and one certainly lived but may not have been a poet (Torf-Einarr, whom I discuss in a subsequent chapter). Thus Snorri places Ragnarr side by side with men whose poetry was well attested in tradition.

The process through which, in Ida Gordon's words, 'the hero who speaks the verse has become the poet who composed it' (1961:76) is illustrated further by the traditions on the hero Starkaðr, as traced by Axel Olrik. In Saxo Grammaticus Starkaðr utters a lengthy exhortation, which is couched in metrical form, representing a Latin translation of a vernacular poem. Here the poetic form of the speech is merely a matter of narrative convention and does not imply that Starkaðr was really a poet: Saxo characterizes him as the stereotypical old warrior. But in poetry subsequent to Saxo the recitation of verse was interpreted as one of Starkaðr's accomplishments, and so he acquired the attributes *skáld* and *þulr*. Hjalti, the hero who speaks the harangue within the poem 'Bjarkamál' (as translated by Saxo), also came to be regarded as a poet (Olrik II 1910:42).

In *Qrvar-Odds saga* and *Hálfs saga* we see a combination of two of the tendencies that I have been documenting in this chapter: namely, the convention of the verse-speaking hero and the *modus operandi* that fragments unitary poems into series of *lausavísur*.

In *Ǫrvar-Odds saga* the hero, like Ragnarr loðbrók, recites a poem about his life (*ævikviða*) before dying. The story is told with apparent attention to antiquarian verisimilitude: Oddr asks some of his men to sit beside him and transcribe his poem on to 'spjǫld' / 'wooden tablets,' a motif that deviates from a more common notion that the listeners memorized poems on a first hearing (as in *Gísla saga* chapter 18 and 'Darraðarljóð' 10). The ensuing *ævikviða* would naturally comprise all Oddr's adventures, but in the best manuscripts of the saga only the last six lines are quoted at this point (1892ed:95). Other manuscripts have a complete, lengthy poem. It includes many stanzas that in all manuscripts have already appeared in earlier episodes. Some of them had been introduced on first appearance with the preface 'þá kvað Oddr' / 'then Oddr said' (ibid 25, 26, 40): in each case Oddr is made to speak the verse immediately after the event it describes, when somebody asks what has happened. Sometimes, however, preference is given to a preface that does not expressly indicate spontaneous composition: 'þar um kvað Oddr þessa vísu' / 'Oddr made up this verse about that' (with variants). In Boer's opinion all the verses, irrespective of the choice of preface, originated in an early form of the death-song of Oddr. Though ostensibly *lausavísur*, the verses prefaced by 'þá kvað' fit naturally into the long, summarizing *ævikviða*: the time adverb in them is invariably 'þá,' not 'nú,' and they cover whole episodes with great brevity (Boer 1892:135). Finnur Jónsson agreed with these views, noting that in the historical sagas verses are occasionally introduced as if they were *lausavísur* although clearly they belong to (extended) poems (II 1923:149–51). He suggested that the *ævikviða* had originally been composed for recitation after a telling of the prose saga. The manuscripts that group all the stanzas in one poem near the end of the saga would therefore be close to the author's original intentions, and very similar is the use of 'Krákumál' in the versions of *Ragnars saga*. As Finnur Jónsson pointed out, a further analogue is contained in *Þorgils saga ok Hafliða* (1952ed:18), with its account of saga recitations at a wedding at Reykjahólar in 1119. One of the guests, Ingimundr Einarsson, relates the story of Ormr Barreyjarskáld, embellishing it with numerous verses and, to conclude, a *flokkr* of Ingimundr's own composition.

In *Hálfs saga*, which, like *Ragnars saga* and *Ǫrvar-Odds saga*, recounts the largely fictive deeds of a hero from the ancient past, we find a verse where king Ǫgvaldr tells how long it is since he became a resident of his burial mound (1909ed:73–4). The same verse, with a few variants, appears, followed by two others, in *Ragnars saga* (1906–8ed:221–2).

On Sámsey, Danish Vikings find a *trémaðr* (a wooden statue of a man). It is large, old, and covered in moss. The Danes wonder who would have sacrificed to it. The *trémaðr* answers with three verses:

1 Þat var fyr lǫngu,   er í leið megir
  Heklings fóru   hlunna †tungum†
  framm of salta   slóð birtinga:
  þá varð ek þessa   þorps ráðandi.
                  (*Skj* A2 241 v 1)

It was a long time ago that the sons of Heklingr sailed their †ships† on their course across the salt sea. I became the possessor of this habitation then.

2 Ok því settumk   svarðmerðlingar
  suðr hjá salti,   synir Loðbrókar:
  þá var ek blótinn   til bana mǫnnum
  í Sámseyju   sunnanverðri.
                  (*Skj* A2 241 v 2)

And to this purpose the Vikings [?], sons of [Ragnarr] loðbrók, set me up, south beside the salt sea; then was I worshipped, in the south of Sámsey, to bring about men's deaths.

3 Þar báðu standa,   meðan strǫnd þolir,
  mann hjá þyrni   ok mosa vaxinn;
  nú skýtr á mik   skýja gráti,
  hlýr hvárki mér   hold né klæði.
                  (*Skj* A2 241–2 v 3)

There they bade the man stand, beside the thorn-bush and overgrown with moss, so long as the shores endure: now the tears of the clouds rain down on me; neither flesh nor clothes protect me.

Heusler-Ranisch took the view that verse 1 originally belonged in *Hálfs saga* and was borrowed by the author of *Ragnars saga* (*Eddica minora* 1903ed:lxxxii). This seems highly implausible. The three verses give excellent narrative progression as they stand in *Ragnars saga*: verse 1 describes the Vikings on their voyage and sums up what will happen ('þá varð ek þessa / þorps ráðandi'); verse 2 follows on with a strong

22 Introduction

syntactic link ('ok því') to explain why the *trémaðr* was erected; and verse 3, implying the departure of the Vikings, laments elegiacally the *trémaðr*'s solitary life. The second and third verses cannot stand independent of the first. Stylistically the three verses are homogeneous, with a liberal use of kennings. The influence of 'Hávamál' 49 and 50 on both verse and prose in *Ragnars saga* has been pointed out by Siegfried Gutenbrunner (1937:139–43):

> Váðir mínar   gaf ec velli at
>   tveim trémǫnnom;
> reccar þat þóttuz,   er þeir rift hǫfðo,
>   neiss er nøcqviðr halr.

I gave my clothes to two *trémenn* in a field. They looked fine men, once they were dressed: a naked man is despised.

> Hrørnar þǫll,   sú er stendr þorpi á,
>   hlýra henni bǫrcr né barr;
> svá er maðr,   sá er mangi ann,
>   hvat scal hann lengi lifa?
>
>   (Neckel-Kuhn ed:24)

The fir-tree that stands on the þorp [?hillside] withers;   neither bark nor needles shield it. Such is a man whom nobody loves; why should he live for long?

The use of the word 'þorp' in verse 1 is clearly part of the general influence of 'Hávamál,' and the same putative sense 'hillside' will do in both contexts. This evidence shows that *Ragnars saga*, with three verses about a *trémaðr*, is primary, and *Hálfs saga*, with one verse about a *haugbúi*, is secondary. Only a fragment of the original poem has found its way into *Hálfs saga* and it has been used in an altogether less appropriate context.

The evidence presented in this chapter shows that a variety of forces worked together to give fragments from poems the semblance of *lausavísur*. A partial explanation might be sought in the existence of a custom of extemporaneous verse-making that thrived in Norway and Iceland through the Middle Ages and that is discouraged, where love poems and satires are concerned, in the law text *Grágás* (1852ed II:183–4).

Knowledge of this custom might have preconditioned prose authors into supposing that verses of other types that came their way were also *lausavísur*. There also existed an apparently long-established literary form that combined prose and verse in a *prosimetrum* (Kuhn 1952:276–7). Verses that had begun life as self-contained poems, independent of any prose contribution, might at a later stage have been incorporated within a prose narrative on the model of genuine *prosimetra*. An additional source of confusion was the drastic abridging process that went on in scribal and probably also oral transmission: eventually a poem might be remembered only by a single prominent stanza, for example the refrain or the first verse. Finally, however, the creative powers of prose authors have, I think, been underestimated: we need to bear in mind especially the tendency for authors, probably already at the oral stage, to invent occasions that purportedly accounted for comments and displays of personal feeling in verses – Sigvatr's alarm, Oddr's grief, Eyvindr's exasperation. The experience encapsulated in the verse is made as *immediate* as possible, and correspondingly the speaker within the verse eclipses the poet: the *prosimetrum* form seen, for example, in *Hervarar saga ok Heiðreks* may have been influential in this. The tendency is to treat verse with a peculiar literal-mindedness, as if, of necessity, it were composed at the time of the events it describes and the speaker within it were the author. When we consider the verses incorporated in prose works we should be alert to this tendency and prepared to entertain the possibility that certain alleged *lausavísur* are in reality excerpts from extended poems.

Excursus: The Present Historic Tense in Poetry

In the previous chapter we saw that *lausavísur* and excerpted verses are not easily distinguished. We also saw that there existed a tendency to interpret verses as if they were composed at the time of the events they describe. This mode of interpretation has resulted in a still-prevalent belief that present-tense narration in poetry is a mark of *lausavísa* style: the poet composes as the events unfold and therefore naturally uses the present tense (cf Finnur Jónsson in *Edda Snorra Sturlusonar* III (1880–7:582). Correspondingly, when present-tense narration occurs in longer poems it is often explained as denoting an enduring or frequentative or perpetual present, or as indicating that the poem in question was assembled from originally free-standing *lausavísur*. Influential in the formation of these views was an article by Axel Åkerblom (1917) where almost all instances of the present historic in skaldic poetry before 1100 and in eddaic poetry are emended or otherwise explained away. Åkerblom noted that the heavy use of the present historic contributed to give Icelandic saga style its vividness and immediacy. The poets, he argued, might also have been expected to alternate present and preterite forms, if only to obtain correct metre and rhyme (ibid 293). But the reality, as he sees it, is a very sharp distinction between prose and poetry on this score. In this chapter I shall introduce new evidence on the present historic and re-examine Åkerblom's conclusions.

Even in the prose the present historic is not uniformly prevalent. Personal taste probably played a large part in its use. In the manuscripts, present and preterite forms are frequently alternative readings, so frequently in some works that such variants are not noted in the apparatus. The abbreviation of *verba dicendi* to their initial letter, 'segir/sagði' to 's' and 'kveðr/kvað' to 'k,' implies a free choice of tense on the part of the reader: it also bedevils attempts to put the analysis of tense usage in the sagas on a statistical basis.

In her monograph of 1951 Ulrike Sprenger illustrated the variety of styles that existed by analysing eight sagas in detail. She saw the differences among them as reflecting the mode and period of composition. First came *Heiđarvíga saga*, which, following Sigurđr Nordal in the íf edition, she saw as early and highly influenced by oral narrative, and then two intermediate sagas, *Hænsa-Þóris saga* and *Gísla saga*. In *Heiđarvíga saga* she found the present historic to be the dominant narrative tense, without restriction to any particular type of situation or semantic groups of verbs. The preterite was used only very sparingly, being appropriate for character introductions and indications of time and perhaps also for climaxes (1951:12–14). *Hænsa-Þóris saga* and *Gísla saga* contained a very similar distribution. The survey continued with the so-called 'book-sagas' *Eyrbyggja saga*, *Egils saga*, *Laxdœla saga*, *Njáls saga*, and *Grettis saga*. In *Egils saga* a dramatic contrast at once became evident in that the preterite was now the standard tense of narration and many chapters contained no instance of the present historic at all (ibid 59). Sprenger thought she could identify a use of the present historic as a prelude to major scenes, the main body of which would be narrated in the preterite (ibid 61). *Eyrbyggja saga* was close to *Egils saga*: verbs of movement and sometimes other actions seemed often to occur in the present (ibid 62–3). The usage in *Laxdœla* was distinct, a mixed dominance of the two tenses, although usually the present (ibid 65–6). *Njáls saga* and *Grettis saga* showed only a sparing use of the present historic (ibid 74–7). It was seen chiefly with verbs of movement and in quasi-formulaic phrases that Sprenger regarded as having descended from the oral phase (ibid 71). In her conclusions Sprenger acknowledged that the exact blend of tenses to be found in the individual sagas depended on the individual author (ibid 119). Peter Hallberg has suggested that genre may also be a factor (1978–9:211–12). So far as we can judge from the extant manuscripts, Sturla used 7 per cent present historic verbs in his *Íslendinga saga*, whereas in *Hákonar saga* he used only 0.6 per cent. Hallberg points out that while *Hákonar saga* is a piece of official historiography, based on Norwegian source material, *Íslendinga saga*, for its part, is a description of contemporary people and events in Iceland, based on the author's firsthand knowledge. This closeness to the material might have called forth a more vivid narrative style, with a greater use of the present historic. Genre considerations of this sort may also have been important in skaldic poetry, as later chapters will suggest.

26 Introduction

If we now turn our attention from the later sagas, especially *Njáls saga* and *Grettis saga*, to the *rímur*, a new type of poetry that seems to have been contemporary with them, we find a generally similar alternation and frequency of tenses. Evolving from skaldic poetry, the *rímur* were long narrative poems that continued the traditional predilection for kennings and other complex forms of diction and for alliteration, while innovating, perhaps with some foreign influence, in rhyme schemes and metre. In their simplicity of word order they resemble prose or eddaic poetry more than skaldic poetry. Most of them are direct versifications of a prose story (Ólafur Halldórsson KLNM '*rímur*'). The earliest of them is the 'Ólafs ríma Haraldssonar,' which was probably composed some two or three decades before being copied into *Flateyjarbók* about 1390. The author, Einar Gilsson, concentrates on the battle of Stiklastaðir and the death and miracles of Óláfr, basing his account on *Heimskringla*, though freely selecting and arranging the material furnished by Snorri (Jónsson III 1924:14). The work is obviously literary rather than popular in character, despite the simplicity of diction (Ólason 1983:55). The standard narrative tense is the preterite, just as in the sagas of the period:

> Ólafr kóngr ǫrr ok fríðr
> *átti* Nóregi at ráða;
> gramr *var* æ við bragna blíðr,
> borinn til sigrs ok náða.
> (*Rimnasafn* 1905–22 ed:1 v 1)

King Óláfr, generous and noble, ruled Norway; the king was always friendly to his men, born to victory and grace.

With verse 4 comes the first example of the present historic, along with the perfect:

> Fimm *hefir* kóngr *kristnat* lǫnd,
> kann ek ǫll at nefna;
> gramr *vill* jafnan rjóða rǫnd
> ok rangan ósið hefna.

The king has made five lands Christian; I can name them all: the king will always redden his shield and punish the wicked heathen practices.

The Present Historic Tense in Poetry

In the *ríma* as a whole, as it stands in *Flateyjarbók*, the ratio of preterite to present historic is about four to one. Occasional stanzas contain only present-tense verbs:

> Bragning *lætr* byrja ferð
> bónda múg í móti;
> hann *vill* jafnan hræra sverð
> ok herða skot með spjóti.
> (*Rimnasafn* 2 v 12)

The king causes an expedition to be commenced against the forces of the free farmers. He will always brandish his sword and shoot powerfully with his spear.

Somewhat more common is a mixture of the two tenses:

> Herrinn *drífr* á hilmis fund
> at heyja ímun stranga;
> svá *var* þrútin þeira lund
> at þraut *varð* fram at ganga.
> (*Rimnasafn* 5 v 33)

The army flocks to meet the king to fight a fierce battle; so heated was their mood that the battle was about to commence.

Usually Einar condenses and rearranges Snorri's text to a degree that makes comparison of tense usage impossible, but here the two texts are close and we find that Einar has the present historic where *Heimskringla*, as represented by the ÍF edition, has the preterite:

> Þá sá þeir her bónda, ok fór þat lið dreift mjǫk ok var svá mikill fjǫldi, at af hverjum stíg *dreif* liðit. (ÍF 27:363)

Then they saw the army of the free farmers, and that army advanced in a great throng and was so numerous that it flocked together from every pathway.

With the 'Grettisrímur,' which Finnur Jónsson dates to around 1400 on metrical and linguistic grounds, a comparison becomes easier because the poem follows the saga text (chs 14–24) in much greater detail (Jóns-

28 Introduction

son III 1924:39). Quite commonly the poem has the present historic where the saga, as represented by the ÍF edition, has the preterite:

> Grettir óx upp at Bjargi, þar til er hann var tíu vetra gamall.
> (ÍF 7:37)

Grettir grew up at Bjarg, until he was ten years old.

> Blíðr upp at Bjargi *vex*
> brjótr orma valla;
> fulla hafði fjóra ok sex
> fengit nǫðru galla.
> (*Rímnasafn* 45 v 16)

The happy boy grows up at Bjarg; he was fully ten years old.

The occurrence of present historic and preterite side by side in the one stanza is quite frequent.

> ... honum *þóttu* ... kjúklingar seinfœrir. Honum *gerði* mjǫk hermt við þessu. (ÍF 7:37)

The chickens seemed to him to be slow. This vexed him greatly.

> Stála Týr, sem stendr greint,
> starfinn tók at leiðaz;
> kjúklingarnir *keifa* seint,
> karli *er búit* at reiðaz.
> (*Rímnasafn* 46 v 23)

The task began to irk the warrior, as has been mentioned; the chickens stumble slowly along; the lad is going into a rage.

> Nokkurri stundu síðar *talaði* Ásmundr til, at Grettir *skyldi* geyma hrossa hans. (ÍF 7:39)

Some time later Ásmundr said that Grettir would have to look after his horses.

garprinn *segir* at Grettir *skal*
geyma hrossa sinna
>   (*Rimnasafn* 48 v 41)

The man says that Grettir must look after his horses.

Grettir kom til hrossahúss, lýkr upp, ok *stód* Kengála fyrir stalli.
>   (íF 7:40)

Grettir came to the stable, opens it, and Kengála stood in front of the stall.

Í hesta hús kom hetjan fús hreysti vendr,
Kengála fyrir stalli *stendr*
>   (*Rimnasafn* 49 v 9)

Into the stable came the eager hero, his mind on brave deeds;
Kengála stands in front of the stall.

These comparisons can only be tentative, in the absence of a full collation of the *Grettis saga* manuscript readings, but they suggest that the present historic was a recognized element in verse style and not merely a characteristic that was mechanically reproduced from the prose.

The blend of present historic and preterite in these *rímur* has a general counterpart in English and Scottish ballad style, as can be seen from the Walter Scott version of 'Sir Patrick Spens' (Child 1882–98 II:26 no 58):

> The king *sits* in Dunfermline town
> Drinking the blude-red wine;
> 'O whare will I get a skeely skipper,
> To sail this new ship of mine!'
>
> O up and *spake* an eldern knight,
> *Sat* at the King's right knee,
> 'Sir Patrick Spens is the best sailor,
> That ever sail'd the sea.'
>
> Our king *has written* a braid letter,
> And seal'd it with his hand,

And sent it to Sir Patrick Spens,
Was walking on the strand.

Here, as in some other ballads, the present historic is confined to the beginning, where the scene is being set: the dominant narrative tense is the preterite. The perfect tense may be used when an interval of time separates one action from the next in the story:

They hoysed their sails on Monenday morn
Wi' a' the speed they may;
They *hae landed* in Noroway
Upon a Wodensday.

In view of this general similarity, one might be tempted to suppose that the *rímur* derive their blend of tenses from some hypothetical prototype of ballad style, reinforced by native prose. Yet the alternation of narrative tenses is a characteristic that could less speculatively be traced back to skaldic style. Björn K. Þórólfsson stressed the great debt owed by *rímur* to the older poetic forms in other stylistic matters, notably diction (1950:181): the elaborate kennings in 'Grettisrímur' are testimony to that. He saw an important contact between the older and the younger form in that two at least of the earliest writers of *rímur* also composed poetry in traditional skaldic metres and rhyme-schemes.

Of these two poets one is Einar Gilsson: aside from his 'Ólafsríma,' he composed various works on the life of Bishop Guðmundr, including two *drápur*, one *dróttkvætt* and the other *hrynhent* (for these terms see Turville-Petre 1976:xxxix, xviii–xxi, and xxxii–xxxiii, respectively). Finnur Jónsson also ascribed the 'Selkolluvísur' to him (III 1924:13). In 'Selkolluvísur' a few examples of the present historic occur amid a dominantly preterite narration. The verb 'kemr' / 'comes' is used twice (vv 4 and 17) and the idea of motion is also contained implicitly in the third example:

Ætla á Hamar, þvíat, humra
hyrbídendur frídir,
þar stód, bings, et blída
bænhús, með sid vænan.

(*Skj* A2 410; B2 437 v 13)

The two fine men with laudable faith propose [to go] to Hamar, because the fair oratory stood there.

On the other hand, verbs of motion are also found in the preterite. Only one example of present historic is found in the *hrynhent* poem:

> Klerka *sendir* meiðir mundar
> mundar grjóts við hlyn til fundar,
> vita skyldi þeir atferð Eldis
> elda vess á Þorláksmessu.
>
> (*Skj* A2 404; B2 430 v 3)

He sends clerks to Guðmundr: they were to observe his conduct on Þorlákr's mass-day.

This verb too is associated with movement. The ratio of preterite to present historic in the two poems is very high, seventeen to one in the *hrynhent* poem and approximately twenty-seven to one in the 'Selkolluvísur.' The other *drápa* contains no examples.

The second poet who we know composed both *rímur* and traditional skaldic verse is Kálfr, a monk who identified himself as *Vitulus vates* 'Kálfr skáld' in both the 'Völsungsrímur fornu' and the 'Kátrínardrápa.' He may, according to Björn K. Þórólfsson, have been a contemporary of Einar Gilsson (1950:182), and certainly he belongs to the fourteenth century rather than the fifteenth (cf Jónsson III 1924:38). The 'Völsungsrímur' exhibit the customary blend of tenses within a predominantly preterite narration. The ratio of preterite to present historic in the first two cantos is approximately five to one, comparable to the four to one in Einar's 'Ólafsríma.' Conversely, the low incidence of the present historic in Einar's *dróttkvætt* and *hrynhent* poetry is matched in Kálfr's 'Kátrínardrápa,' whose fifty-one stanzas provide only five instances. These, unlike the examples in Einar, have a broad range of meanings: only one could be termed a verb of motion:

> Keisarans tók kvón at fýsaz
> Kátrínu at tjá iðran sína;
> bragnar *vísa* at byrgðu húsi
> bauga Hlǫkk á grímu dǫkkri.
>
> (*Skj* A2 521; B2 574 v 22)

The emperor's wife became eager to express her remorse to Catherine: men direct her to the locked house in the dark night.

32 Introduction

Other fourteenth-century poets who continue the traditional skaldic poetry make a less sparing use of the present historic. Poems in which it is well represented, though always in second place to the preterite, are the 'Vitnisvísur,' the 'Máríuvísur' I and III, the 'Heilagra Manna Drápa,' and – by far the most prodigal in this respect – the 'Pétrsdrápa.' This evidence suggests that present historic narration was a recognized option in late skaldic style, but that considerations of genre or decorum kept the incidence lower than in contemporary *rímur*: individual taste alone does not account for the distribution.

The pattern is similar in the so-called eddaic poems. Six examples of the present historic are with verbs of movement. One stanza is exceptional in containing two instances ('Helgakviða Hundingsbana' I:13):

> *Fara* hildingar   hiǫrstefno til,
> þeirar er lǫgðo   at Logafiǫllom;
> sleit Fróða frið   fiánda á milli,
> *fara* Viðris grey   valgiǫrn um ey.
> (Neckel-Kuhn ed:132)

> The warriors go to the battle which they waged at Logafjǫll:
> Fróði's peace was broken between the foes; wolves stalk
> around the island, eager for dead bodies.

In 'Sigurðarkviða in skamma' 8 the motivation for the abnormal form is clearer, since, as Sprenger points out, the action is frequentative (1951:111). Here we find three present-tense verbs:

> Opt *gengr* hon innan,   illz um fyld,
> ísa oc iǫcla,   aptan hvern,
> er þau Guðrún   *ganga* á beð
> oc hana Sigurðr   *sveipr* í ripti ...
> (Neckel-Kuhn ed:208)

> Often she goes within, filled with evil, ice and icicles, every
> evening, when he and Guðrún go to bed and Sigurðr drapes
> her in linen.

Occasionally the present historic seems to be used to signal an important new action, as in 'Grípisspá' 5:

The Present Historic Tense in Poetry   33

> *Gengr* ór scála   scatna dróttinn
> oc *heilsar* vel   hilmi komnom ...
>   (Neckel-Kuhn ed:165)

The lord of the warriors goes out of the hall and greets the newly arrived prince cordially.

The two instances in 'Vǫlundarkviða' seem also to mark a new turn in the narrative:

> Þat *spyrr* Níðuðr,   Niára dróttinn,
> at einn Vǫlundr   sat í Úlfdǫlom
>   (Neckel-Kuhn ed:118 v 6)

Níðuðr, king of the Niárar, hears that Vǫlundr remained alone in Úlfdalir.

The other example is like this and indeed nearly all the eddaic examples in being prominently placed at the beginning of the stanza:

> Úti *stendr* kunnig   qván Níðaðar,
> oc hon inn um gecc   endlangan sal
>   (Neckel-Kuhn ed:122 v 30)

Outside stands the wise queen of Níðuðr, and she went inside along the hall.

Although 'gecc' is a verb of motion, it is not attracted into the present by the preceding 'stendr'; and indeed verbs of this type are almost always in the preterite. The pattern with *verba dicendi* is the same: the two likely examples are 'Rígsþula' 36 and 'Helgakviða Hjǫrvarðssonar' 36. Bugge advocated emendation in the latter case, from 'biðr' / 'bids' to 'bið' (with þú' understood), but on insufficient grounds (1867:177). Of the mythological poems only 'Þrymskviða' contains the present historic, here too with a verb of motion (v 12):

> *Ganga* þeir fagra   Freyio at hitta
>   (Neckel-Kuhn ed:112)

They go to meet beautiful Freyja.

Earlier in the same poem (v 3), the preterite had been used in a very similar line:

Gengo þeir fagra   Freyio túna
(Neckel-Kuhn ed:111)

They went to the beautiful dwellings of Freyja.

Here again emendation has been proposed to remove this isolated occurrence of the present tense (Sijmons-Gering 1903–6 I:144), but the combination of variation with repetition in verse 12 is an unexceptionable element in Norse poetic style.

My conclusion from the eddaic evidence is that although it is scanty it cannot be emended away. On the other hand, we do not know when these poems were composed and we cannot assume that they remained immutable until being set down on parchment. The examples of the present historic contained in them do not necessarily antedate the mid-thirteenth century.

In Snorri's *Háttatal*, the sheer rarity of the present historic seems to be operating as a possible cause of misinterpretation. *Háttatal* divides into three sections, the first in praise of King Hákon and the second and third in praise of Skúli jarl. Much of the poem deals not with specific historical events but with permanent characteristics of the two rulers, especially their readiness to undertake expeditions, their bravery in battle, and their generosity to their followers. In describing these permanent attributes Snorri naturally uses the habitual present tense, which Fidjestøl sees as especially characteristic of *Háttatal* (1982:252). Where narrative technique is concerned, the second section of the poem is of greatest interest. It divides, as Möbius pointed out, into three parts, the first (vv 32–9) historical, the second (vv 41–62) habitual, and the third (vv 63–6) historical once more (1879–81 ed I:41–2). The third part is narrated entirely in the preterite, but the first part is not so straightforward. It begins by describing Skúli's participation in the battle that saw the crushing of a rebellion against his brother, King Ingi, in 1213 (ibid I:39). Then follows Ingi's expedition to Vágsbrú, to subdue an insurrection in Trøndelag. The earl is seen manning and equipping his ships, sailing across a routinely stormy sea, and precipitating a flight on the part of the rebels (vv 34–5). Some evidently linger to fight, and they are dealt with mercilessly (vv 36–7). All these events of 1213 and 1214 are narrated in the preterite, except for one present-tense main clause in verse 37:

> ... kann virðum banna
> vald ... hǫfundr aldar
> ... sá's bil lestir
>
> (*Skj* A 2:62; B 2:71)

The earl, who curbs vacillation, is able to deny power to [these] men.

Interpretation here is difficult: the main clause verb might be present historic, referring to the same battle as the other (preterite) verbs in the stanza, or it might be habitual present, indicating that Skúli is always swift to check insurrection. Either way, it provides a transition to verse 38, which, describing Skúli's return voyage from Trøndelag, is clearly in the present historic.

> Farar snarar fylkir byrjar,
> freka breka lemr á snekkjum,
> vaka taka vísa rekkar,
> viðar skriðar at þat biðja;
> svipa skipa sýjur hepnar
> sǫmum þrǫmum í byr rǫmmum;
> Haka skaka hrannir blǫkkum
> hliðar; miðar und kjǫl niðri.
>
> (*Skj* A2:62–3; B 2:71; *NN* 1312)

The earl begins his speedy voyage; devouring waves crash against the ships; the leader's men begin to wake and call for the departure of [their] ship; the ships' planks, with their securely fitting edges, glide gladly along, in a strongly blowing fair wind; the breakers shake the ships' sides; beneath the keel a mark [ie the wake] is made.

In verse 39, where Skúli gains an earldom as a reward for his efforts, the tenses revert to a mixture of preterite and present.

Ok hjaldrreifan hófu
hoddstiklanda miklir –
morðflýtir kná mœta
malmskúrar dyn – jalmar,
hjaldrs þá's hilmir foldar
hugfœrum gaf stœri –
ógnsvellir fær allan –
jarldóm – gǫfugr sóma.

(Skj A 2:63; B 2:71; NN 1314)

And the great battles exalted the generous leader, who rejoices in the fray – the warrior is able to endure combat – when the king of the land [Ingi] gave the brave warrior the title of earl; the noble warrior has all honour bestowed upon him.

As in verse 37, the exact temporal significance of the present-tense verbs is difficult to determine.

In spite of these transitional present-tense forms in verses 37 and 39, the present historic in verse 38 is unexpected. The manuscripts show uncertainty as to the correct place for this stanza. Only in manuscript U is it placed as here and in the editions: in W it stands between verses 54 and 55, while in R it is appended at the conclusion of the entire poem, and in T, where the end of *Háttatal* is lost, it is missing altogether. The correctness of the arrangement in U is, however, not in doubt. Möbius convincingly ascribed the misplacement in the other manuscripts to two factors: the metre in verse 38 looks like *hrynhent* although it is actually *dróttkvætt*; the stanza is not mentioned in the prose commentary to *Háttatal* (1879–81 ed I:64; II:68–9). It seems to me probable that a third factor also contributed to the misplacement, namely the deviant present-tense narration in an almost entirely preterite environment. On superficial inspection verse 38 seems more at home between verses 54–5, where the context is wholly present tense. The present historic, used in verse, was apparently deviant enough to be capable of confusing copyists. They sought to foster clarity in communication by using the preterite for past events and by restricting the present to continuing or habitual events.

The present historic has a more prominent role in Gunnlaugr Leifsson's translation of the 'Prophetiae Merlini.' The *Historia Regum Britanniae* of Geoffrey of Monmouth, to which the 'Prophetiae' belong, seems to have been completed not later than 1138–9, and Gunnlaugr's death occurred in 1218–19: a precise dating of the translation is not possible. Gunnlaugr follows the Latin text fairly closely, except that occasionally he inserts extra stanzas and half stanzas, in particular so as to amplify on the battle descriptions in typical skaldic style (Jakob Benediktsson KLNM 'Merlínússpá'). Most of the poem is of course concerned with the future, but the beginning of the second section of the translation is an account of the historical events that led up to Merlin's prophecies, abridging the account in Geoffrey's *Historia* (Eysteinsson 1953–7:97). A detailed analysis of this part of Gunnlaugr's poem seems justified, because the distribution of tenses to be observed here strongly resembles that seen in the poems to be discussed in later chapters.

Gunnlaugr was obviously steeped in the vernacular poetry of his native Iceland. According to Benediktsson the poet's handling of metre and diction reveals the influence of 'Vǫluspá' in particular, along with two other poems containing prophecy, the 'Grípisspá' and the 'Fáfnismál.' The 'Darraðarljóð,' part of which is also prophetic, could be added to the list. His familiarity with the more complex type of poetry that we term 'skaldic' is especially evident in his liberal use of kennings (eg *Skj* B2 17 v 34). He employs a wide range of kenning types, from the virtually formulaic pronoun-substitute 'spillir bauga' / 'destroyer of rings,' ie 'man' (cf Eysteinsson 1953–7:97) to a fully imagistic combination of two base-words and verb.

bregðr benlogi
byggðum hjarna   (v 35)

the flame of battle [sword] destroys the dwellings of brains [heads]

Skaldic effects are also attempted with end-rhyme (v 36) and word order: in verse 13 the reader or listener has to wait four lines for the phrase 'veitið vatni' / 'drain the pool' to be completed by 'niðr ór fjalli' / 'down from the mountain'; in verse 14 the corresponding words are brought into their natural order.

Beginning the historical prelude to the prophecies, Gunnlaugr has five stanzas of preterite narration recounting how Vortigernus was overpowered by the invasion of Angles and Saxons: this represents a very condensed and free summary of the *Historia* VI:9–16 (Geoffrey 1911–29 ed chs 92–105). In verse 6 comes a new initiative on Vortigernus' part, one that seems to be emphasized by a change of tense:

38 Introduction

> En hertogi
> hœlis *leitar*,
> *gerisk* traustan turn
> tyggi at smíða;
> ok þangat til
> þeirar gerðar
> *samnar* mǫrgum
> mildingr smiðum.
>
> > (Skj A2 22; B2 25)

But the leader of the army seeks a refuge, the king prepares to build a strong tower; and there for that enterprise the prince assembles many masons.

Very striking, set against the poetry so far discussed in this chapter, is the consistent use of the present historic throughout the stanza. It cannot be due to a slavish adherence to Geoffrey's Latin, because there the verbs are clearly either preterite (perfect) or imperfect (*Historia* VI:17 Geoffrey 1911–29 ed ch 106):

> Qui [ie Vortigernus' wise men] *dixerunt* ut *ædificaret* sibi turrim fortissimam, quæ sibi tutamen *foret*, cum ceteras munitiones *amisisset*. Peragratis ergo quibusque locis ... *venit* tandem ad montem Erir, ubi, coadunatis ex diversis patriis cæmentariis, *jussit* turrem construere. (Here and below I use the 1911–29 edition [Faral], checked against the 1929 edition [Griscom].)

Aside from the tenses, Gunnlaugr's translation is now quite close and detailed.

Following this, we have a block of three stanzas where the narration, like Geoffrey's, is preterite throughout   (Skj A2 23; B2 25–6):

> Kómu til smíðar
> spakir vǫlundar –
> þat es ýtum sagt –
> uppi í fjalli;
> en þat's drengir
> á degi gerðu
> sá þess engan stað
> annan morgin.

Able smiths came to the work up on the mountain – so people
are told, but what the men did by day was nowhere to be seen
the next morning.

Convenientes itaque lapidarii coeperunt eam fundare. Sed quic-
quid una die operabantur, absorbebat tellus illud in altera, ita ut
nescirent quorsum opus suum evanesceret.

Kalla lét fylkir
fróða seggi;
frá gunnþorinn
gramr hvat olli,
es gǫrla hvarf
grundvǫllr sá brott
sem grund gǫmul
gleypði steina ...

The king had the wise men called; brave in battle, he enquired
what the cause was that the foundations vanished away totally,
as if the old earth swallowed stones ... (For an attempt to restore
and explicate the very obscure last two lines see Kock NN 1282
and Kock II 1949:16.)

Cumque id Vortegirno nuntiatum fuisset, consuluit iterum
magos suos, ut causam rei indicarent.

Einn vas maðr sá,
es myrkva frétt
fyr skata skýrum
skynja kunni;
hét yngva vinr
Ambrósiús,
en enn ágæti
ǫðru nafni
Merlínús sá
maðr kallaðisk.

There was one man alone who could explain the dark portent
to the wise king; the prince's friend was called Ambrosius but
the excellent man was called by another name, Merlinus.

40 Introduction

> Tunc ait Merlinus, qui et Ambrosius dicebatur ... (*Historia* VI:19 Geoffrey 1911–29 ed ch 108)

Then, in verse 10, at a dramatic moment, we have a brief excursion into the present historic (*Skj* A2 23; B2 26):

Þat kvað valda
verdags hǫtuðr,
at þar undir vas
ólítit vatn;
bauð grund grafa
gumna stjóri,
reynisk spaklig
spámanns saga.

The man said the cause was that underneath lay a large body of water; the king bade that the ground be excavated: the prophet's story is proved to be wise.

'Domine mi rex, voca operarios tuos, et jube fodere terram, et invenies stagnum sub ea, quod turrim stare non permittit.' Quod cum factum fuisset, repertum est stagnum sub terra, quod eam instabilem fecerat.

In the next stanza there is a return to unmixed preterite narration:

Ok enn fróði halr
frétti lofða,
hvat und vatni
væri niðri;
ok es engi þat
annarr vissi
sagði fylki
fleinþollr spǫkum:

And the wise man asked the men what might be beneath the water; and when nobody else knew that he told the wise prince.

Accessit iterum Ambrosius Merlinus ad magos et ait: 'Dicite mihi, mendaces adulatores, quid sub stagno est.' Nec unum verbum respondentes obmutuerunt.

The two stanzas of direct speech that ensue are not relevant to my purpose here; in verse 14 the narrative resumes, once more in the preterite:

Gerðu greppar
þat's gumnum bauð,
varð vatni niðr
veitt ór fjalli,
ok seimgefendr
snáka þekðu
tryggðarlausa,
sem Týr firum
hafði Hristar
hugspár sagat.

The men did what he bade them, the water was drained down from the mountain, and the men saw the treacherous snakes, as the prophet had said.

Credidit rex verbis ejus, quia verum dixerat de stagno, et jussit illud hauriri, et Merlinum super omnia admirabatur. Admirabantur etiam cuncti qui astabant tantam in eo sapientiam, existimantes numen esse in illo.

With the waking of the two dragons, the narrative quickens in pace and shifts into the present historic (v 15):

Ok drjúgligir
drekar vǫknuðu,
gerðusk báðir
brott ór rúmi;
rennask síðan
snart at móti
fróns fásýnir
frœknir baugar.

And the mighty dragons awoke and issued forth from their lairs; then the fierce serpents, rarely seen, instantly rush at each other.

... Egressi sunt duo dracones, quorum unus erat albus, et alter rubeus. Cumque alter alteri appropinquasset ...
(*Historia* VII:3 Geoffrey 1911–29 ed ch 111)

In describing the frenetic activity that ensues, Gunnlaugr makes heavy, though not exclusive, use of the present historic (*Skj* A2 24; B2 27 vv 16–18). By contrast, Geoffrey's verbs are uniformly perfect or imperfect.

Gerisk sókn mikil
snáka tveggja,
gapa grimliga
grundar belti,
hǫggvask hœknir
hauðrs gyrðingar,
blásask eitri á
ok blóm eldi.

A great battle breaks out between the reptiles, the snakes gape hideously, the dragons strike each other savagely, blow venom and dark fire on each other.

... commiserunt diram pugnam et ignem anhelitu procreabant.

Forflótti vas
fránn enn rauði,
bar enn ljósi hann
liðr at bakka;
en hann hagliga
hrøkkr at móti,
elti hann enn hvíta
hugtrúr dreka.

The red serpent fled, the white one drove him to the edge; but nimbly he turns to attack; steadfastly he pursued the white dragon.

The Present Historic Tense in Poetry 43

Prævalebat autem albus draco rubeumque usque ad extremitatem lacus fugabat. At ille, cum se expulsum doluisset, impetum fecit in album ipsumque retroire coegit.

Þeir víg *gera*
vats farveg í,
ok lengi hvatt
linnar *berjask*;
mega ormar þar
ýmsir meira
ok ýmsir þeir
undan *leggja*.

They make war in the channel from the pool, and the snakes fight long and bitterly; now the one dragon prevails, now the other, now the one flees, now the other.

Ipsis ergo in hunc modum pugnantibus ...

By the standards of most of the poems discussed so far, this part of 'Merlínússpá' is exceptional for the high incidence of present historic (a ratio of preterite 3.5 to present historic 1, approximately).

The present historic is idiomatic in Latin, from Plautus onwards. Thus although Gunnlaugr did not use it in direct imitation of Geoffrey, one might perhaps argue that he was influenced by his general training and reading in Latin. Certain other syntactic and stylistic traits in Old Norse prose have been ascribed to Latin influence on clerical writers (Nygaard 1896, Kristjánsson 1981). But it seems unlikely that in such imitation clerical writers went completely against the grain of their own language. Frederick Amory has contended that 'there were linguistic limits to what clerical stylists might do with the vernacular' (1978–9:69). In his opinion 'the Latin reading of the clerical class in Iceland and Norway would not have prompted the more independent-minded members who wrote in the vernacular to adapt Old Norse to certain Latin turns of speech unless their native tongue were in fact easily conformable to these, and conceivably these alone.' As an example of what might have been possible, Amory suggested that the 'periphrastic oddities of style' in *Fóstbrœdra saga* might have resulted from the combined influence of Latin style and skaldic style.

Students of 'learned style' have not classed the present historic among idioms that were regarded as totally foreign to Old Norse and imported from Latin. Marius Nygaard thought merely that this idiom was on the whole more common in learned style than in popular style (1916:30). We know that Gunnlaugr's literary training and experience embraced skaldic style as well as Latin style. Probably, then, he inherited the present historic idiom from skaldic and other vernacular poetry, while his knowledge of Latin served, if anything, to reinforce it.

Gunnlaugr, as we have seen, does not make uniform use of the present historic. Sometimes it is interspersed with the preterite, sometimes it is used alone. In the three stanzas where all the verbs are present-tense (vv 6, 16 and 18), the illusion develops that the speaker is commenting on events as they occur. This uninterrupted use of present historic comes close to 'running commentary.' A modern example is the sports commentary, where the commentator's description of the football match or horse race or other event keeps pace with the action as it proceeds. In a sports commentary heavy use is made of the present tense because the action is present and continuing. In the running commentary type of poem the present-tense verbs foster an illusion that the action is present and continuing. We shall see further examples of this technique later.

The examples of the present historic examined so far in this chapter are, I have been arguing, an accepted stylism in the tradition of skaldic poetry. If I am correct in this contention, we should expect comparable examples to occur in pre-1100 skaldic verse, precisely the corpus of poetry that Åkerblom regarded as characterized exclusively by the preterite. In identifying these examples I shall begin with Bragi, concentrating on that well-known genre where a shield or other visual artwork is described.

In Bragi's 'Ragnarsdrápa,' which describes a shield, three apparent examples are to be found, the first of them in verse 5 (Turville-Petre 1976:3; the translation is his):

Þar, svá at gerðu gyrðan
golfhǫlkvis sá fylkis,
segls naglfara siglur
saums andvanar *standa* ...

(Skj A 2)

There, as they encircled the vessel of the prince's floor-horse [ie house?], stand masts of the sail of the sword [ie warriors] without nails ...

The problem is to determine whether 'standa' is finite (third person plural present indicative) or an infinitive, and in the absence of a secure interpretation of the four lines as a whole certainty is not within our grasp. The word 'sá' has been taken as the accusative of 'sár' / 'large vessel, vat, tub' and in combination with 'golfholkvis' / 'house' interpreted as a kenning for 'bed' or 'sleeping apartment' (LP 'sár'). Turville-Petre seems to suggest taking the word literally: 'since the legless, armless Jǫrmunrekkr seems to have fallen on his head, it may be that he fell into a beer-tub like King Fjǫlnir [in *Ynglinga saga* ch 11]. His warriors would surround the tub ['gerðu gyrðan'] to pull him out' (1976:3). Unfortunately, our other sources leave us uncertain as to how and where the final actions in the legend took place (cf de Boor [1951] 1966:187). Meanwhile, the word 'fylkis' is the reading of one manuscript for 'fylkir' in the other two (*Skj* A 2). Possibly, therefore, we should read 'sá fylkir' / 'the king saw' with 'siglur standa' as the accusative and infinitive governed by 'sá.' Other difficulties, however, would remain unsolved and the majority opinion is that 'standa' is a finite verb (Jónsson in *Skj* B 2, Kock NN 2720, Turville-Petre 1976:3, and Marold 1983:71 and 74n44).

A second possible example of the present historic occurs in verse 10 (Marold 1983:82–3):

> *Lætrat* lýða stillir
> landa vanr á sandi –
> þá svall heipt í Hǫgna –
> Hǫð-Glamma mun stǫðva ...
>
> (*Skj* A 3)

On the sand the landless leader of men [ie the sea-king] does nothing to check the wishes of the warlike Glammar: then rage swelled up in Hǫgni ...

This half-stanza has caused many difficulties, but they have been swept away by Marold's recognition of 'glamma' as the name of a people. The element 'hǫð-' / 'war' in such a compound is paralleled in *Beowulf* by 'Heaþo-Scilfingas' (cf 'Scylfingas' in the same poem) and 'Heaþoræmas' (cf Old Norse 'Raumar'). The present-tense verb that begins the sentence is an emendation for 'letr' / 'hinders' in the manuscripts (Gering 1886:20, Kock NN 156, Krause 1925:136): Finnur Jónsson retains 'letr,' translating 'fraråder' (*Skj* B 2–3). Åkerblom's tentative emendation to the preterite 'lét' has not found support (1917:297n1).

The third possible example occurs in verse 6:

ok bláserkja(r) birkis
bǫll fagrgǫtu allir
ennihǫgg ok eggjar
Jónakrs sonum *launa*

(*Skj* A 2)

and all of them repay the sons of Jónakr for the mighty blows to the forehead ['bǫll ennihǫgg'] and the sword-wounds ['fagrgǫtu eggjar' / 'beautiful paths of the blade'] of the king.

As in verse 5, the problem is to know whether 'launa' is finite or infinitive. Finnur Jónsson thought finite ('er i færd med at lönne': *Skj* B 2), but Kock (NN 215 and 2002), followed by Reichardt (1928:23–4 and Turville-Petre (1976:4), have taken 'launa' as an infinitive, governed by the emended form 'gǫtu' (an auxiliary). Marold rejected the emendation (1983:74). I believe that manuscript 'fagr' – ousted in the editions by the emendation 'fǫgr' – should also be restored: with Finnur Jónsson, but against the manuscripts, I should attach it to '-gǫtu,' not to 'bǫll-/ball-.' I regard 'bláserkja(r) birkis' as an irregular kenning for 'warrior,' with neuter base-word: interpretation as a kenning for 'sword' leads to duplication with 'eggjar' and is unnecessary in view of the parallels for the warrior kenning cited by Reichardt (1928:24). The genitive case is objective: thus 'the blows and wounds inflicted on the warrior,' who, of course, is King Jǫrmunrekkr. In this interpretation, as in Finnur Jónsson's and Marold's, 'launa' is construed as a present indicative form. Åkerblom prefers to construe it as an infinitive: his interpretation will be discussed presently.

In his article Åkerblom accepts some use of the present tense in 'Ragnarsdrápa' but explains it in terms of the genre of the poem. Evidently the composition of the poem was inspired by the gift of a shield from one Ragnarr, who may have been identical with Ragnarr loðbrók (Turville-Petre 1976:xxiii). The shield seems to have been decorated with a series of scenes from myth and legend. In Åkerblom's opinion, limitations of space on the shield would have dictated that each myth or legend was represented by a single scene, which would have shown one situation from the story. In the poem, on the other hand, Bragi's retelling of the stories is not subject to these constraints. Åkerblom speculates that when Bragi uses the preterite he is describing events not shown on the shield (relying on his independent knowledge of the story), whereas when he uses the present he is indicating an event depicted there by the artist (1917:297). Thus Åkerblom reads 'þar standa' in verse 5 as Bragi's gesture towards the scene depicted on the shield (cf Marold 1983:100).

The present tense is not, however, so simply accounted for. The actions denoted by the verbs 'standa' / 'stand' and '*gørva gyrðan' / 'encircle' are necessarily one and the same and, if depicted, would have been depicted in the one scene. Therefore, following Åkerblom, 'gerðu' ought to be present tense: in fact, of course, it is preterite. Moreover, there is not necessarily an association between the deictic word 'þar' in verse 5 and the use of the present tense there, since in verse 14 we find the phrase 'þat erum sýnt' (a clear reference to the artist's depiction) in combination with the preterite (*Skj* B 3). We should also note that Bragi gives another indication of what could be seen on the shield in verse 12: 'þá má sókn á Svǫlnis / salpenningi kenna' / 'that battle can be seen on the shield.' The word 'sókn' here evidently refers back to the verb 'sóttu' in verse 10, suggesting that the action denoted by this verb, despite its preterite form, was portrayed on the shield. When Åkerblom identifies 'lætrat stǫðva' in verse 10 as indicating, with the present tense, the sole aspect of the 'Hjaðningavíg' to be depicted, he is obliged to ignore Bragi's express indications that the artist's treatment of the legend was more comprehensive.

In the 'Haustlǫng' the pattern is similar: a statement that such and such a scene can be found depicted on the shield is followed by preterite narration when the scene in question is put into words. In verses 1–2, after a statement that he can see the dealings of the gods with Þjazi depicted on the shield, Þjóðólfr immediately launches into the preterite to describe those dealings. Similarly in verse 14:

    Eðr of sér, es jǫtna
    ótti lét of sóttan ...
        (*Skj* A 19; B 17)

48   Introduction

Moreover, one can see when Þórr attacked ...

In verse 20 the poet indicates that the representations on the shield were not restricted to a single isolated incident from each of the two myths depicted:

> Gǫrla lítk á Geitis
> garði þær of farðir
>
>   (Skj A 20; B 18)

I see those events clearly [or completely?] upon the shield.

The one clear example of the present tense, relating to a past event, in the poem occurs in verse 13 (on the present tense in verse 7 see Marold 1983:198).

> Hófu skjótt, en skófu
> skǫpt ginnregin, brinna,
> en sonr biðils *sviðnar*
> (sveipr varð í fǫr) Greipar:
> þat's of fát á fjalla
> Finns ilja brú minni;
> baugs þá'k bifum fáða
> bifkleif at Þorleifi.
>   (Skj A 19; Holtsmark 1956:127)

They started burning at once, and the gods cut shavings from shafts, and the son of Greip's suitor is singed: his journey came to a halt. That story ['minni'] is painted on the shield. I received a shield, painted with colours [?], from Þorleifr.

Here, certainly, the present-tense verb precedes a statement that something was painted on the shield, and it might therefore be construed as indicating that Þjóðólfr is gesturing towards the scene. But such a conclusion would be premature. All four actions or events mentioned in the first *helmingr* (half-stanza) could have been shown together in one picture, as is indicated by the *hysteron proteron* in the first two lines (on which see Skj B 19, Kock NN 225 and 1811, and Holtsmark 1956:127–9). Certainly Þjazi's burning and the end of his flight are simultaneous. Yet only the verb 'sviðnar' is present, while the other three (including 'varð,' of the end of the flight) are preterite. Furthermore, the statement in the second *helmingr* that something is painted on the shield seems to refer not merely to the whole of the preceding *helmingr* but beyond that to the entire story told in verses 1–13: the verbal recapitulation of verse 1 signals that the story taken up there has now been completed. This is reinforced if, as in 'Húsdrápa,' the word 'minni' means 'tradition, memory,' hence 'traditional story, myth, legend,' following the neuter article 'þat,' rather than 'my' (dative case), agreeing with 'brú.' In the absence of archaeological evidence we cannot say for sure just how detailed shield pictures might have been. Anne Holtsmark pointed out that even one picture could cover a good deal of the story (1956:130). For example, a scene covering the early part of the story might contain multiple representations of the eagle, showing him first sitting in the tree above the gods, then snatching a morsel of their meal and being struck by Loki, and finally flying off with Loki in tow. A pictorial narrative technique of the sort reconstructed by Holtsmark is to be seen on the Bayeux Tapestry and indeed very commonly in medieval art.

Noting that 'sviðnar' is the sole instance of a possible present historic in 'Haustlǫng,' Åkerblom speculated that the final '-r' was a scribal addition, altering 'sviðna', which would be governed by 'hóf,' understood from 'hófu,' the plural form at the beginning of the stanza (1971:296). This is very similar to his suggestion for 'Ragnarsdrápa' 6, where he takes 'launa' as an infinitive governed by 'létu,' which is understood from the singular form 'lét' in the previous *helmingr* (ibid 295–6). These interpretations, while not impossible, are syntactically awkward because of the change of number in each case. A circularity of argument is involved, since Åkerblom construes as he does solely in order to eliminate a possible example of the present historic (ibid 296). Neither interpretation has found favour with subsequent commentators on Bragi and Þjóðólfr.

There are good reasons, as we shall see, for thinking that the next extant poem in the descriptive genre is the 'Sigurðardrápa' of Kormakr. Kormakr's poem was delivered before Sigurðr's death in 962, though perhaps not much before, and one stanza from it is cited in *Heimskringla* (ÍF 26:168). The stanza is formally remarkable because each *helmingr* contains two entirely different topics: the first three lines and the first syllable of the fourth are devoted to Sigurðr (his hospitality and protection of the heathen rites), while the final five syllables of the fourth line are on mythological or legendary subjects. Clearly mythological is 'véltu goð Þjaza' / 'the gods tricked Þjazi' (referring to the story we have seen in 'Haustlǫng'). The counterpart in the second *helmingr*, 'vá Gramr til menja' / 'Gramr won treasure in battle,' is more obscure, but might allude to the sword of Sigurðr Fáfnisbani – appropriately because the earl being honoured in the poem was his namesake (Fidjestøl 1982:94). In the commentary to *Háttatal* this type of intercalation is termed *hjástælt* (*Snorra Edda* 1931ed:221–2), presumably meaning 'forged on,' like the steel ('stál') cutting edge on iron knives and swords. In the opinion of Helmut de Boor, these *stál*, or intercalations, consist of brief descriptions of scenes carved in Sigurðr's hall or embroidered on tapestries there, analogous to 'Húsdrápa' ([1930] 1964 I:229); see also Schier 1976A: 440).

Also attributed to Kormakr are six *helmingar*, quoted without indication of their source in 'Skáldskaparmál.' Four of them contain a *stál* identical in form to the two mentioned above (*Skj* B 69–70):

'seið Yggr til Rindar' (v 3) / 'Yggr won Rindr through magic'
'komsk Urðr ór brunni' (v 4) 'Urðr came out of the spring'
'*sitr Þórr í reiðu*' (v 5) / 'Þórr sits in the wagon'
'fór Hroptr með Gungni' (v 7) / 'Hroptr went with Gungnir'

The formal resemblance is so striking and the *hjástælt* form so rare that one might naturally conclude, with Kurt Schier (1976A: 440) and Turville-Petre (1976:45), that all eight *helmingar* belong to the same poem. But, as shown by Cecil Wood, two of the *helmingar* refer not to Sigurðr but to his son Hákon. In the majority of manuscripts the *helmingr* containing the intercalation 'sitr Þórr í reiðu' mentions a 'mǫg Sigrøðar' or 'Sigraðar'; only in AM 748 is the subject 'mǫg Hákonar.' The former can be taken as Hákon jarl, Sigurðr's successor, if 'Sigrøðar/Sigraðar' may be equated with 'Sigurðar' (as is implied by the reading 'Sigurðr' in U). The latter is Sigurðr himself (son of an earlier Hákon), and AM 748 here seems to have the secondary reading, one designed to make the *helmingr* explicable as part of the 'Sigurðardrápa' (Wood 1959:311). The other *helmingr*, which has no *stál*, refers to the patron with the circumlocution 'Haralds sannreynis sonr' / 'son of the true tester of Haraldr [gráfeldr]': Wood interprets this as 'the son of Sigurðr jarl' (ibid 307), using Snorri's explanation in 'Skáldskaparmál' (*Snorra Edda* 1931ed:163). Wood goes on to divide the extant fragments among a 'Hákonardrápa,' where each *stál* had to do with specific mythological figures, a first 'Sigurðardrápa,' where each *stál* had to do with the gods in general, and a second 'Sigurðardrápa,' where each *stál* had to do with the legend of Sigurðr Fáfnisbani (1959:318–19). This, however, is to make too fine a distinction among the different types of 'forn minni' / ' old traditions': the decorator of the hall at Hlaðir might have combined mythological and legendary material just as the craftsman of Bragi's shield did in depicting Þórr, Hymir, and the Miðgarðsormr alongside Hamðir, Sǫrli, Jǫrmunrekkr, Heðinn, Hǫgni, and Hildr. Fidjestøl advocates taking all eight *helmingar* together as a 'Hlaðajarladrápa,' recited to Hákon, the son, but composed in praise of Sigurðr, the father (1982:93; cf. *ÍF* 8:ciii). A second possibility is a poem addressed principally to Sigurðr but with some praise of Hákon, the rising young man. This would fit with the name of the poem in *Heimskringla* and with information in *Skáldatal*, which lists Kormakr as skald to Sigurðr jarl and Haraldr gráfeldr but not to Hákon jarl (*Edda Snorra Sturlusonar* III 1880–7:253, 256, 261, 265, 266). I shall try to show in a later chapter that 'Liðsmannaflokkr' is another poem in praise of two leaders both of whom are still alive at the time of the poem's composition.

Probably, therefore, all the intercalated sentences belong in the one poem. If we consider these sentences we note that one of them, 'sitr Þórr í reiðu,' contains a verb in the present tense, whereas the others have a preterite verb. Cecil Wood sees 'sitr Þórr' as belonging with 'komsk Urðr' and 'fór Hroptr' in a 'Hákonardrápa,' so whether we adopt his reconstruction of the fragments or that of most other scholars a shift in tense is entailed. The shift would be particularly conspicuous if, as Fidjestøl thinks, the 'seið' and 'sitr' sentences belong in one stanza (1982:94). According to de Boor's view of the poem's origin, each *stál* describes a scene visible in the hall at Hlaðir. Preterite and present are used indifferently in these *stál*, which suggests once more that Åkerblom was wrong to ascribe any special deictic function to present-tense verbs in poems of the descriptive genre. The occurrence of preterite forms side by side with the present in these poems also rules out the possibility that the present forms connote an enduring or permanent state, of objects permanently visible on the shield or wall: if that explanation were correct all the verbs would have to be present. The present historic seems the natural classification, and the sparing use of it fits with what we have seen in the later poetry.

'Húsdrápa,' composed by the Icelandic poet Ulfr Uggason in the 980s, seems, as I have noted, to reflect the influence of 'Sigurðardrápa.' Kurt Schier has pointed out that Óláfr pái, the patron complimented in 'Húsdrápa,' was in some measure a client of Sigurðr's son, Hákon jarl; according to *Laxdœla saga*, Óláfr spent several months with Hákon while obtaining wood in Norway for his new hall. Schier envisages a simultaneous transmission of literary and iconographic traditions from Norway to Iceland: just as Ulfr was influenced by Kormakr, so the decoration of Óláfr's hall was influenced by Hákon's, formerly Sigurðr's (1976A:441–3).

The surviving fragments of the 'Húsdrápa' show the usual mixture of present and preterite verbs. Although the preterite is dominant, the present, used of past events, has a much greater importance than we have seen elsewhere, the ratio being about two to one.

The one full stanza extant contains what is in Schier's opinion a version of a highly archaic creation myth (ibid 427). It tells of a battle between Loki and Heimdallr, in the heathen mythology an event that Schier considers took place near the time of the world's creation. The present tense in this stanza can therefore not be an instance of present substituting for future, as in the prophetic parts of 'Vǫluspá' and other poems. Some problems of text and interpretation exist, but since these do not affect the tense of the verbs I shall use Schier's recent reconstitution of the stanza and refer the reader to his detailed discussion of previous work on it (1976B:578–81).

> Ráðgegninn *bregðr* ragna
> reinar at Singasteina
> frægr við firna slœgjan
> Fárbauta mǫg vári:
> móðǫflugr *ræðr* mœðra
> mǫgr hafnýra fǫgru –
> kynnik – áðr ok einnar
> átta – mærðar þóttum.
>
> (Skj A 136–7 v 2)

The celebrated guardian of the rainbow [Heimdallr], resourceful in counsel, moves against the exceedingly crafty son of Fárbauti [Loki] at Singasteinn: soon the brave strong son of nine mothers [Heimdallr] has control of the beautiful stone; I make it known through the episodes of my poem.

Further stanzas on the creation story have not been preserved. Of the popular story concerning Þórr and the Miðgarðsormr five *helmingar* survive. Schier suggests that the graphic descriptions of Þórr's blows on the heads of Hymir and the Miðgarðsormr enable us to recognize with special clarity the pictorial source from which Ulfr was working (1976A:427). Perhaps contrary to expectation, the tense of narration is preterite throughout the Þórr fragments, with the possible exception of 'kvezk' in verse 3. Here manuscripts R and W read 'qvađ,' against U 'qvez.' R and W also differ from U in attributing the *helmingr* to Bragi, not Ulfr, but the patterns of internal rhyme point strongly to the later poet's authorship.

> Þjokkvaxinn *kvezk* þykkja
> þiklingr firinmikla
> hafra njóts at hǫfgum
> hætting megindrætti.
> (*Skj* A 137; B 128)

The stoutly grown thick creature [the giant] says he sees extremely great danger in Þórr's heavy and mighty catch.

An episode from the story of Baldr is told in a further five *helmingar*, four of which describe the procession of gods and other mythical beings to the pyre and the fifth the launching of the funerary ship. It might be supposed that only the more incidental parts of the story are preserved here and that Ulfr must have elaborated, in stanzas no longer extant, on the nowadays better-known episodes of the Baldr myth, but Jan de Vries has made a case for regarding the funeral of Baldr as a key part of the myth, with its own independent significance (1955:41–60). The handling of tenses in this section of the 'Húsdrápa' is decidedly unusual: three *helmingar* are in the present, one is accusative-and-infinitive dependent on 'hykk' / 'I believe,' and only one is preterite. The *helmingar* with present tense are as follows:

> *Ríđr* á bǫrg til borgar
> bǫđfróđr sonar Óđins
> Freyr ok folkum *stýrir*
> fyrstr enum golli byrsta.
> (*Skj* A 137; B 129 v 7)

Freyr, experienced in battle, rides in front on a boar with golden bristles to Óđinn's son's stronghold [the pyre], and directs the warrior-hosts.

> *Ríđr* at vilgi víđu
> víđfrægr, en mér líđa,

Hroptatýr, of hvápta
hróðrmǫl, sonar báli.
(Skj A 137; B 129 V 8)

Óðinn, renowned far and wide, rides to the great pyre of his son, and words of eulogy issue from my mouth.

Kostigr *ríðr* at kesti,
kynfróðs þeim's goð hlóðu
Hrafnfreistaðar, hesti
Heimdallr, at mǫg fallinn.
(Skj A 138; B 129 V 10)

The excellent Heimdallr rides his horse to the pyre which the gods heaped up for the fallen son of the wise Óðinn.

Laxdœla saga chapter 29 offers information about the occasion of recitation. Shortly after being built, Óláfr's new hall Hjarðarholt was the scene of his daughter's marriage to a Norwegian, an occasion at which many were present including Ulfr, who presented a poem about Óláfr and the stories depicted in his hall. In the opinion of Kurt Schier, the 'Húsdrápa' retells only those parts of the stories that could be seen depicted in the carvings (1976A:429; cf Frank 1978:111). Åkerblom took the same line as with 'Ragnarsdrápa': present tense was used to indicate what could actually be seen, whereas the preterite signalled actions that were filled in by the poet from his own independent knowledge. He regarded the much heavier use of the present in 'Húsdrápa' as reflecting the greater amount of space available to the artist. With so much of the stories visible to his audience and therefore appropriately described in the present, Ulfr had less opportunity than Bragi to fill in missing sections with preterite narration. This theory obliged Åkerblom to assume that the surviving fragments represent illustrated portions of the Baldr and Loki/ Heimdallr stories but non-illustrated portions of the Þórr story (1917:298). Since the Þórr fragments cover most of the story – and certainly the most dramatic part – Åkerblom's argument lacks credibility. It also fails to account for the *helmingr* where Þórr material is juxtaposed with the refrain (Skj B 129; Finnur Jónsson combines this with another *helmingr* to produce a complete stanza, following the U manuscript, but cf. Frank 1978:111):

Víðgymnir laust Vimrar
vaðs af frónum naðri
hlusta grunn við hrǫnnum.
Hlaut innan svá minnum.
(Skj A 137 v 6)

Þórr struck the head from the gleaming serpent against the waves. Inside thus, with old stories, was [the hall decorated].

Although the last line here represents only a part of the refrain, which would have been completed elsewhere in the poem, the adverb 'svá' is sufficient to show that what the poet has just described, along with the rest of the episode, was to be seen in the hall (cf Frank 1978:111–12). In my view, then, Åkerblom's arguments cannot hold, and 'Húsdrápa' becomes another instance of a poem where preterite and present historic narration were combined. The shift of tenses in the Baldr story is especially noteworthy: if the fragments originally ran in chronological order, as Finnur Jónsson has them (Skj B 129–30), we have a sequence (present historic followed by preterite) to which we shall find parallels in the poems to be discussed in later chapters.

The evidence presented in these two chapters establishes two important points. First, there was a tendency for originally unitary poems to become fragmented in transmission, whether through attrition or through special interpretations. Second, the present historic tense could be used alongside the preterite in Old Norse–Icelandic poetry, regardless of the genre or the period. Two different kinds of use can be distinguished: sometimes we find an isolated occurrence of one or two present-tense verbs in a generally preterite environment; sometimes the pattern is that of a sustained incidence of present-tense verbs through one or more stanzas, without any preterite ingredient, so that the effect becomes that of a running commentary. The assertion that the present tense, in either of these distributions, is a hallmark of a specifically *lausavísa* discourse has been shown to be without foundation. What should rather be said is that the comparative rarity of this stylism seems to have opened the way for various types of misinterpretation.

In the next four chapters I shall turn to our major narrative poems, in the attempt to show that they have all, in one way or another, been the subject of misinterpretation on this score. Indeed, only one of them,

'Darraðarljóð,' has consistently been recognized and analysed as a unitary poem, and even here it is my contention that the narrative technique has been misunderstood in some of its detail. I shall begin with two relatively straightforward works, moving then to the very complex 'Liðsmannaflokkr' and 'Darraðarljóð.'

THE POEMS

Þjóðólfr Arnórsson: The Battle of the River Nissa (from *Sexstefja*)

1 Skeið sák framm at flœði,
  fagrt sprund, ór ǫ́ hrundit;
  kenndu, hvar liggr fyr landi
  lǫng súð dreka ens prúða:
  orms glóar fax of farmi
  fráns, síz ýtt vas hǫnum –
  bǫ́ru búnir svírar
  brunnit gull – af hlunni.
                (ÍF 28:141; Skj A 381, v 18)

Fair lady, I saw the ship launched out of the river into the high tide; you see where the long clinker-planking of the proud dragon [ie the longship] lies before the land. The mane of the shining serpent glistens above the cargo, since the ship was launched from the roller; the ornamented stem bore pure gold.

2 Slyngr laugardag lǫngu
  lið-Baldr af sér tjaldi,
  út þar's ekkjur líta
  orms súð ór bœ prúðar:
  vestr réð ór Nið næsta
  nýri skeið at stýra
  ungr – en árar drengja –
  allvaldr – í sjá falla.
                (ÍF 28:142; Skj A 381 v 19)

The warrior flings the long awning out of the way on Saturday, out where the proud widows gaze on the serpent's clinker-planking from the town. The young king steered the brand new ship west out of the [River] Nið, and the men's oars plunge into the sea.

3 Rétt kann rœði slíta
ræsis herr ór verri;
ekkjan stendr ok undrask
árar burð sem furðu:
ært mun, snót, áðr sortuð
sæfǫng í tvau ganga;
þǫll leggr við frið fullan
ferkleyf á þat leyfi.
(ÍF 28:142–3; Skj A 381 v 20)

The king's army knows how to lift the oar straight from the stroke; the widow stands and marvels at the handling of the oars, as a miracle. Lady, there will be rowing [indeed] before the tarred oars split in two; the four-edged timber [the oar] grants leave for that [ie hard rowing] with full indemnity.

4 Sorgar veit, áðr slíti
sæfǫng ór mar strǫngum
herr, þar's heldr til varra
hár sjau tøgum ára;
norðmeðr róa naðri
negldum straum enn heglda –
út es sem innan líti
arnar væng – með jarni.
(ÍF 28:143; Skj A 381–2 v 21)

The army knows sorrow, before they lift the oars out of the mighty sea [ie end their expedition], where the rowlock guides seventy oars toward the water. The Norwegians row with the hail-spattered current in their iron-nailed dragon [ship]; out there it is like looking at the under side of an eagle's wing [ie the motion of the oars resembles the motion of a wing in flight].

5 Eigu skjól und skógi
skafnir snekkju stafnar;
læsir leiðangrs vísi

lǫnd herskipa brǫndum:
almenningr liggr innan –
eið láta sér skeiðar
hóbrynjaðar hlýja –
hverja vík í skerjum.

           (ÍF 28:143–4; Skj A 382 v 22)

The planed prows of the ship have shelter under the woods; the leader of the expedition forms a barrage round his lands with the stems of the warships. The levy [of ships] lies inside each inlet amidst the skerries; the ships, with their high shields, let the spits of land provide protection.

6 Hléseyjar lemr hǫvan
   hryngarð konungr barði;
   neytir þá til þrautar
   þengill snekkju strengja:
   eigi es jarni bjúgu
   indæll skaði lindis;
   gnegr af gaddi digrum
   grjót ok veðr en ljótu.

           (ÍF 28:144; Skj A 382 v 23)

The king smashes the high tumbling walls of Hlésey [ie the sea] with his prow; he relies on the ship's cables to the limit of their strength. The foe of the lime-tree [ie the wind] is not gentle to the curved iron [ie the anchor]; rocks and the ugly weather gnaw away at the sturdy fluke.

7 Haraldr þeysti nú hraustla
   helfning sinn at Elfi;
   náttar Nóregs dróttinn
   nær at landamæri:
   gramr á þing við Þumla:
   þar's eindagaðr Sveini,
   hrafni skyldr, nema haldi,
   hans fundr, Danir undan.

           (ÍF 28:144–5; Skj A 382–3 v 24)

Haraldr now impelled his war-band valiantly to the [River] Göta Älv; the ruler of Norway spends the night near the frontier. The king has a meeting at Þumla: an encounter, the raven's due, is there appointed with him for Sveinn, unless the Danes flee.

8 Lét vingjafa veitir,
varghollr, dreka skolla
lystr fyr leiðangrs brjósti –
liðs oddr vas þat – miðju.
(ÍF 28:146; Skj A 371 v 12)

The dispenser of gifts to friends, beneficent to the wolf, eagerly positioned his dragon [ship] to hover in front of the centre of the fleet; it was the vanguard of the force.

9 Fast bað fylking hrausta
friðvandr jǫfurr standa;
hamalt sýndisk mér hǫmlur
hildings vinir skilda:
ramsyndan lauk rǫndum
ráðandi manndáða
nýtr fyr Nizi útan
naðr, svá't hver tók aðra.
(ÍF 28:146; Skj A 371–2 v 13)

The peace-loving king commanded his brave army to stand fast; I saw the leader's comrades place their shields to overlap above the rowlocks. Off the coast from the [River] Nissa, the valiant instigator of manly deeds fortified the powerfully swimming dragon [ship] with shields, so that each shield touched the next.

10 Alm dró upplenzkr hilmir
alla nótt, enn snjalli;
hremsur lét á hvítar
hlífr landreki drífa:
brynmǫnnum smó benjar
blóðugr oddr, þar's stóðu –
flugr óx Fáfnis vigra –
Finna gjǫld í skjǫldum.
(ÍF 28:149–50; Skj A 372 v 14)

The valiant king of Uppland drew his bow all night; the lord caused arrows to shower against the white shields. The blood-

drenched point inflicted wounds upon the mail-shirted men,
where arrows lodged in shields; the volley of spears from the
dragon [ship] increased.

11 Flest vas hirð, sú's hraustum
hrafns fœði vel tœði,
dauð, áðr dǫglingr næði,
døkks, á land at støkkva:
skóp furðu þá skerði –
skipum ǫll vas þá – snjǫllum
hrings – til heljar gengin –
hverr fótr konungs Jóta.

(*Skj* A 372 v 15)

Most of the war-band, who supported the valiant feeder of the
dark raven well, was dead before the king [Sveinn] succeeded in
fleeing to land. Each of the king of Jutland's feet performed a
miracle then for the brave giver of rings: his entire following had
made their way to Hell [ie had perished].

12 Sogns kvǫðu gram gegnan
glæst, sjau tøgu et fæsta,
senn á svipstund einni
Sveins þjóðar skip hrjóða.

(ÍF 28:151; *Skj* A 372 v 16)

It was said that immediately, in one fell swoop, the brave king of
Sogn [Haraldr] cleared Sveinn's men's splendid ships, at least seventy [of them].

13 Sveinn át sigr at launa
sex, þeim es hvǫt vexa
innan eina gunni
ǫrleiks, Dana jǫrlum:
varð, sá's vildit forða,
vígbjartr, snǫru hjarta,
í fylkingu fenginn
Fiðr Árnason miðri.

(ÍF 28: 151–2; *Skj* A 373 v 17)

The six Danish earls, who spur on the fighting in one battle, do
not need to be rewarded for victory by Sveinn. Finnr Árnasson,

splendid in battle, who did not wish to save his bold heart [ie his life], was captured in the centre of the force.

In the editions these stanzas are divided into two groups: verses 8–13 are assigned to Þjóðólfr's *Sexstefja*, a partially preserved poem in praise of Haraldr harðráði, while verses 1–7 are explained as *lausavísur* 'free-standing (improvisatory) verses.' For reasons I shall discuss presently, the status of the latter verses has remained uncertain. The editors of *Edda Snorra Sturlusonar* comment: 'Fortasse rectius hæ septem strophæ ad unum carmen non intercalare referendæ sunt (III 1880–7:589). Bjarne Fidjestøl has tentatively suggested that verses 1–7, like the others, formed part of *Sexstefja* (1982:237–9). He places especial weight on stylistic criteria. I should like to begin the present analysis by demonstrating how little warrant the medieval prose sources provide for modern editorial dismemberment of this sequence of verses.

In discussing the handling of these verses in the medieval historical compilations I shall begin with *Heimskringla*, because this work preserves more verses than the others that antedate it (at least, as now extant). *Hulda/Hrokkinskinna*, a conflation of *Heimskringla* and *Morkinskinna*, will need little separate comment. In chapter 60 of the relevant part of *Heimskringla* (ÍF 28:141), Snorri describes how Haraldr harðráði calls out his fleet and has his new, specially built ship launched into the River Nið. Then verse 1 is quoted, and in all manuscripts but one it is prefaced with the words 'þá kvað Þjóðólfr skáld' / 'then Þjóðólfr the skald said,' a formula that identifies the verse as a *lausavísa*, one composed expressly for this occasion and recited extemporaneously. In the one dissenting manuscript (F) the prefatory words are 'svá segir' / 'thus says' (1893–1901ed III:156), indicating that the verse in question is regarded not as an impromptu composition but as part of a poem composed retrospectively. I shall discuss this disagreement among the manuscripts presently. Snorri goes on to recount briefly how Haraldr steered his ship out of the river and corroborates his story by quoting verses 2–4. The prefatory formula here and with subsequent stanzas is 'svá segir Þjóðólfr': in other words, Snorri most probably thought he was dealing with a narrative poem, not with a series of unconnected occasional verses. In *Hulda/Hrokkinskinna* the last sentence before verse 2 in *Heimskringla* – 'þar var vandaðr róðr mjǫk' / 'the rowing was very difficult there' – is slightly reworded and transposed so as to follow verse 2 and preface verse 3, where the first hint of difficult times for the oarsmen actually occurs

(Louis-Jensen 1977:169). This is not the only place where we see the *Hulda/Hrokkinskinna* redactor outdoing Snorri in his care to match the content and lexicon of the prose narrative and its supporting verses. Their interpretation seems to be guided by criteria of relevance: whereas the verse expresses confidence that the oars will withstand all the trials to ensue during the expedition, the effect of the prose commentary is to restrict this statement to the occasion of launching. As the *Heimskringla* narrative continues, the incidence of verses remains abnormally high. They are very obviously the backbone of Snorri's account. A brief passage prefacing verse 5 tells how Haraldr sails south, collecting his fleet, and then east, encountering bad weather in Viken and taking shelter. A sentence of comment on the excellence of the anchor on the new ship is followed by verse 6. A further sentence, bringing Haraldr to the Göta Älv, is followed by verse 7. The comment in this verse about the possible flight of the Danes anticipates the ensuing events: Snorri's next chapter, opening with a more substantial prose passage, tells how Sveinn's army fled when they heard of his enemy's approach, causing Haraldr to disband part of his forces. With the remainder he raided in Danish territory until intercepted by Sveinn, whose men had meanwhile regrouped; badly outnumbered, some of the Norwegians advocated flight. For a memorable version of Haraldr's reply, Snorri uses a verse from a second skaldic source, Steinn Herdísarson's 'Nizarvísur.' But in his account of the preparations for battle Snorri returns to Þjóðólfr, and once more his narrative is a paraphrase of the following verse (v 8). Another sentence, describing how Haraldr's ships were readied, leads into verse 9 rather irrelevantly. In *Hulda/Hrokkinskinna* the correspondence between verse and prose is again tightened up. Snorri's account of the commencement of the battle draws on further verses by Steinn Herdísarson, returning to Þjóðólfr (v 10) where he describes how the battle lasted all night. A stanza or two by Þjóðólfr, on the start of the battle, may well have been omitted here. Such an omission certainly occurs in Snorri's ensuing prose narrative, recounting Hákon jarl's part in the battle and the slaughter or flight of the Danes. Here a verse by Arnórr jarlaskáld is cited in corroboration; a Þjóðólfr verse of very similar content (v 11) is absent from *Heimskringla* but cited in *Morkinskinna*. After some further detail on the rout of the Danes, Snorri returns to Þjóðólfr, quoting verse 12 and finally, after three sentences on the capture of the Danish earl Finnr Árnason, verse 13. The narration that follows is without skaldic corroboration for some chapters, until we reach chapter 71 and an anonymous set of verses describing peace negotiations between Haraldr and Sveinn (to be dealt with in the next chapter under the name 'Friðgerðarflokkr').

In summary, the Þjóðólfr verses in this part of *Heimskringla* are neatly demarcated at beginning and end. They form the backbone of the story, though with some supplementation from Steinn Herdísarson and Arnórr jarlaskáld. The prose provides no evidence whatever that at some point one poem by Þjóðólfr stops and another one starts. In particular, the break after verse 7 assumed in modern editions is unjustified, because, as has been noted, this stanza looks forward to the next stage of the story.

Snorri derives this part of his *Haralds saga Sigurðarson* (the constituent saga in *Heimskringla*) from the partially extant *Hákonar saga Ívarssonar*, following it from chapter 39 until chapter 75, with the exclusion of chapters 54–7 (ÍF 28:xxii). *Hákonar saga* is thought to have been written some time during the first two decades of the thirteenth century, roughly contemporaneously with *Morkinskinna* and *Orkneyinga saga* (1952ed: xxvii). Unfortunately, the unique manuscript is in a highly fragmentary state; the surviving material corresponds to Snorri's chapters 39–44, 47–9, 60–1, and 67–9 (ÍF 28:xxii). At the outset, paraphrasing verse 1, the compiler adopts a more laborious approach than Snorri, carefully explaining the deviant lexicon with the comment that ships were formerly termed 'dreki' (v 1) or 'skeið' (v 2). He seems to be using the reading 'logn' in line 4 of verse 1 (for 'lǫng' in the other redactions) when he mentions 'logn ok sólskin' / 'calm weather and sunshine' (1952ed: 23). The formula preceding verse 1 is 'þá kvað'; before the other verses we find 'svá kvað; so here Snorri has merely reproduced what he found in his source. Verses 2–4 are used much as in Snorri. Verses 5–7, by contrast, are not cited. Nonetheless, the redactor seems to have known them, because his narrative appears to be a close paraphrase. Verse 5 is clearly the source for *Hákonar saga*'s 'Hafði úti almenning at skipum ok liði ... Lá herrinn víða um fjǫrðu ok eyjar' / 'He had out a general levy for the ships and army ... The army was widely dispersed round the fiords and islands.' Similarly, verse 6 must lie behind the saga statements that 'þurfti skipit góðra grunnfœra' / 'the ship needed good anchor-cables' and 'fá þeir andviðri stór' / 'they ran into a severe storm.' Finally, verse 7 must be the source for the saga's 'helt konungr her þessum austr með landi til Elfi ok kom þar at kveldi dags' / 'the king brought this army eastwards along the coast and arrived there in the evening' (ibid 25). In view of these verbal correspondences it seems most probable that the version of *Hákonar saga* used by Snorri contained verses 5–7 and that the fragments of the saga extant in the unique manuscript AM 570a 4to represent an abridgment. Abridgment in this redaction can be established elsewhere by comparison with the Latin summary of *Hákonar saga* that survives in the hand of A.S. Vedel (ibid xxvii). Although Jón Helgason and Jakob Benediktsson have argued that Snorri added the verses, the assumption that these already stood in *Hákonar saga* seems more economical and quite as plausible (ibid xxi). In the ensuing narrative verse 8 is used as in Snorri, whereas verse 9 is missing. Again, however, the prose in *Hákonar saga* seems to be based upon the missing verse: 'var þat skip allvel búit' / 'the ship was very well prepared' and 'eggjaði konungr þá mjǫk at berjask frœknliga' / 'the king strongly urged them to fight fiercely' (ibid 27). This fragment of *Hákonar saga* ends abruptly just before the start of the battle, and the next fragment takes up the story after the battle, at a point in the chronology just before Snorri's chapter 67. We therefore cannot tell if (or how) the rest of Þjóðólfr's verses were used in *Hákonar saga*. So far as I can see, the Latin summary contains nothing that will help here (ibid 39–40).

Morkinskinna, at least as now extant, does not use any of Þjóðólfr's verses until verse 10 (1932ed:209). The prefatory formula 'sem Þjóðólfr segir' appears with all stanzas except verse 13, where the formula is 'sem hér vísar til' / 'as is shown here,' without mention of the name of the poet (ibid 213). The preparation of the fleet, launching of the king's ship, and voyage to meet Sveinn figure only in the brief and colourless words 'Haraldr konungr stefnir nú saman ǫllu liði sínu' / 'now King Haraldr called his entire army together' (ibid 207). The account of the battle begins with verses by Steinn Herdísarson, continues with Þjóðólfr's verse 10 and another citation from Steinn, and then adds Þjóðólfr's verse 11, a stanza that, as we saw, does not appear in *Heimskringla* or *Hulda/Hrokkinskinna*. Only the first line is included in the extant manuscript, but since the entire stanza appears in *Fagrskinna* it presumably also appeared in the archetype of *Morkinskinna*. The account in *Morkinskinna* differs from Snorri's in one further particular: after verse 11 it continues 'hér segir ok þat at Sveinn konungr flýði á land upp með skútu einni er flotit hafði við lyptingina' / 'here it is also stated that King Sveinn fled to shore using a cutter that had drifted against the stern [of his ship].' This information is not given in verse 11 and could conceivably derive from a lost stanza. Verses 12 and 13 are used much as in Snorri.

The relationship between *Hákonar saga Ívarssonar* and *Morkinskinna* is controversial. Jón Helgason and Jakob Benediktsson discounted any scribal or literary connection between these redactions, explaining the similarities as due to separate indebtedness to the same mass of oral traditions (1952ed:xxxix). This view has recently been challenged by Bjarne Fidjestøl, who suggests that *Hákonar saga Ívarssonar* was written by an author who knew *Morkinskinna* in a form older than now extant; this author adapted his source so as to give Hákon, not Haraldr harðráði, the lion's share of the attention, adding skaldic verses and perhaps other narrative material that were not present in his source (1982:16–17). It is also possible that all thirteen stanzas cited above were included in the older *Morkinskinna* and that subsequent redactions have used them more or less selectively.

Although there is much here that must remain uncertain, this examination of Snorri's proximate source (*Hákonar saga Ívarssonar*) and probable ultimate source (the older *Morkinskinna*) agrees with our analysis of *Heimskringla* in failing to establish any evidential basis for separating the thirteen stanzas out into two different groups after the style of modern skaldic editions. The only basis for so doing must be internal evidence from the verses themselves. The shift between present and preterite might seem to constitute such evidence, but in fact it will not withstand scrutiny. While it is true that the narration in verses 8–13 is consistently preterite, there are also enough preterite verbs in the previous stanzas to establish that the speaker's point of view is retrospective throughout. In verse 1 we find 'glóar fax' and 'svírar báru brunnit gull,' the one verb in the present historic and the other in the preterite, but describing the same feature without apparent difference in meaning. Although a complete analysis is not feasible, because of the possibility of lost stanzas, the narrative technique in what survives resembles that of 'Merlínússpá,' *Háttatal*, and 'Húsdrápa,' with sudden shifts of tense. But in these other poems the preterite seemed to be the staple tense of narration, with the present conspicuous because of its relative scarcity, while in the Nissa verses the balance is more even.

As previously noted, verses 8–13 of the Nissa stanzas have been editorially assigned to Þjóðólfr's *Sexstefja*. Our source for the name and contents of this poem is Snorri's separate *Óláfs saga helga*, where the Þjóðólfr stanza beginning 'Hvasst frák Haugi et næsta' is mentioned as belonging 'í drápu þeiri, er [Þjóðólfr] orti um Harald konung, er kǫlluð er Sexstefja' / 'in the *drápa* entitled *Sexstefja* which Þjóðólfr composed about King Haraldr' (ÍF 27:439). In *Heimskringla* the same stanza is used at the opening of the *Haralds saga Sigurðarsonar*, although without mention of the title. With the exception of one genuine-seeming impromptu verse (ÍF

28:109), it is economical and not implausible to assume that all succeeding Þjóðólfr verses in this saga about Haraldr belong to the same poem about him. Only two verses out of our thirteen are in any way problematic in this respect. The status of verse 13 is questionable because *Morkinskinna* leaves the author unidentified. Here, though, there is no obstacle to assuming that the ascriptions to Þjóðólfr in *Fagrskinna* (1902–3ed:271) and *Heimskringla* go back ultimately to the older *Morkinskinna*. The other problematic stanza is verse 1, whose prefatory formula in all but one manuscript establishes it as a *lausavísa*, or separately composed occasional verse. This formula seems due to a simple kind of error. The compiler of the original *Morkinskinna* or his source inferred from the vocative 'fagrt sprund' and the present tense that this verse was literally addressed to a lady by the poet as Haraldr's ship rowed by. Strangely enough, the parallel features in verse 3 seem to have been ignored by the medieval narrators; only in modern times was the treatment of verse 3 (and the other verses up to verse 7) brought into conformity with that of verse 1. It was left to the copyist of manuscript F of *Heimskringla* to make the simpler emendation in the other direction, an example that I think future editions of Þjóðólfr should follow.

The excerpt from *Sexstefja* discussed here has a marked artistic unity, arising from the use of a device known as concatenation. Lexical concatenation (the linking of successive stanzas by word or other lexical repetition) is strongly evident and is supplemented by phonological concatenation (stanza linking by means of phonological repetition). A complete analysis would be tedious, so rich is the incidence of these and other features, and so I shall content myself with a few examples.

Lexical concatenation was obviously an exceedingly important device. The only two pairs of stanzas not to be lexically linked at all, so far as I can see, are verses 6 and 7 and verses 7 and 8, where 8 is represented by only one *helmingr*. Furthermore, in successive stanzas where the link is a lexical one, repetition is seldom confined to one lexical item. Probably the weakest linking in this respect is between verses 11 and 12, where the only shared lexical item is 'skipun/skip' respectively; but then, once more, half of verse 12 is lost. Some stanzas are extremely heavily concatenated; verses 1 and 2 have four lexical links, likewise verses 3 and 4. Parallelism in position within the stanza can strengthen these repetitions. Between verses 9 and 10, for example, the repetition of the relatively colourless verb 'standa' is lent a certain prominence by placement at line ends in the symmetrically placed lines 2 and 6, respectively: I say 'symmetrically placed' because 'standa' ends the first *vísuorð* of the first *helmingr* in vese 9 while 'stóðu' ends the first *vísuorð* of the second *helmingr* in verse 10.

Frequently, too, lexical repetition is combined with phonological repetition (for a classification of this kind of concatenation see McKenzie 1981). Lexical repetition combined with identical *hendingar* and placement at a symmetrical point in the stanza links verses 1 and 2 ('súð:prúða[r]') and verses 10 and 11 ('[allr]:snj[allr]'). Verses 12 and 13 are linked by the repetition of 'Svein[n] and 'ein[n],' which rhyme but which, instead of being used in a regular *aðalhending* in either stanza (as in verse 7), contribute to rather more diffuse echoic effects. Another of these more elusive effects occurs in verses 5 and 6, where 5.7–8 ('hóbrynjaðar hlýja') is echoed in 6.1–2 ('Hléseyjar lemr hóvan / hryngarð ... '), via the main consonance or rhyme respectively but also via the reappearance of the non-rhyming syllable '-yn-.'

Lexical repetition often goes hand in hand with a carry-over of alliteration. Indeed, a fascinating aspect of concatenation is the multiplicity of possible combinations and permutations of linking devices. Thus the words 'ekkj[a]' and 'árar' are associated with a set of vowel alliterations in verses 2 and 3, but alliterative carry-over occurs independent of lexical carry-over between verses 6 and 7, which are not lexically linked; here we see twofold alliterative linking, again with associated symmetries of placement. Martin Chase has analysed several major twelfth-century poems for alliterative carry-over between stanzas and has ventured the opinion that kindred devices would have been used in some – though not necessarily all – earlier poems (1985). This view seems correct, as will appear from further analyses later in this book; it might be added that even within the individual poem the repertoire of concatenating devices may vary. I have not considered all the subtler types of repetition detected by Chase and McKenzie, because a statistical analysis of the possibility of random repetition seems to me to be a necessary preliminary.

Aside from the concatenation of adjacent and near-adjacent stanzas, other forms of patterning appear. These include the linking of groups of three stanzas. Here verses 2–4 are of special interest, with the repetition of the lexical pair 'út:lít[a]' in *skothendingar* in verses 2 and 4, echoed in the rhyming repetition of 'slít[a]' at the end of the first line in verses 3 and 4. This pattern is further strengthened by the carry-over of alliteration.

Stanzas near the opening may also be linked with ones near the close. Especially significant is the repetition in unusual contexts of the unusual word 'furð[a]' (vv 3 and 11), equidistant from the beginning and end of the verse sequence, as now extant. (On this type of repetition and its function see Poole 1985B:273–8). In verse 3 the watching 'widow' 'marvels' at the oarsmanship, as at a 'miracle,' in what seems to be a systematic use of a lexical set from the Christian religion. In a roughly contemporary poem by Arnórr Þórðarson the king's fleet is said, in a more explicit deployment of the same hyperbole, to resemble an angel host (*Skj* B 310 v 18; Turville-Petre 1968:8). In verse 11 the 'furða,' or 'miracle,' appears by contrast to be a distinctly ignoble one; the feet of the Danish king perform a miracle for him by enabling him to flee the scene of action. The postponement of the grammatical subject, 'fótr' in my interpretation, to the final line delays the identification of the beneficent miracle-worker, and so creates a nice bathos: while Kock's interpretation of 'skóp' as an impersonal verb is also syntactically possible, it leaves 'fótr' and its adjuncts without any clear function in the sentence (*NN* 860).

The word 'friðr,' used in verses 3 and 9, seems to contribute to a similar kind of effect. As used in verse 3, the word is memorable because it occurs in a context of extreme skaldic playfulness. The essential idea seems to be that the oars of Haraldr's fleet are strong enough to withstand hard usage and not break. Such an idea may have been a poetic commonplace. A description of the failure of nautical gear under the stress of too-arduous rowing is found in 'Atlamál' 37; here the oar-loops, the thole-pins, and even the keel are damaged (though the oars themselves are not mentioned). Þjóðólfr speaks of the oar metaphorically as an authority figure, which grants leave for hard rowing with the assurance that the rower will not suffer any penalty. He uses a lexical set that belongs in the laws regarding safe conduct and personal sanctuary: 'slíta' / 'break,' 'friðr' / 'peace, safe conduct, immunity from penalty,' and 'leyfi' / 'leave, permission.' This lexical set, along with its Old English equivalents, has been the subject of a valuable article by Christine Fell (1982–3). The legal vocabulary provides an appropriate vehicle for the metaphor because provisions concerning safe conduct and sanctuary must often have been invoked when travel or an expedition (as in these verses) was being planned.

To summarize: The verses analysed in this chapter emerge as a well-rounded whole, in respect of both narrative technique and concatenation; a further analysis, to show how they integrate with the other remains of *Sexstefja*, would be a worthwhile exercise but beyond the scope of this book, since the present historic is not elsewhere a feature of the narrative technique in that poem.

'Friðgerðarflokkr': The Peace Negotiations between Haraldr and Sveinn

In *Heimskringla* Snorri tells how Haraldr harðráði and Sveinn Úlfsson met off the coast of modern-day Sweden, after years of war between their countries, to negotiate a peace. When these negotiations were crowned with success, a poet commemorated them in six stanzas, which Snorri quoted in the course of his own narrative:

1 Norðr lykr gramr, sá's gerðir
   grund, frá Eyrarsundi –
   hrafngœlir sparn hæli
   hǫfn – langskipa stǫfnum:
   rísta gulli glæstir
   gjalfr, en hlýður skjalfa,
   hvasst und her fyr vestan
   Hallandi framm brandar.

   (ÍF 28:159 v 138; Skj A 401)

'The king [Sveinn], who blocks access to his land, forms a barrage with the prows of his longships north of Øresund. The warrior trod the harbour with the heel [of the ships' keels]. The gold-encrusted bows slice their way keenly through the seas west of Halland, with an army on board, and the wash-strakes tremble.'

2 Gerðir opt fyr jǫrðu
   eiðfastr Haraldr skeiðum;
   Sveinn skerr ok til annars
   eysund konungs fundar:
   út hefra lið lítit

    lofsnjallr Dana allra,
    hinn es hvern vág sunnan,
    hrafngrennir, lykr stǫfnum.
                    (ÍF 28:159 v 139; Skj A 401)

Haraldr, a man true to his oath often forms a barrage before his land with his ships. Sveinn, too, sails through the sound, with its islands, to meet the other king. That famed warrior, who blocks off every inlet from the south with his prows, brings a great army of all the Danes.'

3   Sýstuð suðr þar's æstu,
    snjallr gramr, Danir allir –
    enn sér eigi minni
    efni – mæltrar stefnu:
    Sveinn tekr norðr at nenna
    nær til landamæris –
    varð fyr víðri jǫrðu
    vindsamt – Harald finna.
                    (ÍF 28:160 v 140; Skj A 402)

You went southwards, brave prince, where the Danes all requested an appointed meeting – the need seems as great as ever. Sveinn ventures northward closer to the border – it was windy off the wide land – to meet Haraldr.

4   Telja hótt, es hittask,
    hvártveggja mjǫk, seggir,
    orð, þau's angra fyrða
    allmjǫk, búendr snjallir:
    láta þeir, es þræta,
    þegnar, allt í gegnum –
    svellr ofrhugi jǫfrum –
    eigi brátt við sóttum.
                    (ÍF 28:160–1 v 141; Skj A 402)

As the men meet, the valiant landed farmers on both sides make loud speeches, which offend people very greatly. Those men, who wrangle unremittingly, are slow to accede to a settlement. A rash attitude builds up in the kings.

5 Ofreiði verðr jǫfra
  allhætt, ef skal sættask;
  menn, þeir's miðla kunnu,
  mǫl ǫll vega í skǫlum:
  dugir siklingum segja
  slíkt allt, es her líkar;
  veldr, ef verr skulu hǫlðar,
  vili girndar því, skiljask.

  (ÍF 28:161 v 142; Skj A 402)

The excessive anger of the kings becomes a menace, if a settlement is to be reached; men who know how to mediate weigh all the issues in the balance. It is right to tell the princes everything that their people wish; if men must part on worse terms, a policy of selfishness is the cause of it.

6 Hitt hefk heyrt, at setti
  Haraldr ok Sveinn við meinum –
  guð sýslir þat – gísla
  glaðr hvárrtveggi ǫðrum;
  þeir haldi svá sœrum –
  sǫtt lauksk þar með vǫttum –
  ok ǫllum frið fullum,
  ferð at hvǫrgi skerði.

  (ÍF 28:161–2 v 143; Skj A 402)

I have heard that Haraldr and Sveinn gladly exchanged hostages as a safeguard against hostilities; that is God's doing. May they keep their oaths and a full and general peace in such a way that neither nation will violate it; a conciliation was concluded there in the presence of witnesses.

In the extant medieval sources this sequence of verses lacks a title and an author. Some convenient label is needed, and 'Friðgerðarflokkr' or 'poem on the making of peace' (in imitation of Snorri's 'friðgerðarsaga') is my suggestion. In *Heimskringla*, as also in *Hulda/Hrokkinskinna*, the maker of the verses figures simply as 'skáldit' / 'the skald.' An ascription to Þjóðólfr Arnórsson is tempting, on stylistic grounds, but Bjarne Fidjestøl has shown that the ascription to Halli stirði that appears in Johann Peringskiöld's edition of *Heimskringla* (Stockholm 1697:II 143) may go back to a lost medieval manuscript (1982:145–6). All we know of Halli stirði (or striði: variant forms of the nickname are preserved) is that he was one of the court poets of Haraldr harðráði. The *flokkr* is credited to Halli in the editions of Finnur Jónsson (*Skj* A 401; B 370–1) and E.A. Kock (I 1946:184–5).

Before discussing the verses as a separate entity we need to note how they are handled in the prose of Snorri and his followers. In this respect *Hulda/Hrokkinskinna* deviate only in relatively minor points from *Heimskringla* (see *Fms* 6:331–3). Snorri quotes verses 1 and 2 as a unit, with the prefatory formula 'segir skáldit' / 'the poet says'; except for verse 5, which follows immediately on verse 4, the remaining stanzas are introduced with the words 'svá sem hér segir' / 'as is said here.' *Hulda/Hrokkinskinna* vary in adding 'ok enn kvað skáldit' / 'and the poet also said' before verse 5 (ibid 332). These meagre formulas offer important information about the verses they preface. As we noted, 'svá sem ... ' normally implies that the verse to be quoted is an excerpt from a poem of some length. In the prose before verse 1 Snorri refers to these verses as a *flokkr* (íf 28:159). *Hulda/Hrokkinskinna* are presumably to be relied on when they add the information that verses 1 and 2 began the *flokkr*: 'hann hefr svá upp' / 'he begins in this way' (*Fms* 6:331). It is relatively seldom that we can be confident that the initial verses of a poem are extant: they were particularly subject to loss.

In *Heimskringla*, as also in *Hulda/Hrokkinskinna*, the prose description of events is so compact and dependent on the six verses that their inner cohesion is not masked. This is a poem, then, which survived the very drastic processes of dispersal and abridgment that normally operated when skaldic poetry was quoted in the kings' sagas. The prose passages between verses 2 and 3 and 3 and 4 are extremely brief (one or two sentences) and work to bring out the meaning of the verses rather than to contribute new information. As noted, no real break occurs between verses 4 and 5. In a more lengthy passage between verses 5 and 6 Snorri outlines the terms of peace (followed by *Hulda/Hrokkinskinna*), introducing information that is not contained in the verses. While he might be summarizing a lost stanza here, the information is of a sort that might have been preserved elsewhere. With verse 6 and a brief sentence mentioning the departure of the kings for their respective countries, the episode and the chapter conclude.

The compiler of *Hulda/Hrokkinskinna* goes somewhat further than Snorri in bringing out the single authorship of the verses. Between verses 1 and 2 he adds the words 'ok enn kvað hann' / 'and also he said,' and this is followed up by the phrase 'ok enn kvað skáldit' before verse 5.

In summary, the verses, taken in themselves, give every impression of belonging to one poem. An apparent exception to this unity is that while in verses 2 and 6 Haraldr is spoken of in the third person, in verse 3 he is addressed directly ('sýstuð suðr'). The same alternation of persons can be found, however, within a single stanza by Þjóðólfr (ÍF 28:82–3):

> Þjóð veit, at hefr háðar
> hvargrimmligar rimmur –
> rofizk hafa opt fyr jǫfri –
> átján Haraldr – sáttir;
> hǫss arnar rauttu hvassar,
> hróðigr konungr, blóði –
> ímr gat krǫs, hvar's kómuð –
> klœr, áðr hingat fœrir.

> The people know that Haraldr has fought eighteen extremely fierce battles; the peace has often been broken by the king: honoured prince, you reddened the grey eagle's sharp claws in blood before you returned here; the wolf received food wherever you went.

A third example occurs in the work of another of Haraldr's poets, Valgarðr (ÍF 28:93).

The style of the *flokkr* is also marked by an alternation of tenses. Although the preterite occurs, far heavier use than normal is made of the present tense. Åkerblom suggested this might mean that each stanza was originally a free-standing composition, or *lausavísa*, composed right at the time of the events it described. In this way the events would be in the here and now so far as the poet was concerned, and therefore he would naturally use the present tense in narrating them. Subsequently, Åkerblom suggested, the skald would have brought his *lausavísur* together to produce a complete poem (1971:301). But Åkerblom also conceded the possibility that the present tense here might represent a present historic.

The evidence, both external and internal, points to the latter explanation as the only admissible one. Snorri, as we noted, does not preface these stanzas with formulas distinctive of *lausavísur*. Åkerblom's idea that the poet composed right in the midst of events also needs careful examination against verses 3–5.

In verse 3 all the actions and events denoted by the verbs, except 'æstu,' are simultaneous. A poet genuinely reporting actions that are still continuing would say 'sýslir' (not 'sýstuð'), 'sér,' 'tekr,' and 'verðr' (not 'varð'). What we actually find in this stanza is an alternation between preterite and present historic, parallel to Gunnlaugr Leifsson's handling of tenses in the preface to Part II of 'Merlínússpá' (vv 10, 15, and 17) or to Þjóðólfr's in *Sexstefja*.

The consistent use of the present tense in verses 4 and 5 is significant too. Here the events the poet reports are not concurrent but successive; each event develops out of the previous one. The encounter between the free farmers is acrimonious, the kings in their turn grow angry, and finally wiser heads mediate between the two sides. With this paraphrase we can compare Snorri's (ÍF 28:160–1):

> En er konungarnir fundusk, tóku menn at røða um sættir konunganna, en þegar þat var í munni haft, þá kærðu margir skaða sinn, er fengit hǫfðu af hernaði, rán ok mannalát. Var þat langa hríð, svá sem hér segir [quotes vv 4 and 5]. Síðan áttu hlut í inir beztu menn ok þeir, er vitrastir váru. Gekk þá saman sætt konunga ...

> And when the kings met, men began to discuss terms of peace between the kings, but as soon as the topic was broached many complained of the harm they had sustained through raiding, plundering, and slaughter. That went on for a long while, as is stated here ... Then the best men and those who were wisest took a part in proceedings. Then terms of peace were concluded between the kings ...

Since not all the actions and events in verses 4 and 5 are simultaneous they cannot all be continuing as the poet speaks. The narrative tense here and in verse 2 is more reasonably explained as a sustained present historic, creating the effect of a running commentary.

The final verse is a step further removed from the action, with a decided air of resolution and summation, together with wishes for the future. One present-tense verb, in the parenthesis 'guð sýslir þat,' breaks the pattern of preterite and perfect-tense narration. If the idea is that God always works peace between opposing factions, 'sýslir' could be regarded as a frequentative or even eternal present. On the other hand, the object pronoun 'þat' suggests that the poet's mind is more particularly on the peace between Haraldr and Sveinn, and so 'sýslir' may be a final instance of the present historic. It leaves us with the impression that the news has reached the poet recently.

Throughout the *flokkr*, as Åkerblom points out (1917:301), the heavy use of the present and the frequency of tense shifting communicate a feeling of suspense and urgency (cf de Vries I 1964:275). The ratio between the tenses is highly unusual: one preterite, approximately, to every four presents, or the inverse of the incidence we have found in poems that themselves ranked as exceptional for the frequent use of the present historic.

We have seen that some of the examples of present historic in Old Norse poetry may originate not with the poet but with modifications in oral or scribal transmission. In 'Friðgerðarflokkr,' however, at least some of the shifts in tense must go back to the poet, because one preterite form ('sýstuð') and two present forms ('skjalfa' and 'sýslir') are guaranteed by rhyme.

The *Hulda/Hrokkinskinna* text provides a sobering reminder of how detail of this sort could be tampered with. Jonna Louis-Jensen reaches a low general estimate of the *Hulda/Hrokkinskinna* compiler's handling of skaldic verse, showing that seemingly better readings in that redaction are liable to be scribal emendations (1977:152–4). In addition to the eccentricities that she mentions, a bias can be detected towards preterite rather than present forms. We find 'ristu' for 'rísta' in verse 1, 'gerðuð' for 'gerðir' in verse 2, and 'góð sýsl var þat' for 'guð sýslir þat' in verse 6 (*Skj* A 401–2): readings normalized by me). Finnur Jónsson adopted the last of these variants (*Skj* B 371), but apparently changed his mind later (LP 1931 'sýsla'): the short syllable 'guð' as first rise is a metrical feature with adequate parallels elsewhere (eg 'Liðsmannaflokkr' 10.8). One wonders if this levelling of preterite forms was practised elsewhere: for a possible example see Bjarni Hallbjarnarson, 'Kalfsflokkr' 2 (Fidjestøl 1982:57).

In their narrative technique 'Friðgerðarflokkr' and the Nissa section of *Sexstefja* sometimes deviate from running-commentary format. A long series of present historic verbs gives immediacy and an illusion that the action happens as the skald speaks, but the preterite forms interspersed through the narrative keep the audience in mind of the poet's true perspective as one who speaks after the event. The result is a blend between 'running commentary' and the more usual preterite-dominant narration. We shall find this mixed type again in 'Liðsmannaflokkr' and possibly also in 'Darraðarljóð.'

'Friðgerðarflokkr' is a poem of peacemaking that starts by communicating, directly and by way of overtones, the danger of war. The poem begins in a tense 'cold war' respite from hostilities. The choice of poetic diction helps to create the right sense of menace. One king is a 'hrafngœlir' / 'one who causes the ravens to sing' (no doubt with joy). The other is a 'hrafngrennir,' which, if 'grennir' is cognate with 'granni,' should mean that he resides in the same place as ravens, or they with him. Ravens, like other scavengers, accompany those who make it worth their while: in 'Haraldskvæði' the victorious career of the king is alluded to when the raven declares that he and his kin have followed Haraldr since they were hatched. The ravens' position is equivalent to that of opportunistic warriors in the comitatus, who traditionally sought out and accompanied only those chieftains who were achieving victory and plunder. The choice of diction here excludes the peace-keeping or law-enforcing or benefacting aspects of royal rule that could relevantly have been mentioned, given the ultimate direction the poem will take. Instead the poet seems to focus on things as they seem at the time, with the fleet called out and the army on board.

Other words seem chosen to suggest speed and urgency, like 'sparn hæli.' Usually here too a martial overtone is evident. The words 'rísta' / 'cut,' normally of ships but occasionally of swords, 'skjalfa' / 'tremble,' often of weapons but here of wash-strakes, 'hvasst' / 'sharply, keenly,' and 'skerr' / 'cuts' would all be at home in descriptions of a battle.

Phrases where 'út' or 'úti' combines with 'ólítill,' or 'lítill' associated with a negative particle, comparable to 'út hefra lið lítit' in this poem (2.5), verge upon the formulaic in battle poetry. In Hallfreðr's 'Hákonardrápa' 8 (*Skj* B 148) we find a conveniently alliterating version of the phrase:

ólítit brestr úti
...
hart á Hamðis skyrtum
hryngráp Egils vápna

out there a great rushing blizzard of arrows smites fiercely against the mailshirts

One of the verses in *Hallfreðar saga* has the same combination in a bathetic context:

sem ólítill úti
alls mest við fǫr gesta
– stœrik brag – fyr búri
búrhundr gamall stúri
                (*Skj* B 157)

as if a big old house dog sulked outside in front of the storehouse, especially with the coming and going of guests: I am making a poem

This satirical piece of *bragr*, the word itself perhaps incongruously imported from another genre, seems to depend on contexts where the enemy threat could not so lightly be discounted. Genre associations provide the humour. Another 'straight' use of the phrase occurs in Þórarinn loftunga's 'Tøgdrápa' 2 (*Skj* B 298):

fœrði ór firði
fimr gramr Lima
út ólítinn
otrheims flota

the able king brought a large fleet out on to the sea from Limafjǫrðr

The phrase 'hefr út' has a close counterpart in 'Vellekla' 7: 'oddneytir úti / eiðvandr flota breiðan / ... hafði' / 'and the warrior, true to his oath, had a large fleet out' (*Skj* B 118). The word 'eiðvandr,' similar in sense to 'eiðfastr,' has an obvious relevance in the martial context of 'Vellekla,' where vengeance is explicitly an obligation (cf v 10). In 'Friðgerðarflokkr' the immediate effect of 'eiðfastr' could be equivalent, suggesting the martial resolution of Haraldr's leadership, though more remotely the word looks forward to verse 6 and the pledges of peace ('þeir haldi svá sœrum ...').

Of necessity, sea battles often begin with the sailing of enemy ships on converging courses; in describing this reality, the skalds, like the poet of 'Friðgerðarflokkr,' often find ways of bringing out the pattern. In 'Eiríksflokkr' Halldórr ókristni sets the leaders' actions apart, with one stanza for each. In the first stanza we hear of Eiríkr jarl: 'út bauð jǫfra hneitir / ... / – sunnr helt gramr til gunnar – / ... lidi miklu' / 'the oppressor of kings called out a large army ... ; the lord set his course south to battle.' The next stanza deals with the matching actions of the opponent, Óláfr

Tryggvason: 'Eyna fór ok einu / ... konungr sunnan / ... sjau tøgum skeiða' / 'the king of the Eynir came from the south ... with 71 ships' (Skj B 193).

Sigvatr's 'Knútsdrápa' 4 is comparable in a different respect:

Þurðu norðan	The cold keels raced
(namsk þat) með gram	from the north (the news spread)
til slétts svalir	with the king
Silunds kilir,	to low-lying Sjælland,
en með annan	while with another
Ǫnundr Dǫnum	Swedish army at the row-locks
á hendr at há	Ǫnundr sails
her sœnskan ferr.	to meet the Danes.
(Skj A 249; B 233)	

This stanza is characterized by a shift in tense of the sort we have found in 'Friðgerðarflokkr' and 'Merlínússpá,' that is to say with verbs of motion and within a single stanza. The *aðalhending* 'her:ferr' is admittedly not an absolute guarantee that we have the line as Sigvatr said it, because he has some *skothendingar* in other even lines of this poem: thus 'ætt:frétt' in 3.2 (Skj B 232; cf ÍF 27:270). But to emend to 'fór' against all the manuscripts, as Åkerblom seems to advocate, and on no stronger grounds than a general suspicion of the present historic, is methodologically unsound (1917:309).

The purpose of these voyages has remained unstated throughout verses 1–3. The words used of the meeting itself, 'fundr' and 'stefna,' can both be applied to hostile engagements as readily as to other kinds of meetings. In verse 4, at the halfway point in this brief poem, the focus shifts from action to talk, but with the irony that the talk is so acrimonious as to threaten renewed hostilities. The very proper decisiveness displayed by the kings in the first three verses, in expediting the meeting, shows up the contrasting reluctance with which the free farmers grudgingly set about the negotiations. The adjective 'snjallir,' which initially appears to be praise for these men (it had been used of Haraldr in the previous stanza), is ironically undercut by 'eigi brátt' in the last line, so that their tardiness and dragging of feet become the dominant impression. A comparable effect is achieved by Þorleikr fagri when he applies the epithets 'hugstinnir' / 'resolute' and 'snarráðir' / 'decisive' to the free farmers in a stanza that expresses scorn at their failure to support Haraldr in battle (ÍF 28:118). This trace of partisanship in the poet is balanced by a hint of censoriousness against the kings, with their susceptibility to hot-headed impatience. The wise mediators, glimpsed metaphorically weighing all grievances in the balance, command the real respect.

As used here, the present historic tense would have heightened the feelings of haste, urgency, energy, uncertainty, and menace that inform the poem. The audience is located in the midst of dramatic events with a perhaps surprising outcome.

Concatenation and allied effects contribute much to the cumulative effect of the poem. Intricate verbal parallels link one stanza with another. The close of verse 4 and opening of verse 5 are an especially thorough working out of the principle of repetition with variation.

> –svellr ofrhugi jǫfrum –
> eigi brátt við sóttum.

> Ofreiði verðr jǫfra
> allhætt, ef skal sættask.

The words at line end are identical ('jǫfr-') or close cognates ('sóttum/ sættask'). The words 'ofrhugi' and 'ofreiði' are similar in position, formation, sense, and prefix. Vowel alliteration and internal rhyme (*hending*) are carried over from one stanza to the next.

Simultaneously, verse 5 is linked forward to verse 6 through 's' alliteration in lines 5–6 and through the etymological play 'sættask/sótt,' a figure that connects all three final stanzas.

The first three stanzas have the same kind of continuity. In verses 1 and 2 the parallels between the first *helmingr* and the last, that is between 1.1–4 and 2.5–8, create a frame: thus 'lykr' in 1.1 and 2.8, 'stǫfnum' in 1.4 and 2.8, and 'hrafn-' in 1.3 and 2.8. These repeated words cluster in the last line of verse 2. The ringing of changes on kennings of identical meaning, 'hrafngœlir' and 'hrafngrennir,' is another instance of repetition with variation; it is worked out with almost obsessive neatness, down to the choice of two agent-nouns beginning with 'g' and ending with '-ir.' The word '-grennir' is perhaps selected because it provides a further consonantal rhyme to the 'hinn:sunnan' *skothending* in the previous line. The result is a restriction of freedom that goes beyond the already very rigid rules of classical *dróttkvætt*.

Other repetitions link the first *helmingr* in each stanza: thus 'gerðir' (1.1 and 2.1), 'Eyrarsundi/eysund' (1.2 and 2.4). These various verbal symmetries are of course a counterpart to the symmetry of the kings' movements as they embark on their voyages to the rendezvous; particularly apposite in this respect is the placing of words to form a chiasmus.

The chiastic effect is continued in verses 2 and 3. The first and last *helmingar* contain mentions of Haraldr (2.2 and 3.8) and Sveinn (2.3 and 3.5), the cognates 'fundar' and 'finna' (2.4 and 3.8), and an amplification of 'fyr jǫrðu' into 'fyr víðri jǫrðu' (2.1 and 3.7). The similarity between the first and last two lines is especially striking. The artful variation of the linking devices themselves can be seen by comparing verses 4 and 5, where, as we saw, it was the exactly opposite set of couplets that provided continuity.

In the other two *helmingar* of verses 2 and 3 similar linking is found: 'sunnan' and 'suðr' represent another etymological figure (2.7 and 3.1), while the line 'lofsnjallr Dana allra' (2.6) begins a series that continues with 'snjallr gramr, Danir allir' (3.2) and ends with 'allmjǫk, búendr snjallir' (4.4). A carry-over of vowel alliteration provides a further link between verses 3 and 4; like the 'h' alliteration in verses 1 and 2, it is placed in the second couplet of all but one of the *helmingar*. In verse 2, lines 3–4 lack this 'h' alliteration, but instead contain the vowel alliteration that will link the stanza onward to verses 3 and 4.

This restriction of choice in alliteration represents a voluntary tightening of the rules. The same kind of thriftiness can be seen in the poet's rhyming habits, so that we find a great deal of non-structural rhyming organized according to a definite pattern. Thus the unrhymed syllable '-fastr' in 2.2 echoes 'hvasst:vestan' in 1.7 and looks forward to 'sýstuð:æstu' in 3.1. The final three stanzas correspondingly make heavy use of *hendingar* in '-tt-,' with an example in the first couplet of each stanza; full rhymes or *aðalhendingar* with 'sótt,' the poem's most significant word, further enrich this pattern in 4.8 and 6.6. Another pattern links an unrhymed syllable in the third line of certain *helmingar*, so that 'her' (1.7) rhymes with 'skerr' (2.3) and, symmetrically, 'sparn' (1.3) with 'hvern' (2.7).

Thus all six stanzas are complexly interconnected. Even in the more colourless vocabulary there is a homogeneity such that the word 'all-' occurs in every verse except the first (twice in verse 4 and three times in verse 5). Though this stylistic monotony may in some poems have resulted from the levelling effect of oral transmission, as suggested by Bjarne Fidjestøl (1982:52 and 58), it was also on occasion exploited by the skalds as an inconspicous unifying device.

The poem is neatly rounded off by the repetition with new meaning of two significant verbs. Haraldr's diligence in seeking the settlement – sýstuð suðr' (3.1) – foreshadows God's providence – 'guð sýslir þat' (6.3) – in bringing it to pass. The verb 'lykr,' used of the defensive manoeuvre that seals off the coast from enemy ships in 1.1 and 2.8, appears in 6.6 in the contrasting context of a peaceful close to the negotiations ('lauksk').

'Liðsmannaflokkr': The Campaigns of Knútr and Þorkell in England

1 Gǫngum upp, áðr Engla
   ættlǫnd farin rǫndu
   morðs ok miklar ferðir
   malmregns stafar fregni:
   verum hugrakkir Hlakkar,
   hristum spjót ok skjótum,
   leggr fyr órum eggjum
   Engla gnótt á flótta.

   (Skj A 422 v 1)

Let us go ashore, before warriors ['malmregns stafar'] and large militias ['morðs ferðir'] learn that the English homelands are being traversed with shields: let us be brave in battle, brandish spears and hurl them; great numbers of the English flee before our swords.

2 Margr ferr Ullr í illan
   oddsennu dag þenna
   frár, þar's fœddir órum,
   fornan serk, ok bornir:
   enn á enskra manna
   ǫlum gjóð Hnikars blóði;
   vart man skald í skyrtu
   skreiðask hamri samða.

   (Skj A 422 v 2)

Many an impetuous warrior ['Ullr oddsennu'] puts on today the ugly old shirt, where we were born and bred: once more let us nourish the raven ['gjóð Hnikars'] on the blood of Englishmen; the cautious poet will slip into that kind of shirt which the hammer sews.

3   Þollr mun glaums of grímu
    gjarn síðarla árna
    randar skóð at rjóða
    rœðinn, sá's mey fœðir:
    berr eigi sá sveigir
    sára lauks í ári
    reiðr til Rínar glóða
    rǫnd upp á Englandi.
                    (Skj A 221 v 5)

That garrulous reveller ['glaums þollr'] who brings the girl up will be eager to make no undue haste to redden his sword ['randar skóð] at night: the warrior ['sveigir sára lauks'] does not carry a shield ashore into English territory at this early hour, enraged, in quest of gold ['Rínar glóða'].

4   Þóttut mér, es ek þátta,
    Þorkels liðar dvelja –
    sǫusk eigi þeir sverða
    sǫng – í folk at ganga,
    áðr an ?hauðr? á heiði
    hríð víkingar kníðu –
    vér hlutum vápna skúrir –
    varð fylkt liði – harða.
                    (Skj A 220 v 2)

Þorkell's men did not seem to me, as I saw [them], to lose time in joining battle – they did not fear the ringing of swords – before the Vikings fought a hard engagement on ?hauðr? heath; we encountered showers of weapons; the warband was in battle formation.

5   Hár þykki mér, hlýra,
    hinn jarl, es brá snarla –
    mær spyrr vitr ef væri
    valkǫstr – ara fǫstu:

en þekkjǫndum þykkir
þunnblás meginásar
hǫrð, sú's hilmir gerði
hríð, á Tempsar síðu.
             (Skj A 422 v 3)

This earl, who briskly broke the ravens' ['ara hlýra'] fast, seems to me outstanding – the clever girl asks if there was carnage – but the battle the king waged, on the bank of the Thames, seems a hard one to the bow-men ['þekkjǫndum þunnblás meginásar'].

6 Einráðit lét áðan
Ul/kell, þar's spjǫr gullu –
hǫrð óx hildar garða
hríð – víkinga at bíða:
ok slíðrhugaðr síðan
sátt á oss hvé mátti
byggs við bitran skeggja
brunns; tveir hugir runnu.
             (Skj A 220 v 3)

Ulfcetel decided beforehand to await the Vikings, where spears made their din – the fighting ['hildar garða hríð'] grew fierce – and you saw from our appearance afterwards how that remorseless man could prevail against the bitter keeper of the stone [stronghold] ['brunns byggs skeggja']; dissent arose.

7 Knútr réð ok bað bíða –
baugstalls – Dani alla –
lundr gekk rǫskr und randir
ríkr – vá herr við díki:
nær vas, sveit þar's sóttum,
Syn, með hjalm ok brynju,
elds sem olmum heldi
elg Rennandi kennir.
             (Skj A 422 v 4)

Knútr decided, and commanded the Danes all to wait – the mighty warrior ['baugstalls lundr'] went bravely into battle – the army fought alongside the moat: lady, where we engaged the enemy forces, with helmets and mailcoats, it was almost as if a man ['elds Rennandi kennir'] held a maddened elk.

8 Út mun ekkja líta –
opt glóa vǫpn á lopti
of hjalmtǫmum hilmi –
hrein sú's býr í steini
hvé sigrfíkinn sœkir
snarla borgar karla –
dynr á brezkum brynjum
blóðíss – Dana vísi.
    (Skj A 422–3 v 5)

The pure widow who lives in the stone [stronghold] will look out – often weapons glitter in the air above the king in his helmet – [to see] how valiantly the Danish leader, eager for victory, assails the city's garrison; the sword ['blóðíss'] rings against British mailcoats.

9 Hvern morgin sér horna
Hlǫkk á Tempsar bakka –
skalat hanga má hungra –
hjalmskóð roðin blóði: (Skj A 423 v 6)
rýðr eigi sá sveigir
sára lauk í ári,
hinn's Grjótvarar gætir,
gunnborðs, fyrir Stað norðan.
    (Skj A 221 v 5n)

Each morning, on the bank of the Thames, the lady ['horna Hlǫkk'] sees swords stained with blood; the raven must not go hungry: the warrior ['sveigir gunnborðs'] who watches over Steinvǫr, north of Stað, does not redden his sword ['sára lauk'] at this early hour.

10 Dag vas hvern þat's Hǫgna
hurð rjóðask nam blóði,
ár þar's úti vǫrum,
Ilmr, í fǫr með hilmi:
kneigum vér, síz vígum
varð nýlokit hǫrðum,

fyllar dags, í fǫgrum
fit, Lundúnum sitja.

(Skj A 423 v 7)

Every day the shield ['Hǫgna hurð'] was stained with blood, [?lady?], where we were out [?early?] on our expedition with the king: now that these hard battles have been recently concluded, we can settle down, lady ['fyllar dags fit'], in beautiful London.

Selected variants and emendations:

v 1 1 'gengom' Delagardie (Del); 2 'fareni' (?) Del; 4 'skafar' *Flateyjarbók* (*Flat*); '-rengs' Del. Cf *Skj* A 422.

v 2 1 'allan' Del; 2 'od-' *Knýtlinga* (*Kn*); '-senni' *Flat*; 3 'frett' Del; 'freyr' *Flat*; 4 'um' *Kn* (for 'ok'); 6 'aulun giods' *Flat*; 7 'ørt' *Kn*; 8 'skødaz' *Kn*; 'søda' *Kn*; 'seida' *Flat* (for 'samða'). Cf *Skj* A 422.

v 3 2 'riða' Del (for 'árna'); 4 'roðenu' Del; 6 'í' *Skj*; 'a' Del, *Flat*; 7 'gloðæ' Del. Cf *Skj* A 221.

v 4 1 'þottoð uier' Del; 5 'aðan er' *Flat* (for 'áðr an'); 'haurd' *Flat*; 7 'sku(ru)' Del; 8 'fylgr' *Flat*. Cf *Skj* A 220.

v 5 3 'at' Del (for 'ef'); 4 '-kǫstr' *Skj*; '-kost' Del; '-kaust' *Flat*; 5 'enn' *Flat*; 6 '-blad' (?) Del; 8 '-aar' Del. Cf *Skj* A 422.

v 6 2 'Ulf-' Del, *Flat*; 6 'sætt- ... motte' Del; 6 'bys' Del. Cf *Skj* A 220.

v 7 8 'elgr ennanda' *Flat*. Cf *Skj* A 422.

v 8 2 'jǫrn' Del (for 'vǫpn'); 5 'sœkir' not in Del; 7 'brezkar bryniur' *Kn*. Cf *Skj* A 422-3.

v 9 3 'skal ... mæy' Del; 4 'hræ-' *Kn* (for 'hjalm-'); 'roðenn' Del; lituð' *Kn*; 7 '-varrar' Del. Cf. *Skj* A 423 (for lines 1-4) and 221 (for lines 5-8).

v 10 2 'hud' Del; 5 'saz vigi' Del; 6 'gny-' Del. Cf *Skj* A 423

The textual history of 'Liðsmannaflokkr' has an important bearing on the structure and attribution of the poem and so must be discussed in detail. 'Liðsmannaflokkr' is found, complete or in part, in three prose compilations. The entire set of ten stanzas is included in two redactions of the saga of Óláfr helgi, these being the *Legendary Saga* (1982ed:48-53; 1922ed:11) and the fragmentarily preserved saga by Styrmir fróði Kárason (*Flateyjarbók* III 1868:237-9). In the third witness, *Knýtlinga saga* (1982ed:116; 1919-25ed:45-6), only two of the above stanzas are found. These are verse 2, as printed above, and a second set of eight lines, which comprises the first half of verse 9 followed by the second half of verse 8. The order is 9.1-4, 8.5-8, and finally 2.

The sources also differ as to the attribution of the *flokkr*. In the Óláfr sagas, Óláfr himself is the speaker, whereas in *Knýtlinga saga* they are a collective effort by the 'liðsmenn' / 'household troops' of Knútr.

The three prose compilations are related to each other through scribal, not oral, transmission, but the exact nature of the relationship is complex and to some extent conjectural. The two Óláfr sagas for their part are independent reworkings of the so-called 'Oldest Saga of St Óláfr,' fragments of which survive, and the *flokkr* is thought to have been incorporated in this work (Fidjestøl 1982:21–2). According to Jónas Kristjánsson the 'Oldest Saga' dates from around the turn of the thirteenth century (1972:223).

The sources of *Knýtlinga saga* have long been controversial. Bjarni Guðnason, following Gustav Albeck (1946), traces it back to a lost *Knúts saga*, which is referred to in *Heimskringla* (ÍF 35:xcii). In his opinion, the compilers of 'Oldest Saga' and *Knýtlinga saga* both obtained their text of 'Liðsmannaflokkr' and their notion of its context from *Knúts saga*. The date of *Knýtlinga saga* is uncertain but lies between 1250 and 1270 (Jónsson II 1923:775–8; Axelson 1959–60:144).

In the two Óláfr sagas, Óláfr's composition of the *flokkr* is associated with the end of Knútr's 1015–16 campaign in England. The Danish leader has won the submission of all England except London, where the garrison is stubbornly resisting him. Óláfr comes to his aid with a stratagem that delivers the city into his hands. In *Legendary Saga* the *flokkr* is then quoted, with the comment 'þenna flokk orti Óláfr eptir atlǫguna' / 'Óláfr made this *flokkr* after the attack' (1982ed:48). Following the *flokkr* is the sentence 'þenna flokk orti Óláfr hinn helgi þá er hann var með Knúti konungi' / 'St Óláfr made this *flokkr* when he was with king Knútr' (ibid 54). Styrmir's version is not preserved independently but can be found incorporated within an interpolation in the *Flateyjarbók* redaction of Snorri's *Óláfs saga helga* (II 1862:22–3; Nordal 1914:118). Although here the story of Knútr's and Óláfr's conquest is fragmented and in part derived from an additional source (A. Campbell 1949:87, 91), it is close to *Legendary Saga* where the *flokkr* is concerned. The verses are preceded by the sentence 'þenna flokk orti Óláfr konungr eptir er hann hafði unnit Lundúna borg' / 'King Óláfr made this *flokkr* after he had conquered London' (*Flateyjarbók* III 1868:237). Thus, so far as the author of *Legendary Saga* and Styrmir knew, the *flokkr* was composed after, not during, the siege of London.

In *Knýtlinga saga* Óláfr and his supposed stratagems play no part in the story, nor is the false assertion made that London was captured during the 1016 campaign (in fact Knútr gained the city as part of an accord with Edmund Ironside). In this account the *flokkr*'s composition seems to be placed during the siege (1919–25ed:45–6):

> Knútr konungr lagði ǫllum herinum upp til Lundúnaborgar ok setti þar um herbúðir sínar; síðan veittu þeir atsókn til borgarinnar, en borgarmenn vǫrðu. Svá segir í flokki þeim, er þá var ortr af liðsmǫnnum [v 9.1–4, 8.5–8]. Ok enn þetta [v 2]. Knútr konungr átti þar marga bardaga ok fekk eigi unnit borgina.

> King Knútr brought his entire army up to London and placed his shelters for the army round the city; then they attacked the city, but the garrison defended it. So it says in the *flokkr* which was made then by the household troops ... And also this ... King Knútr had many battles there and failed to capture the city.

Gustav Albeck thought that the author of *Knýtlinga saga* had reached the correct assessment of Knútr's success with the London siege fortuitously, in the course of eliminating Óláfr from the story (1946:34). But in a different context *Legendary Saga* also notes that Knútr did not manage to take London (1982ed:44). Bjarni Guðnason is therefore surely right in arguing that the *Knýtlinga* and alternative *Legendary Saga* accounts stem from *Knúts saga* (ÍF 35:xciv).

As we have seen, *Knýtlinga saga* does not credit Óláfr with any part of Knútr's 1016 campaign. Óláfr's movements at this period have proved difficult to reconstruct from the various sources. He was certainly in England in 1014, assisting Ethelred to regain his throne (Johnsen 1916:13–14). A year later (autumn 1015) Knútr began his invasion, having secured the aid, so Ove Moberg thinks, of the earl Eiríkr Hákonarson, who joined him with ships from Norway. Óláfr saw this for the opportunity it was and returned to Norway to claim the kingship, perhaps with Knútr's express sanction (Moberg 1941:28–30). Soon after the time, however, a tradition grew up that Óláfr had fought in England in 1016 as Knútr's ally. This tradition can be traced from William of Jumièges and Adam of Bremen to Saxo's *Gesta Danorum* and the brief Norwegian histories *Historia Norwegiae* and *Ágrip*, and thence to the sagas of Óláfr, where his part in the conquest was exaggerated out of recognition in the way we have seen. Moberg thought the tradition might have had its root in some service rendered to Knútr by Óláfr before the return to Norway, but that is hard to believe, because Óláfr's last actions in England, as recorded by Sigvatr in 'Víkingarvísur' and by Óttarr svarti in 'Hǫfuðlausn,' seem to have been fought on Ethelred's side and to have included a raid against the people of Lindsey in punishment for their having assisted Knútr (Poole 1980:275). Admittedly, our sources are far from full, even the *Anglo-Saxon Chronicle*, and no doubt more was going on during 1015–16 than can now be reconstructed. Even so, it seems very unlikely that having established a toe-hold on Norway Óláfr would have been in a position to return to England in 1016 to help Knútr with his siege (A. Campbell 1949:79). *Knýtlinga saga* is likely, then, to be historically accurate and faithfully reproducing *Knúts saga* material when it offers an account of Knútr's 1016 campaign that excludes Óláfr.

Óláfr is therefore unlikely to have been on the spot to compose the 'Liðsmannaflokkr,' or at least those verses in it that deal with the London siege. Recognizing this, Finnur Jónsson tried to solve the resulting problem of attribution by dividing the *flokkr* into two groups of stanzas. He identified one group as a series of *lausavísur* made by Óláfr during 1009–12 while campaigning in England in alliance with the Danish warlord Þorkell inn hávi. The other group he took to be a short *flokkr* composed by Knútr's men in 1016 (I 1920:459). To the 1009–12 group Jónsson assigned verse 3, which refers to a Norwegian girl-friend, verse 4, a description of the battle at 'Hringmaraheiðr' / 'Ringmere heath' in 1010, verse 6, which describes a battle against Ulfcetel (evidently the military commander in East Anglia), and the second *helmingr* of verse 9, which again refers to the Norwegian girl-friend. Admitting that the allocation of stanzas between the two groups was to some degree arbitrary, Jónsson dallied with the possibility that further, unspecified stanzas should be transferred from the 1016 to the 1009–12 group. Jónsson's distribution was adopted by Margaret Ashdown in her edition, but she remarked that the curtailed version of the *flokkr* was 'exceedingly puzzling' and that possibly 'further expurgation' was needed – again without specifying how that would be achieved (1930:206).

The text of the *flokkr*, as presented in *Skjaldedigtning*, is certainly incoherent. If we read verse 5 as it stands there (B 392 v 3) we find ourselves left in the dark as to who 'hinn jarl' / 'this earl' is: the reference might be to Eiríkr jarl of Hlaðir or to Þorkell inn hávi. But if we read the stanza in its context (as presented above and in the editions of *Legendary Saga* and *Flateyjarbók*) the earl is clearly identified as Þorkell by the mention of his name in the preceding stanza. The natural course, therefore, would be to group verse 4 with verse 5, rather than as a separate composition, printed 182 pages earlier (*Skj* B 210 v 2).

Finnur Jónsson's 'judgment of Solomon' does such violence to the text and produces such poor results that we must question its necessity. Various scholars, notably Gustav Albeck (1946:35), Anne Holtsmark (1954:104–5), Dietrich Hofmann (1955:61), and Jan de Vries (I 1964:281), have expressed doubts about it, but without attempting a systematic explanation of the *Legendary Saga* and *Flateyjarbók* text. Some have tried to remove part of the basis for Jónsson's division by casting doubts on one or both of the variant attributions. Albeck believed that the attribution in *Knýtlinga saga* had no independent authority, being the result of a deliberate suppression of the Óláfr attribution by a compiler who thought it historically incorrect (1946:34–5): similarly Alistair Campbell (1946–53:247). Moberg suggested that the *Knýtlinga saga* compiler dropped the Óláfr ascription because he knew that Knútr and Óláfr were on terms of hostility for most of their lives (1941:86n56): Anne Holtsmark also thought political reasoning of some kind had been involved (1954:105). Dietrich Hofmann was more inclined to give credence to *Knýtlinga saga* as an independent source (1955:60): he doubted that Óláfr was the author, but as a tentative compromise suggested that verse 4 might originally have been of Óláfr's composition and then subsequently absorbed into the ten-stanza work composed collectively by Knútr's soldiers (ibid 61). He believed that this ten-stanza version should be treated as a single poem and not tampered with editorially (ibid 62). Bjarni Guðnason goes a step further by firmly rejecting Óláfr's authorship. He argues that *Knýtlinga saga* faithfully reproduces *Knúts saga* in crediting Knútr's *liðsmenn* with the poem; the ascription to Óláfr in the sagas of that king represents an innovation that is in keeping with the general tendency for stories to cluster round his name (*ÍF* 35:xcv). Bjarni does, however, leave open the possibility of composition by a single *liðsmann*. Jan de Vries is exceptional in rejecting both attributions: he explained the mixture of Þorkell and Knútr material in the poem as pointing to late (twelfth-century) composition from a source where the events of 1009–10 and 1016 had become confused (I 1964:281). But the linguistic evidence is rather for composition in the eleventh century in an Anglo-Scandinavian milieu (Poole 1987:284–6).

The variant attributions, even if more firmly substantiated, would not in themselves prove that two originally separate sets of stanzas had been conflated in 'Oldest Saga.' Disagreements between sources about the authorship of verse are a familiar phenomenon: examples of rival 'claimants' are Eyvindr skáldaspillir and Þorgeirr høggvinkinni (*Skj* A 71), Kormakr and Gunnlaugr ormstunga (*Skj* A 80; Poole 1981:481–2), and Þorleifr skúma Þorkelsson and Vígfúss Vígaglúmsson (*Skj* A 117). Two similarly named men, Hrómundr inn halti and Hávarðr halti, vie for two *helmingar*; one of these *helmingar* has yet a third claimant, Þorbjǫrn þyna (*ÍF* 6:321n). Also three-cornered and especially relevant here because it occurs in the Óláfr sagas is the competition for a stanza that the 'Oldest Saga' and *Legendary Saga* give to Óttarr svarti, Styrmir to Bersi Skáldtorfuson, and Snorri to Sigvatr (*Skj* A 277: Bersi *lv*.1; cf Nordal 1914:110 and Fidjestøl 1982:23).

Although the variant attributions are not sufficient grounds for a dismemberment of the *flokkr*, a complicating factor is the mention of the Norwegian girl-friend in two of the ten verses. The girl-friend is named as Grjótvǫr, an *ofljóst* (or synonym-substituting) form of the familiar name Steinvǫr. The speaker of verses 3 and 9 reproaches Steinvǫr's father or guardian for his unwillingness to join the present expedition and his jealous possessiveness concerning his daughter or ward, at home 'north of Staðr' (this presumably being Cape Stad in Norway). In another of the *Flateyjarbók* excerpts from Styrmir's saga of Óláfr, the king makes a verse about the loss of a girl-friend where also there is mention of Staðr' and a play on the idea of stones (III 1868:239–40): the name of the woman is not given. The text is difficult (see *Skj* B 211 v 7, Kock NN 1110 and 2773, Kock I 1946: 110 v 7, Einarsson 1961:25, and Mundal 1984 [draft version]). If we believe that this verse is really of Óláfr's making and that the woman referred to there is the same as in 'Liðsmannaflokkr' 3 and 9, then conceivably verses 3 and 9 (and perhaps other stanzas) should be seen as correctly ascribed to Óláfr in 'Oldest Saga.'

The alternative, however, as Bjarni Guðnason has indicated, is to look sceptically at the Óláfr attributions, which are the source of our difficulties. A variety of love verses and love stories are attached to Óláfr, but they seem apocryphal (Poole 1985C; cf Hofmann 1955:60). The association of 'Liðsmannaflokkr' and the Staðr *lausavísa* with him is not difficult to account for. A very well-attested event in his early career is his participation in an attack on London in 1009. The *Anglo-Saxon Chronicle* includes the attack in its account of the doings of Þorkell's army, with which we know Óláfr was involved, and his participation is confirmed by Sigvatr's 'Víkingarvísur.' But the most famous siege of London took place in 1016, and from quite early confusion arose as to who had taken part in the two different campaigns. Some muddlement can perhaps already be detected in Sigvatr's mention of a 'díki' / 'ditch, earthwork,' describing the 1009 action, because it was evidently in 1016 that circumvallation played a prominent part in the Viking offensive (A. Campbell 1949:77n4). Out of a confusion of this sort, Óláfr became credited in tradition with a part in the 1016 siege and in the imaginary storming of the city. Because the 'Liðsmannaflokkr' mentions the siege and occupation of London it could very readily have become attracted to Óláfr's name at this stage. The attribution to him might have been felt to be not an innovation but a mere particularization of the individual confederate of Knútr who was responsible for the poem's composition. The mention of Þorkell in the *flokkr* may also have helped in this process: side by side with the traditions that Óláfr assisted Knútr in 1015–16 existed better-supported traditions, to be discussed presently, to the effect that Þorkell had done so as well. Óláfr and Þorkell's well-known alliance of 1009–12 could therefore be imagined as continuing into 1015–16. The attribution of the Staðr *lausavísa* to Óláfr and probably also the composition of the verse would follow at a later stage. The *lausavísa* can be seen as a mere elaboration of verses 3 and 9 in the *flokkr*. Steinvǫr is not heard of elsewhere and may have been no more than the stereotypical 'girl back home.'

I have already noted that *Knýtlinga saga* and the two Óláfr sagas are not agreed on the arrangement of the *helmingar* in verses 8 and 9. Remarkably enough, the effect of the arrangement in *Knýtlinga saga* is to exclude any mention of Steinvǫr and Staðr; instead of this material we have further detail of the fighting (8.5–8). Finnur Jónsson believed that here *Knýtlinga saga* preserved the original state of the *flokkr* and that 9.1–4 and 5–8 could not belong together (I 1920:459). In fact, though, the stanza as organized in 'Oldest Saga' reads coherently. The words 'hjalmskóð roðin blóði' in 9.4 evidently prepare for 'rýðr ... / sára lauk' in 9.5–6. Also to be borne in mind is the syntax of 'líta' in verse 8. This verb may take an object : 'hvé' in 8.5, introducing a noun clause, supplies the object, whereas 9.5–8 cannot have that function. Conversely, 'sér' in verse 9 has its object in 9.4: it is therefore not in need of the second object that comes with 8.5–8, but combines naturally with 9.5–8. The arrangement in 'Oldest Saga' therefore seems preferable.

Finnur Jónsson explained 9.5–8 away as a mere duplicate of 3.5–8, originating in oral tradition, but the view that the poet deliberately repeated himself is more reasonable (Hofmann 1955:61). Bjarne Fidjestøl points out that verse 9 contains other repetitions as well; the motif of a woman watching is repeated from verse 8, as we saw, and 'á Tempsar bakka' is similar to 'á Tempsar síðu' in verse 5. The function of verse 9 in structural terms is to recapitulate material used earlier in the poem. This evidence points to abridgment in *Knýtlinga saga*, not interpolation in 'Oldest Saga' (Fidjestøl 1982:61). As Fidjestøl points out, heavy repetition seems to have led to similar telescoping in the transmission of the Hrómundr halti verses (ibid 63).

The telescoped version in *Knýtlinga saga* might be due to a memorial or scribal lapse. It is also possible, though, that the redactor purposely avoided 3.5–8 and 9.5–8 because he knew the love verse with the Staðr allusion, which Styrmir had included in his saga of Óláfr, and felt that the present Steinvǫr references pointed too directly to Óláfr, whom he had otherwise carefully kept out of the story. Snorri himself was capable of omitting verses that did not agree with his other material, as we shall see in studying the history of the Torf-Einarr *flokkr* (cf also Fidjestøl 1982:41–2).

Bjarni Guðnason implies that *Knúts saga* contained all ten verses of the 'Liðsmannaflokkr' (ÍF 35:xciv–xcvi). This is plausible because, as we have seen, *Legendary Saga* reproduces *Knúts saga* material (the statement that Knútr never captured London) at just that point in the chronology. Much of the content of the *flokkr* is of course directly relevant to a biography of Knútr. The Þorkell content can be compared, where relevance to a life of Knútr is concerned, with the information on Úlfr jarl that apparently was also included in *Knúts saga* (and from there taken over into *Fagrskinna*).

Although only four *helmingar* of the *flokkr* appear in *Knýtlinga saga*, as against twenty in 'Oldest Saga,' that again is no indication of interpolation in the latter source. The *Knýtlinga saga* compiler makes clear that the verses cited are merely excerpts from a longer work: 'svá segir í flokki þeim, er þá var ortr af liðsmǫnnum' / 'so it says in the *flokkr* which was then made by the *liðsmenn*' (ÍF 35:116).

Zealous abridgment is one of the hallmarks of *Knýtlinga saga* (eg ÍF 35:cx and 130). Bjarni Guðnason suggested that the life of Knútr's saintly namesake was intended as the focus of the saga and the lives of previous kings as a mere introduction to it (xciii). The compiler cuts most ruthlessly when the same episode had already been dealt with in *Heimskringla*, as is often the case, but even where it was not covered in Snorri's work the material may be abridged, though less severely, and skaldic verses omitted. This is best seen where *Knýtlinga saga* and *Fagrskinna* are both borrowing from *Knúts saga*, as in the account of Knútr's pilgrimage to Rome, which Snorri omits entirely (ÍF 35:123 and

Fagrskinna 1902–3ed:188–9, respectively). In the *Fagrskinna* narrative of the Rome journey a verse from Sigvatr's *Knútsdrápa* (v 10) is cited: it is missing from *Knýtlinga saga*, although not already cited by Snorri in *Heimskringla*. Additionally, important information is omitted when the *Knýtlinga saga* compiler neglects to explain that Knútr was in company for part of his journey with the emperor Conrad: this omission leaves the subsequent statement that the emperor made money available to Knútr unprepared for. By contrast, *Fagrskinna* covers both these points (Albeck 1946:72n47). The supposed connection between Knútr's journey and the marriage of his daughter Gunnhildr to Henry, the future emperor, is not noted in *Knýtlinga saga*. Although historically false, the connection was made by writers as early as Adam of Bremen and Henry of Huntingdon: the allusion to it in *Fagrskinna* is therefore presumably another instance where that text reproduces *Knúts saga* more faithfully than does *Knýtlinga saga* (íF 35:cv). The brevity of *Knýtlinga saga* compared to *Fagrskinna* on the Rome journey, an important enterprise on the king's part, is the more striking when one recalls that *Fagrskinna* itself is not noted for diffuseness. The only obvious example of a detail present in *Knýtlinga saga* but missing from *Fagrskinna* is the information that Knútr's route to Rome took in Flanders, which can be traced back through *Knúts saga* to the *Encomium Emmæ* (cf Moberg 1945:22). This, along with other considerations, excludes the possibility that *Knýtlinga saga* derived its account of the Rome journey from *Fagrskinna* (íF 35:xcii).

The *Knýtlinga saga* compiler was sometimes disorganized in the presentation of material. The statement that Knútr went to Rome by way of Flanders is placed at the end of a description of Knútr's generosity en route instead of in its natural place at the beginning, in association with the words 'fór hann suðr til Róms' / 'he went south to Rome.'

The almost total silence concerning Þorkell inn hávi seems more calculated. He crops up only once in *Knýtlinga saga*, far less than his historical importance would warrant (íF 35:103). In an episode that Styrmir and *Knýtlinga saga* both have (*Flateyjarbók* II 1862:23 and íF 35:108, respectively) and that seems to go back to *Knúts saga* (íF 35:xcvi), the *Knýtlinga saga* compiler has apparently dropped Þorkell from the story. If that was a policy, it could account for the omission of Þorkell verses from the *flokkr*.

In sum, these parallels justify us in positing an abridgment and rearrangement of 'Liðsmannaflokkr' in *Knýtlinga saga*. They eliminate any need to suppose that the *flokkr* in 'Oldest Saga' represents a conflation of two originally separate groups of verses.

The result is that 'Oldest Saga' is to be preferred for its disposition of the *flokkr* and *Knýtlinga saga* for its attribution; neither redaction has reproduced the material in *Knúts saga* with total faithfulness. As to the attribution, we cannot establish definitively whether the *flokkr* was composed collectively by *liðsmenn* or singly by a spokesman for them. What can be shown is that, however produced, the constituent verses, taken together, have the continuity and cohesion of a poem. The *flokkr* is recognizably in the same genre as 'Friðgerðarflokkr' and the Nissa section of *Sexstefja*. Furthermore, the mixing of Knútr and Þorkell material need not be an outcome of late or multiple composition: it can be explained, as I shall show presently, as a reflex of the politics of England in the second decade of the eleventh century. 'Liðsmannaflokkr' reads quite differently from a seemingly genuine collective composition in *Sturlunga saga*, commenting on the attack on Sturla's household by the Vatnsfirðingar. Although these verses on the Sauðafellsfǫr display some stylistic unity there is little narrative progress; instead, some of the verses are intended as a reply to others, and they show the outcome of the battle in a variety of different partisan lights (1946ed 1:329–32).

A source of apparent disunity in the poem, as already noted, is the presence of praises to both Knútr and Þorkell. The shift of subject from one leader to the other comes just before the midpoint of the *flokkr*, with the second *helmingr* of verse 5 functioning as a linking passage. Knútr is not identified immediately, but the word 'hilmir' must refer to him in the light of its subsequent use in 8.3 and 10.4. The stanza begins by calling Þorkell 'hár' and alluding to the heavy toll of English dead at his battle and then proceeds, via the conjunction 'en,' to the statement that Knútr's battle struck his comrades as 'hǫrð.' The honourable general epithet 'hár,' for Þorkell, will be matched soon, in 7.4, by the similar epithet 'ríkr,' for Knútr; these adjectives either already were or else later became the standing nicknames for these two leaders: Þorkell hávi, Knútr ríki. When Knútr's battle is called 'hǫrð' that is precisely the rather colourless adjective applied to Þorkell's battle on the heath in 4.8. The motif of Þorkell feeding ravens in 5.2–4 is matched for Knútr in 9.3. Some weighing of the merits of the two men seems to be going on, but it is curiously even-handed, as if there were a fear of exalting one at the expense of the other. The conjunction 'en,' though translated 'but' above, need not be strongly adversative and here could be rendered as 'and.' Nonetheless, beneath this superficial impartiality, one senses that Knútr is being given pride of place: he has a slight advantage in the stanza allocation – eleven *helmingar* to Þorkell's nine. With greater partisanship, all but one of his stanzas mention his personal participation in the fighting, whereas Þorkell's is mentioned in only two of his stanzas.

Praise poems normally praise one patron at a time. Different ways of explaining the divided attention here have been, or can be, contemplated. As we have seen, Finnur Jónsson saw the Þorkell stanzas as chiefly of Óláfr's composition, while the Knútr stanzas were the work of the *liðsmenn*. Even with Óláfr eliminated from authorship one might see the Þorkell verses as produced by one faction among the *liðsmenn* and the Knútr verses by another, being subsequently amalgamated to form a collective composition. We have also seen that Jan de Vries regarded the *flokkr* as a late, antiquarian effort. But the exclusive concentration on Þorkell and Knútr seems strange if we imagine this poem as an effusion in the style of 'Jómsvíkingadrápa'; such a poem would have been likely to concern itself also with the other Scandinavian participants in the English campaigns, notably Sveinn of Denmark, Eiríkr jarl of Hlaðir, and Óláfr helgi. The deliberate association of Knútr and Þorkell that we instead find can be construed as indicating an awareness of English politics in the second decade of the eleventh century – something natural not in an antiquarian poem but in a contemporary work, produced in England.

An examination of Þorkell's part in the English campaigns and his relations with Knútr goes far, I think, to explain the peculiar distribution of material in the 'Liðsmannaflokkr.' Þorkell first came to England in 1009, as a Viking raider, and from then until 1012 he fought a number of actions against the English, including London and Ringmere ('Hringmaraheiðr'). His standing as a leader can be gauged from Simon Keynes's comment that the arrival of his 'immense raiding army ... can probably be regarded as one of the most catastrophic events of Ethelred's reign' (1980:216–17). In Keynes's opinion, Ethelred's reaction included the Agnus Dei coinage, a special issue (Dolley 1978:127), and a 'remarkable programme of public prayer.' 'It is apparent also from the *Anglo-Saxon Chronicle* that the invading army, in its size and organization, was quite unlike any that had previously ravaged in the country' (1980:219). 'There can be little doubt that the period when Thorkell's army was ravaging the country was the turning-point in the history of King Ethelred's struggles against the Vikings ... The events of 1009–12 ... seriously damaged the will of the English to resist and indeed their capacity for resistance at all' (ibid 221–2).

Although Þorkell was a Dane, we should not think of this campaign as an attempt to aid the Danish royal house in its designs upon England.

Norse tradition, notably *Jómsvíkinga saga*, makes Þorkell the brother of Sigvaldi, earl of Jómsborg, and it may have been there that Þorkell had his power base. However, he also had a measure of power in Denmark. According to the *Encomium Emmæ* Þorkell was Sveinn's military commander and took a large part of the Danish army to England in 1009 (ibid 219), along with men from elsewhere in Scandinavia. In 1012 Þorkell showed his independence from Sveinn by going over to Ethelred: he became a valuable, if unpopular, ally of the English royal house, checking the progress of the Danish king's invasion in 1013. But the *Anglo-Saxon Chronicle* narrative for the year 1013 shows that Þorkell's army, like Sveinn's, ravaged the country 'as often as they pleased' (EHD 246), in spite of Ethelred's payments and supplying of provisions: Plummer commented that Þorkell's forty-five ships seem 'to have been scarcely less fatal to the English now than in the days of their avowed hostility' (*Anglo-Saxon Chronicle* 1892-9 II:191). Whichever side he fought on, Þorkell was an independent war-lord first and an ally or subject second.

Early in 1014 Ethelred fled the country, but Sveinn's death on 3 February of that year gave him an opportunity to return, assisted, as we have seen, by Óláfr and Þorkell: Knútr, who had accompanied Sveinn, was forced by the severity of their campaign to flee to Denmark. The *Encomium Emmæ*, from its own partisan position, offers some interesting but rather equivocal information on Þorkell's thinking and activities during the confused period that followed. According to the encomiast Þorkell stayed on in England after Knútr's forced departure: he chose to 'make peace with the natives rather than to return home like one who had, in the end, been expelled' (1949ed:16–17). In his next words the encomiast tacitly concedes that in doing so Þorkell left his loyalty to Knútr open to suspicion, even if an honourable interpretation could be placed on his behaviour: 'And, according to some ['ut quidam aiunt'], he did not do this because he despised his lord, but in order that when Knútr returned with renewed forces and his brother's help to subdue the kingdom, he might either incline the chief men of the kingdom to surrender by his counsel, or if this plan were not a success, attack the incautious enemy from behind as they fought against his lord. And the truth of this is apparent from the fact that he kept with him a very great part of the soldiers, and that the king did not let more than sixty ships depart in company with himself' (ibid). These words suggest a 'secret arrangement' between Knútr and Þorkell (EHD 138), but they are contradicted in the speech that almost immediately after is assigned to Knútr.

The king tells his brother Haraldr that Þorkell, 'deserting us as he did our father, has settled in [England], keeping with him a large part of our ships, and I believe that he will be against us, but nevertheless he will not prevail' (*Encomium Emmae* 1949 ed:17). Dorothy Whitelock suggested that in the aftermath some of Þorkell's contemporaries were favourably disposed to him and others not; the encomiast, not certain what to believe, did not trouble to reconcile the different views (EHD 138–9). Alistair Campbell's view was that the encomiast had blundered in his attempts to depict Þorkell as a consistent supporter of the Danish royal house (1949:lv). It seems reasonable to conclude that relations between Knútr and Þorkell were very strained, perhaps even hostile, in the latter part of 1014.

Discussing Þorkell's role during the next two years, Campbell argued that 'there is absolutely no evidence that Thorkell was not true to the English cause all through until ... he automatically became Knútr's subject, when the latter became king of all England in 1017' (ibid 75). But more prevalent among historians has been the view of Freeman that Þorkell was 'prominent' on Knútr's side during the war with Edmund Ironside, the son of Ethelred. Freeman suggested that he might have changed sides after Ethelred's death, at the Southampton election of Knútr, or when the ealdormann Eadric Streona 'seduced forty ships from the [English] king, and then went over to Cnut' (Freeman 1877 I:670). This statement in the *Anglo-Saxon Chronicle* entry for 1015 is supplemented by Florence of Worcester with the information that the ships were 'manned by Danish soldiers' (EHD 248 and n1). Campbell comments that 'it is usually assumed that these were the remains of the forty-five ships of Thorkell's fleet, which entered English service in 1012' and that this assumption is 'highly probable, for it seems unlikely that a native English fleet of such size was then in being.' He concedes that 'it is open to those who so wish to assume that Thorkell went over to Knútr with these ships' (1949:74n3). The main source for the idea that Þorkell supported Knútr during 1015–16 is once again the *Encomium Emmæ*. The encomiast makes Þorkell have a change of heart, sailing to Denmark in quest of a reconciliation. During a stay of more than a month he urges Knútr 'to return to England, saying that he could easily overcome people whose country was known far and wide to both of them. In particular, he said that he had left thirty ships in England with a most faithful army, who would receive them with honour when they came, and would conduct them through the whole extent of the country' (1949ed:18–19). Add to these thirty ships the nine ships that brought

Þorkell and his men to Denmark for this visit, and it looks likely that the encomiast, with his thirty-nine ships, and the chronicler, with his forty ships, are talking about the same fleet. Furthermore, it looks likely that Eadric was at the head of the 'most faithful army' who would receive Knútr and his Danish confederates 'with honour.' Subsequently, the encomiast shows Þorkell preparing the way for Knútr in a battle at Sherston and fighting as Knútr's ally 'in Aesceneduno loco,' ie at the battle of Assandun (ibid 24). At Sherston Þorkell takes charge at a time that he judges opportune to 'demonstrate his fidelity to his lord' (ibid 21). 'The English, indeed, were the more bold at first, and cut down the Danes with terrible slaughter, to such an extent that they nearly won the victory and would have compelled their enemies to flee, if the latter, held back by their leader's [ie Þorkell's] words and being mindful of their own bravery, had not regarded flight with shame ... This was the first honour which Thorkell brought to the arms of Knútr, and for this he afterwards received a large part of the country' (ibid 21–3). When Þorkell is mentioned as a participant at Assandun he appears in a somewhat legendary context. The Danes possess a miraculous banner, normally of plain white silk but at times auspicious for victory displaying a raven 'opening its beak, flapping its wings, and restive on its feet, but very subdued and drooping with its whole body when they were defeated. Looking out for this, Thorkell, who had fought the first battle, said: "Let us fight manfully, comrades, for no danger threatens us: for to this the restive raven of the prophetic banner bears witness." When the Danes heard this, they were rendered bolder, and clad with suits of mail, encountered the enemy' (ibid 25). Although Þorkell is not mentioned in the lengthy battle description that ensues, the harangue quoted above is sufficient to give him a more salient part in the narrative than Knútr, who is merely noted as having the victory (ibid 27).

The *Anglo-Saxon Chronicle*, like almost all the other sources, is silent on Þorkell's doings between 1014 and 1017. The *Encomium Emmæ* is supported in its account of Þorkell's aid to Knútr in 1015–16 only by somewhat marginal sources. In his *L'Estoire des Engleis* Gaimar gives Þorkell a leading role at the battle of Sherston (1960ed:134):

E il vait mult Kenut guerriant
Tant que Daneis sunt asemblez.
Od ost sunt sur lui alez.
Li cuens Turkil cest ost menad,

Le fiz del rei encuntre alad.
Dunc vindrent a [Escorestan]
L'endemain de saint Johan.

And [Edmund] goes on fighting Knútr for a long time, until the Danes are assembled. With their host they came against him. Earl Þorkell led that host; the king's son advanced to meet him. Then they came to Sherston the day after St John's Day.

Gaimar places Eadric's desertion of Edmund at this period, though, as Bell comments, 'it is not quite clear whether Gaimar thought that he changed sides during the battle or that the defection had taken place earlier' (1960ed:255). Although the basis of Gaimar's work is a lost version of the *Anglo-Saxon Chronicle*, from the reign of Edgar it becomes a compilation from a variety of unknown sources (ibid lxvii). In spite of the low general standing of *L'Estoire des Engleis* as a historical source (Gransden 1974:209 and 212), significance has been attached to a few of Gaimar's statements (Lloyd 1939 I:202 and n32, Gransden 1974:212).

The other sources on Þorkell's aid to Knútr in 1015–16 are Scandinavian. Of these the fullest is the epilogue to *Jómsvíkinga saga* that occurs only in *Flateyjarbók* (I 1860:203–5). Here Þorkell, Knútr, and Eiríkr (meaning Eadric Streona?) depart from Denmark with 'eight hundred' ships (ie probably 960). Þorkell, with thirty ships, kills Ulfcetel; Knútr takes London. Þorkell intercepts Queen Emma as she tries to escape in a ship and encourages Knútr to marry her, advice that leads to a later falling-out between the two men. Campbell was sceptical of the authority of this text, classing it with 'works like *Yngvars saga [víðfǫrla]*, where a solemn historical background is provided for legends of the wildest type' (A. Campbell 1949:91). *Knýtlinga saga* states merely that Þorkell accompanied Knútr to England (1919–25ed:36), while *Legendary Saga* notes that he was with Knútr during the siege of London, again perhaps confusing the 1009 and 1016 actions (1982ed:46).

Although any conclusion from evidence such as the foregoing is bound to be unsafe, the tradition that Þorkell helped Knútr in England is not confined to the *Encomium Emmæ* and may have had a basis in fact. If we wish to connect Þorkell's help with Eadric's desertion of Edmund, then following the *Anglo-Saxon Chronicle* we must date it to late 1015, a considerable time after Knútr's return to England. Alternatively, we can keep Þorkell's and Eadric's initiatives separate, believing that Þorkell visited Denmark to pledge his help and accompanied Knútr in his return to England (following the *Encomium Emmæ*). Eric John accords great importance to Þorkell's participation, crediting to him and Eiríkr jarl jointly the feat of having 'masterminded Cnut's bid for the crown; [Eiríkr] and Thorkell seem to have won the battles' (*The Anglo-Saxons* 199). In his view, Knútr 'was a winner rather than a conqueror'; 'the Encomiast's picture of Cnut in general is no more than polite ... he gives [Þorkell and Eiríkr] the credit for the victorious campaign. He also makes it clear that the campaign was a costly one for the Danes as well as the English, and that Cnut had to take this into account in choosing his policies. Certainly Cnut conducted himself like a man with debts to pay' (ibid 208).

After this obscure phase, Þorkell achieves new prominence in the *Anglo-Saxon Chronicle* with his appointment as earl of East Anglia in 1017. A.E. Christensen notes that this elevation, as with Eadric Streona, was certainly more a result of political necessity than an expression of trust on the king's part: the careers of both earls were correspondingly short-lived (1969:261). On the other hand, Þorkell was able to eclipse Eiríkr. Alistair Campbell suggested that the wane of Eiríkr's importance came about because of the 'remote situation' of his Northumbrian earldom (1949:70); it may also have been especially difficult to govern, because of competition from the brother of the previous earl (*The Anglo-Saxons* 199). The *Encomium Emmæ* makes specific note of Þorkell's knowledge of England, and this too might have given him an advantage over Eiríkr (Larson 1909–10:723). Whatever the causes, Þorkell invariably signs 'first of the *duces*' in witnessing Knútr's charters from the earliest ones issued till 1019 (A. Campbell 1949:75). His name heads the lists of Knútr's earls in the Thorney *Liber Vitæ* (Whitelock 1937–45:131–2). He is the only magnate actually named by Knútr in his 'letter to the people of England,' which was written, according to Dorothy Whitelock, from Denmark at the end of 1019 or the beginning of 1020 (*EHD* 452). Whitelock points out that 'since only Earl Thorkel is instructed to deal with those who defy the laws, it seems probable that the letter was sent to him while he was acting as regent in Cnut's absence' (ibid). Clauses 9 and 10 in particular indicate a close collaboration between king and earl: 'If anyone, ecclesiastic or layman, Dane or Englishman, is so presumptuous as to defy God's law and my royal authority or the secular law, and he will not make amends and desist according to the direction of my bishops, I then pray, and also command, Earl Thorkel, if he can, to cause the evil-doer to do right. If he cannot, then it is my will that with the power of us both he shall destroy him in the land or drive him out of the land, whether he be of high or low rank' (ibid 453). Near in time to this (1020) is an interesting event recorded by Florence of Worcester (ibid 313): 'In the same year the church which King Cnut and Earl Thorkel had erected on the hill which is called [Assandun] was dedicated with great ceremony and glory in their presence by Wulfstan, archbishop of York, and many other bishops.' In the following year Þorkell was banished from the English kingdom for reasons that have never been clearly established (M.W. Campbell 1971:70). The final mention of him comes in the C manuscript of the *Anglo-Saxon Chronicle*, which states that Knútr made Þorkell governor of Denmark and guardian of his son, in exchange taking Þorkell's son back to England (entry for 1023). As M.W. Campbell has emphasized, there are reasons for doubting the correctness of this report, which may stem from a confusion with Ulfr jarl (1971:71–2).

This evidence suggests cumulatively that English subjects would have seen Knútr's and Þorkell's fortunes as closely intertwined right through the historical period covered in 'Liðsmannaflokkr' and, indeed, well beyond the time of that poem's composition.

Any Viking who had fought right through the English campaigns, from 1009 to 1016, would have had additional reason to associate Þorkell and Knútr – as distributors of the Danegeld. A rune-stone at Yttergärde, in Uppland, Sweden, commemorates a warrior-turned-farmer named Ulfr who had taken three Danegelds in England. The first was distributed by Tosti (probably Skǫglar-Tósti, a Swedish war-lord), the second by Þorkell, presumably in 1012, and the third by Knútr, presumably in 1018 (von Friesen 1909:60, 66–73). Somebody in Ulfr's position would have had ample reason to applaud the sentiments of 'Liðsmannaflokkr' when it praises both Danish leaders.

The events of the years 1009 to 1016 and the complex relationship between Knútr and Þorkell would have imposed special demands and constraints on a skald charged with the task of commemorating their deeds. The double focus of the poem arises from the fact that Knútr and Þorkell could be seen as joint rulers of England; the third possible contender for praise, Eiríkr, had been relegated to a subordinate position in England and ousted from his original power base in Norway. Þorkell's position, by contrast, was not clearly subordinate: to some degree he possessed an independent power base, one 'out of Cnut's control as king of both England and Denmark' (*The Anglo-Saxons* 208). In practical terms, Knútr may have been more Þorkell's overlord than his king. The poet presumably also had to cope with the uncomfortable truth that

Þorkell was a more accomplished military leader than the king. Although his alliance with Ethelred between 1012 and 1014 rendered him a suspect ally from Knútr's point of view, Þorkell essentially made the English wars winnable through his devastating campaign of 1009 to 1012. There is also the less-well-substantiated tradition that Þorkell, along with Eiríkr, won the 1015–16 campaign for Knútr. In a poem about the eventual Danish success in the English wars Knútr's prowess could be magnified, for instance by the implication that the siege of London led directly to the occupation of the city, the siege being clearly marked as a strategy of Knútr's choosing ('Knútr réð ok bað bíða / ... Dani alla'). As we have seen, Knútr is accorded slightly more lines and a more active fighting role than Þorkell. By contrast, Þorkell's role is downplayed: the opening three stanzas and even verse 4 are vague as to the location and outcome of the fighting and as to Þorkell's role as leader. The *Encomium Emmæ* shows how a dominant contribution could be ascribed to Þorkell by a near-contemporary writer with suitable motivation and informants. Even in the 'Liðsmannaflokkr,' which is evidently partisan to Knútr, the king's dependence on Þorkell, though it might be downplayed, could not be ignored. In sum, the apparent disunity of the poem, as to topic, is a reflex of the complex politics of its time.

Again, although at first blush this poem appears chaotic in its narrative technique, there are parallels to hand in other poems of this genre. The use of tenses in 'Liðsmannaflokkr' is similar to what we saw in 'Friðgerðarflokkr.' The poem begins (vv 1–3) with a series of verbs in the present tense. Although manuscript forms can be misleading (Delagardie has the preterite 'gengom,' instead of present 'gǫngum,' in the very first line), there is at least substantial agreement among the manuscripts, and some forms are guaranteed by the *hendingar* ('fregni' in 1.4 and 'leggr' in 1.7). The first stanza begins as a harangue, and the present-tense verbs are imperatives ('let us go,' 'let us be,' 'let us brandish'). The speaker is imagined urging on his comrades. But after this the present-tense verbs are mostly indicative and carry the narrative forwards: thus 'leggr ... Engla gnótt' and 'margr ferr Ullr.' The transition from harangue to narrative is so imperceptible that 'ǫlum' in 2.6 could as well be translated 'we nourish' as 'let us nourish.'

In verse 4 we are confronted abruptly with preterite narration: 'varð' (4.8) and 'kníðu' (4.6) are guaranteed by *aðalhendingar*. The landing, the preparation for battle, and apparently the battle itself are now over and in the past. The speaker surveys the course of events with satisfaction –

the advance of Þorkell's army, the marshalling into battle formation, and the actual engagement with the enemy.

In the first three stanzas the illusion is created that the speaker is describing the events as they occur. When the process ends and the speaker begins to look back on events, as if from a fixed point, there is a shift from present tense to preterite. In verse 5 the preterite is again used of the battle that has been fought ('væri' being guaranteed by rhyme). But in an abruptly introduced parenthesis a new use of the present is made: 'mær spyrr vitr ef væri / valkǫstr.' We have to wait until verse 10 to appreciate that this present tense relates to the end of all the fighting, Knútr's as well as Þorkell's.

When the poem goes on to describe Knútr's battles, the preterite continues at first to be the narrative tense: guaranteed forms are 'gerði' (5.7), 'gullu' (6.2), 'sátt' and 'mátti' (6.6), and 'runnu' (6.8). But in verses 8 and 9 a switch to present tense occurs: the guaranteed forms are 'sœkir' (8.5) and 'dynr' (8.7). The adverbial expressions 'opt' and 'hvern morgin' add to the sense that the actions denoted by the verbs are part of a continuing process. But, once more, we realize when we encounter the preterite verbs of verse 10 ('vǫrum' and 'varð' guaranteed by rhyme) that the feeling that the siege is in the here and now is an illusion. The true present, from which the speaker speaks, is after the siege ('kneigum vér ... sitja'); he is to be imagined as telling the tale of his brave deeds to a female companion, presumably the 'mær' mentioned in verse 5. The references to her underline the division of the *flokkr* into a Þorkell half followed by a Knútr half, with the first mention of her neatly just before the dividing point.

The narrative scheme of 'Liðsmannaflokkr' is therefore two 'running commentaries' interspersed with some preterite narration. Margaret Ashdown noticed the peculiar sequence of tenses in the Finnur Jónsson truncated version of the poem, commenting that 'the implication of the last stanza is that the fighting is over, while stanza one suggests the beginning of a raid' (1930:206). She thought that if, 'as seems probable, the poem was composed almost immediately after the event, such change of tense is not inexplicable, and may even be regarded as an artistic device, helping the hearers of the poem to see the succession of events as if they were themselves taking part in the drama.' This view holds good of the complete, ten-stanza text, except that I would not press the notion that the poem was composed 'immediately after the event.' A date in 1017 is quite as likely as one in late 1016. While certainly the speaker of the poem does his speaking shortly after the end of the campaign (note the adverbial modifier in 'nýlokit'), we should not assume that speaker and poet are identical. Previous chapters in this book have demonstrated that the feeling of immediacy in poems like 'Liðsmannaflokkr' is to be seen as a genre characteristic. In its narrative technique, 'Liðsmannaflokkr' belongs in the same group as 'Merlínússpá,' 'Húsdrápa,' the Nissa section of *Sexstefja*, and 'Friðgerðarflokkr.'

My arguments thus far have been directed at dispelling the impressions of disunity that arise from the poem's textual history, attributions, topic, and narrative technique. Where the phonological and lexical organization of the poem is concerned, the dominant impression is by contrast one of unity and homogeneity.

In the organization of lexical features we see the same two seemingly opposed stylistic principles as in the poems examined in previous chapters: a principle of repetition set against a principle of variation. As we saw, the bold variation of *heiti* for 'ship' in the Nissa section of *Sexstefja* elicited comment from the compiler of *Hákonar saga Ívarssonar*. In 'Liðsmannaflokkr' the principle of variation is observed in the naming of persons: the name is given once, and once only; if the person concerned is referred to again it is by a kenning or by a general word such as 'jarl' or 'vísi.' The specific reference can be postponed, as with Knútr, who is first referred to vaguely as 'hilmir,' or [Stein]vǫr, who is simply 'mey' in verse 3.

Most of the national or place names, on the other hand, show the principle of repetition. As with our previous poems, the repetition usually appears to involve a pattern. Thus 'Engla' (1.1, 1.8), 'enskra' (2.5), and 'Englandi' (3.8) occur in successive stanzas and nowhere else; the pattern of distribution is first or last line within the individual stanza, together with the midpoint of the set of three stanzas (2.5). Another national name, 'Dani/Dana,' occurs twice, also in successive stanzas (vv 7 and 8), combining with other vocabulary repetition and carry-over of alliteration and rhyming syllables to form the chiastic type of symmetry seen in 'Friðgerðarflokkr.' A mention of setting, 'á Tempsar síðu' (v 5), is, as we have seen, repeated with variation in 'á Tempsar bakka' (v 9); here again the repetition seems not to be random or chance but part of a pattern. The other names, 'brezkum,' 'Stað,' and 'Lundúnum,' appear once only. The two occurrences of the Valkyrie name 'Hlǫkk' seem to link the beginning of the poem with the end: the other mythological or legendary names are used once only ('Ullr,' 'Hnikars,' 'Ilmr,' 'Hǫgna,' 'Syn').

The style of the *flokkr* is characterized by a certain monotony in vocabulary. A few favourite words are repeated insistently. Among them are 'rǫnd' / 'shield' (four times), 'hríð' / 'battle' (three times, always in association with 'hǫrð' / 'hard'), and 'harðr' itself (four times). The kenning 'randar skóð' / 'injurer of the shield' (v 3) has a close counterpart in 'hjalmskóð' / 'injurer of the helmet' (v 9), both meaning 'sword.' The word 'hjalmr' had been used in the immediately preceding stanzas (vv 7 and 8). The word 'víkingar' appears twice, 'blóð' / 'blood' four times, and 'rjóða' / 'redden' also four times, two of them in rhyme with 'skóð.'

Restriction of vocabulary and verbal repetition function to confer unity upon the poem as a whole. The repetitions, as we have seen, appear not random but designed to produce patterns of various kinds, most conspicuously the linking of successive stanzas. Thus:

hríð víkingar kníðu / ... harða (4.6–8)
hǫrð, sú's hilmir gerði / hríð (5.7–8)
hǫrð óx hildar garða / hríð – víkinga at bíða (6.3–4)

This sequence then links with a new one:

einráðit lét áðan / Ulfkell ... / ... víkinga at bíða (6.1–4)
Knútr réð ok bað bíða / ... Dani alla (7.1–2)

In turn verse 7 is linked on to verse 8 by the words 'hjalmr' and 'brynja,' along with 'Dani/Dana,' as noted; 'hjalmr' continues on into verse 9, supplemented by 'blóð.' Very conspicuous is the link between verses 9 and 10:

hvern morgin sér horna / Hlǫkk ... / hjalmskóð roðin blóði (9.1–4)
dag vas hvern þat's Hǫgna / hurð rjóðask nam blóði (10.1–2)

The parallels in the placing of these linking words and clauses within the *helmingr* or the stanza are also noteworthy.

If we consider stanzas that are not adjacent, the most overt repetition is between verse 3 – 'berr eigi sá sveigir / sára lauks í ári / ... rǫnd upp á Englandi' – and verse 9 – 'rýðr eigi sá sveigir / sára lauk í ári /... gunnborðs.' The reasons for not putting this resemblance down to duplication in oral tradition have already been noted. What instead we seem to be confronting is a refrain on a 'mansǫngr' / 'love-song' theme, as in the 'Jómsvíkingadrápa.' The first occurrence stands near the opening of the *flokkr* and the other near its close, which corresponds well, when allowances are made for the brevity of this poem, with the placing of the *stef* (refrain) in the formal *drápa*. As befits this less formal type of poem, the repetition is not of the verbatim sort we find in 'Jómsvíkingadrápa' and elsewhere, but incorporates a variation, so that the 'sword' and 'shield' elements exchange places in the clause.

Interstanzaic linking by the carry-over of rhyme and alliteration can also be found. For example, complicated patterns of alliterative carry-over link verses 4 to 8. Sometimes unrhymed syllables in successive stanzas seem to have a linking function too. The clearest examples are 'miklar' (1.3): 'Hnikars' (2.6), 'vitr' (5.3): 'bitran' (6.7), and 'rǫskr' (7.3): 'brezkum' (8.7). Each of these words forms the second rise in the line, and the symmetry of placing within the stanzas as a whole is striking too. This fondness for embedding a rhyming link in the second-last line of the *helmingr* has already been observed in 'Friðgerðarflokkr,' but here the pattern is more sustained, so that a chain of rhyming syllables links a succession of five stanzas:

4.3 sǫusk eigi þeir sverða
5.7 hǫrð, sú's hilmir gerði
6.3 hǫrð óx hildar garða
7.7 elds sem olmum heldi
8.3 of hjalmtǫmum hilmi

Finnur Jónsson's reorganization of the *flokkr* cuts across some clear examples of linked stanzas, namely verses 2 and 3, verses 4 and 5, verses 5 and 6, and verses 6 and 7, and this further militates against his views, even when due allowance is made for possible accidental repetition of words, alliteration, and rhyming syllables.

The poetic 'voice' that is heard in 'Liðsmannaflokkr' is distinguished by a cryptic wit, bordering on whimsy and sometimes elusive because of uncertainties attaching to the text. The method is partly indirection, through brief allusions to persons whose actions or inaction contrast with those of the speaker or of the *liðsmenn* in general. In the refrain the gallantry of the speaker and his comrades is contrasted with the pusillanimous inaction of a father or guardian in Norway. Such contrasts are characteristic of Old Norse voyage and battle poetry (Perkins 1969:96n7). In 'Liðsmannaflokkr,' as occasionally elsewhere, the stay-at-home's being at home has some kind of bearing on the speaker's amours. As a guardian and evidently a defender of female virtue he is eventually allowed the dignity of a proper warrior kenning, but first the speaker indicates his contempt in the irregular kenning 'glaums þollr' / 'tree of conviviality,' suggesting his enjoyment of the hall when he ought to be out in the world. The kenning is rather a witty one, because convention would lead the audience to expect completion with an element like 'sverðs' / 'of the sword': a 'tree of the merriment of the sword' (ie 'of battle') would be a warrior. And indeed a suitable word crops up in the shape of 'randar' / 'of the shield.' But if we are tempted to link 'randar' back to 'þollr glaums,' the word that follows, 'skóð' / 'injurer,' comes as a check, because 'randar' will combine naturally with it to form a kenning for 'sword,' as already noted: 'skóð' on its own is not impossible, but compare 'hjalmskóð' in verse 9 and Kock NN 596. The insult is subtle and fugitive: its detection involves a firm grasp of the rules.

In verse 2 the strategy is again contrast. As the men ready themselves for battle some of them are described as donning an 'ugly old shirt, where we were born and bred.' Holtsmark identified the 'shirt' with the caul or amnion and showed that according to superstitions formerly current in Scandinavia and England somebody born with a caul would be lucky and invulnerable in battle as an adult (1954:107). Evincing distaste for the custom, perhaps because it smacked of heathendom, the speaker instead slips on a coat of mail. The speaker's mockery of his comrades combines with some kind of self-characterization, which is obscured by different readings in the manuscripts: a 'skald,' he may be variously 'vart' / 'cautious' or 'ǫrt' / 'swift, fierce.' A cavalier attitude to armour is familiar from the traditions about berserks and from a verse purportedly spoken by Haraldr harðráði, where he remarks nonchalantly that he and his men are advancing without helmets and mail-coats, which have been left behind on the ships (ÍF 28:187–8, Turville-Petre 1968:19). Yet the possession of a mail-coat could also be a sign of superior status, in England at any rate. Whereas the freeman there had to manage with only a shield and spear, the 'þegn' rejoiced in the possession of a sword, helmet, and mail-coat, thanks to the military provisions of King Ethelred (Brooks 1978:83, 90, and 93). Thietmar of Merseburg makes special mention of a vast number of 'loricæ' / 'coats of mail' stockpiled in London during the final siege (1889ed:217). Whether the speaker is deprecating his own caution or congratulating himself on his prestigious equipment is hard to say.

More than most battle poems, 'Liðsmannaflokkr' is composed from the viewpoint of the following, which coincides with the story in *Knýtlinga saga* crediting the *liðsmenn* with authorship. Evaluations of the leaders are attributed not merely to the speaker, as would be routine (4.1–4 and 5.1–4), but to the following in general (5.5–8). Surprisingly frank is verse 6, which implies that Ulfcetel nearly proved more than a match for the invaders and that they for their part subsequently disagreed about the best course to adopt. The opening words in verse 7, 'Knútr réd,' carry the distinct implication that somebody, presumably Þorkell or Eiríkr, was overruled: if so, the naming of names is diplomatically avoided. Especially in the last three stanzas it is the continuing process of the campaign, not merely its outcome, that holds the speaker's attention. There is fitting emphasis on two great rewards of the mercenary, plunder and women, though not on Danegeld. Knútr's coming reward may be hinted at in verse 8, where a widow (Ethelred's?) watches as heroically he attacks the garrison or the relieving forces, his shining weapons brandished over his helmeted head. The *flokkr* suggests an *esprit de corps*, combined with a capacity to criticize and evaluate. Such a cohesion and professionalism appear to have been characteristic of the *lidsmenn* as an institution, although their history is obscure (John 1977:173–6 and 191; cf Hollister 1962:12–16).

The 'ekkja' / 'widow' (or perhaps merely 'single woman,' as sometimes in poetic usage) is said to be 'living in stone.' I take 'in stone' to mean 'behind stone walls': though London was not at that time well endowed with stone buildings, stone sections of the Roman wall survived and Scandinavians in England might well have found such constructions a noteworthy part of the local scene. This reference to stone follows and may have helped to explicate a more enigmatic and witty reference in verse 6. There a man (I think Ulfcetel) is alluded to through the kenning 'brunns byggs skeggja' / 'inhabitant of the barley of the spring/well.' Finnur Jónsson's interpretation is 'islander' (*Skj* B 210 and *LP* 1931 'skeggi'; cf Schier 1976B:583). But 'barley of the spring' must mean 'stone,' not 'island,' with a close counterpart in 'fjardbygg' / 'barley of the fiord' (Meissner 1921:90). A '*stein-skeggi' is a 'dweller in stone,' just as 'hraunskeggi' is somebody living on a lava-field ('hraun'). No doubt Ulfcetel is being envisaged as 'occupying a stone fortification.' Normally only giants would be denoted by a kenning of that sort, being archetypally dwellers in (or on) stones, rocks, or mountains. Used of a man, the kenning is incongruous and may provide a touch of humour. It also anticipates very oddly the maiden named Grjótvǫr in verse 9, where the 'stone' element in the name is emphasized by 'ofljóst.'

Another fanciful touch can be detected in verse 7. Here too interpretation is difficult. The word 'kennir' / 'knower' is characteristically the base-word of a kenning (in spite of Kock, NN 906) and can best be combined with 'elds Rennandi' / 'fire of the river' – ie 'gold' – to yield the standard 'gulls kennir' expression for '(munificent) man' (Meissner 1921:297). The possibility that instead 'syn' combines, by tmesis, with 'elds' to mean 'fire of the mail-coat' – ie 'sword' – and this in turn with 'kennir' to mean 'warrior' ('sverðs kennir') is remote, partly because of the tmesis and partly because 'syn' / 'coat of mail' is probably a mere ghost-word (Skj A 668, B 683). The word is more straightforwardly taken as 'Syn,' a goddess and hence a *heiti* (poetic name) for 'woman,' parallel to 'Ilmr' in verse 10. The result is that 'Rennandi' cannot be combined with the preceding word 'elg[r]' / 'elk' to mean 'ship'; 'elk' must be taken literally. The fierce fighting around the circumvallation ('díki') is being compared with the wild tussle between an elk and its captor. Elk-hunting was a time-honoured pursuit in medieval Norway and Sweden and the object was sometimes to capture the animal alive (John Bernström KLNM 'älg,' Gösta Berg KLNM, 'älgjakt'). A related simile occurs in *Grettis saga* chapter 15, where, after the hero's fight with Auðunn, the two combatants are forcibly separated (ÍF 7:44):

Grettir kvað ekki þurfa at halda á sér sem ólmum hundi

Grettir said that there was no need to hold on to him as though he were a wild dog.

The poet is, I think, influenced by a very similar *helmingr* in the 'Glymdrápa' of Þórbjǫrn hornklofi (Skj B 21 v 6; ÍF 26:113):

ok hjalmtamiðr hilmir
holmreyðar lét olman
lindihjǫrt fyr landi
lundprúðr við stik bundinn.

the proud king, in his helmet, caused his impetuous dragon?-ship ['lindihjǫrt' / 'hart of the linden mast'] to be secured to stakes offshore from the land ['holmreyðar' / 'serpent's' is normally construed with 'hjalm'].

The parallels to 'Liðsmannaflokkr' 7 will be obvious, but they extend also to verse 8: with 'hjalmtamiðr hilmir' compare 'hjalmtǫmum hilmi.' In both poems we see a play on the antitheses 'olmr/tamr' / 'wild/tame,' the king being literally 'tamed to the helmet,' that is, accustomed to wearing it. In 'Glymdrápa' the antithetical words are placed in proximity, while in 'Liðsmannaflokkr' they are given prominence by being placed in lines that are linked:

elds sem olmum heldi (7.7)
of hjalmtǫmum hilmi (8.3)

Each of these two adjectives occupies the second rise in its line. The difference between 'Glymdrápa' and 'Liðsmannaflokkr' is that whereas 'hart' is part of a kenning for 'ship,' 'elk' cannot be: the departure from the model and the trick of word order that places 'Rennandi' after 'elg,' as if to form a kenning, imparts a certain wit to the verse for an initiated audience.

'Liðsmannaflokkr' is no methodical forced march through the long course of the English wars. A vast amount is omitted, as comparison with the *Anglo-Saxon Chronicle* will show (Poole 1987). The method is to concentrate on a few scenes – a landing, a battle on the heath, a hard-won battle against Ulfcetel, the siege of London, and finally the occupation of that city. If two alone of the Viking leaders are mentioned, that is, I think, for special reasons. On the English side, Ethelred and his son Edmund are completely ignored in favour of Ulfcetel: an awareness that from the outset he was the Vikings' staunchest and ablest opponent may be implied (cf the *Anglo-Saxon Chronicle* entry for 1004 and Keynes 1978:230). The fluidity of narrative technique and the touches of fugitive wit make this a text that challenges, more than any other dealt with in this book, conventional ideas about narrativity.

'Darrađarljóđ': A Viking Victory over the Irish

1. Vítt er orpit
   fyrir valfalli
   rifs reiđiský:
   rignir blóđi.
   Nú er fyrir geirum
   grár upp kominn
   vefr verþjóđar,
   er vinur fylla
   rauđum vepti
   Randvés bana.

   Far and wide
   with the fall of the dead
   a warp ['rifs reiđiský'] is set up:
   blood rains down.
   Now, with the spears,
   a grey woven fabric
   of warriors is formed,
   which women friends
   ?of Randvér's killer?
   complete with a red weft.

2. Sjá er orpinn vefr
   ýta þǫrmum
   ok harđkljáđr
   hǫfđum manna;
   eru dreyrrekin
   dǫrr at skǫptum,
   járnvarđr yllir
   en ǫrum ?hælađr?.
   Skulum slá sverđum
   sigrvef þenna.

   The fabric is warped
   with men's intestines
   and firmly weighted
   with men's heads;
   bloodstained spears serve
   as heddle rods,
   the shed rod is ironclad
   and ?pegged? with arrows.
   With our swords we must strike
   this fabric of victory.

3. Gengr Hildr vefa
   ok Hjǫrþrimul,
   Sanngríđr, Svipul,
   sverđum tognum:

   Hildr goes to weave
   and Hjǫrþrimul,
   Sanngríđr, Svipul,
   with unsheathed swords:

	skapt mun gnesta, skjǫldr mun bresta, mun hjalmgagarr í hlíf koma.	the shaft will break, the shield will shatter, the sword will pierce armour.
4	Vindum vindum vef darraðar ?þann? er ungr konungr átti fyrri: fram skulum ganga ok í folk vaða þar er vinir várir vápnum skipta.	Let us wind, let us wind the weaving of the ?pennant? ?which? the young king had before: we must go and advance into the throng where our friends set weapon against weapon.
5	Vindum vindum vef darraðar ok siklingi síðan fylgjum: þar sá ?bragna? blóðgar randir Gunnr ok Gǫndul þær er grami hlífðu.	Let us wind, let us wind the weaving of the ?pennant? and follow the prince afterwards: there Gunnr and Gǫndul, who protected the king, saw ?men's? shields covered in blood.
6	Vindum vindum vef darraðar þar er vé vaða vígra manna: látum eigi líf hans farask; eiga valkyrjur vals um kosti.	Let us wind, let us wind the weaving of the ?pennant? there where the standards of fighting men go forth: let us not permit his life to be lost; the Valkyries have their choice of the slain.
7	Þeir munu lýðir lǫndum ráða er útskaga áðr um byggðu: kveð ek ríkum gram ráðinn dauða; nú er fyrir oddum jarlmaðr hniginn.	Those men will rule the lands who dwelt until this time on the outlying headlands: I say that death is decreed for the mighty king; now the earl has sunk down before the spears.

8   Ok munu Írar
    angr um bíða
    þat er aldri mun
    ýtum fyrnask:
    Nú er vefr ofinn
    en vǫllr roðinn;
    mun um land fara
    læspjǫll gota.

    And the Irish will
    undergo grief
    which will never fade
    in men's memories;
    now the fabric is woven
    and the field dyed red;
    the tidings of men's destruction
    will travel throughout the land.

9   Nú er ógurligt
    um at lítask
    er dreyrug ský
    dregr með himni:
    mun lopt litat
    lýða blóði
    er ?spár várar
    springa? kunnu.

    Now it is fearsome
    to gaze around
    as blood-red clouds
    gather in the sky:
    the heavens will be stained
    with men's blood
    when ?our prophecies?
    can ?spread abroad?.

10 Vel kváðu vér
    um konung ungan;
    sigrljóða fjǫld
    syngjum heilar:
    en hinn nemi,
    er heyrir á,
    ?geirljóða fjǫld?
    ok gumum skemti.

    We spoke well
    of the young king;
    let us sing with good fortune
    many songs of victory:
    and let him
    who listens
    learn ?many a spear-song?
    and entertain men.

11 Ríðum hestum
    hart út berum
    brugðnum sverðum
    á braut heðan.

    Let us ride out fast
    on our bare-backed horses,
    away from here
    with brandished swords.

Selected variants and emendations (cf *Skj* A 419–21):

1.8 'er'] 'þer' *Reykjabók* (R), *Oddabók* (O); 'þer er' *Mǫðruvallabók* (M), *Gráskinnuauki* (Ga)

1.10 'randversk' R; 'randverks' O; 'bla' R, O; 'lika' Ga

2.8 'hæladr'] 'hrelar' R; 'hræladr' O, M, Ga. (For the emendation see Poole 1985A.)

4.3 'þann' Ga; 'sa' R, O, M

5.5 'sa' M; 'sia' R, O, Ga; 'bragnar' R, O; 'bara' M; 'bera' Ga

5.8 'hlífđu'] 'fylgđv' R
9.7-8 'er spar varđar syngia' M; 'þa er soknvardar syngia kvnnv' Ga
10.1 'kvađ-' R, O; 'kveđ-' M, Ga
10.3 '-hliođa' O, M, Ga; '-hliđa' R; 'fliođ' O, Ga
10.7 '-hliođa' R, O; '-flioda' Ga; 'fliod' O; 'hliod' Ga
10.8 'skemti'] 'segi' M, Ga

This poem, editorially entitled 'Darrađarljóđ,' is preserved only in *Njáls saga*. Towards the end of the saga some of the characters participate in the famous Battle of Clontarf, which was fought in 1014. The compiler of the saga follows up his account of the battle with a series of supernatural events that occurred in association with it. The first of these involves a man named Dǫrruđr:

> Fǫstumorgininn varđ sá atburđr á Katanesi, at mađr sá, er Dǫrruđr hét, gekk út. Hann sá, at menn riđu tólf saman til dyngju nǫkkurrar ok hurfu þar allir. Hann gekk til dyngjunnar ok sá inn í glugg einn, er á var, ok sá, at þar váru konur inni ok hǫfđu vef upp fœrđan. Mannahǫfuđ váru fyrir kljána, en þarmar ór mǫnnum fyrir viptu ok garn, sverđ var fyrir skeiđ, en ǫr fyrir hræl. Þær kváđu þá vísur nǫkkurar ... Rifu þær þá ofan vefinn ok í sundr, ok hafđi hver þat, er helt á. Gekk hann þá í braut frá glugginum ok heim, en þær stigu á hesta sína, ok riđu sex í suđr, en ađrar sex í norđr (ÍF 12:454-9).

> On the morning of Good Friday, this event occurred at Caithness, that a man called Dǫrruđr went out. He saw that twelve persons ['menn'] rode together to a certain outhouse and there all of them disappeared. He went to the outhouse and looked in through a window which was set in it, and saw that women were inside and had set up their weaving. Men's heads served as loomweights and intestines from men as weft and warp, a sword as the sword-beater and an arrow as the pin-beater. Then they spoke some verses ... Then they tore the weaving down and ripped it apart, each one retaining the piece which she was holding. Then he left the window and went back home, while they mounted their horses and rode six to the south and the other six to the north.

The verses recited by these women as they weave are the poem 'Darrađarljóđ.'

Although nobody, I think, would accept the entire foregoing account as historical truth, the question of where to draw the line between fact and fiction is not easily decided. In general *Njáls saga* is not regarded as trustworthy where the attribution of verses to characters is concerned: Finnur Jónsson himself accepted that many of the *lausavísur* in it are spurious (1904:93–7) and 1912:5). I shall discuss here three major problems that arise from the *Njáls saga* account of 'Darraðarljóð.'

In the first place, 'Darraðarljóð,' as an account of the battle, diverges markedly from the rest of *Njáls saga*. The poem presents a 'young king' who evidently presided over an Irish defeat. Other than in his citation of 'Darraðarljóð,' however, the compiler of *Njáls saga* treats the battle as an Irish victory; he identifies the king who joins battle against the Irish as Sigtryggr silkiskegg and shows him being put to flight by followers of Brian boru, the Irish high king.

In spite of various attempts, the disagreement over the outcome of the battle is difficult to explain away. Sophus Bugge suggested that the poem was composed very shortly after the battle, while the Norsemen in Scotland were taking comfort from the fact that Brian had been killed whereas Sigtryggr was still alive: the poem would reflect hopes that the whole of Ireland would be united under Norse rule (1901:76). Heusler-Ranisch objected that the severity of the Norse defeat combined with the loss of Sigurðr jarl would have dampened any jubilation or ambitions for the future among the Norse in Scotland (1903:xlix). On the other hand, Heusler-Ranisch saw a possible intimation of Irish victory in the poem, applying to the Irish the reference to those who previously ruled the coastal headlands but now rule all the land. But this leaves other features of 'Darraðarljóð' unexplained, notably the mention of Irish grief in verse 8. Goedheer noted that the idea of the confinement of the Irish to coastal areas seemed quite out of keeping with the very localized nature of Viking power in Ireland at this period (1938:75). Goedheer's approach was to try to minimize the Viking defeat at Clontarf. 'The battle did not cause the defeat of the Dublin kingdom; Sigtryggr remained king, while his great opponent was slain, and among the Irish there arose new troubles in the contest for the hegemony. There is no reason to suppose that the death of so many Viking chiefs caused great affliction among the dispersed Norse settlers. No traces of national or racial feeling are found; Norsemen fought at Clontarf in the ranks of Brian just as there were Irish allies of Sigtryggr. To the Norsemen outside Ireland the battle meant no defeat' (ibid 76; cf 119–21). But although these arguments may tone down the Norse defeat at Clontarf they cannot transmute it into the victory that is mentioned explicitly and triumphantly in 'Darraðarljóð.'

It is also very difficult to make the young king's glorious battle, as described in 'Darraðarljóð,' square with the prose account in *Njáls saga* of Sigtryggr's conduct. In Icelandic tradition a development can be traced from *Þorsteins saga*, which does not mention Sigtryggr in its report of the battle, to *Njáls saga* and the *Flateyjarbók* text of *Orkneyinga saga*, where he is described as fleeing, and finally to the first Danish translation of *Orkneyinga saga*, where it is stated that Sigtryggr 'vant priiss' / 'won the victory': this final elaboration may reflect the influence of 'Darraðarljóð' on a version of *Orkneyinga saga* (íf 34:xxvii). On the whole the relatively cautious account of Sigtryggr in the *Njáls saga* prose agrees better with the Irish sources, which, Nora Kershaw points out, are both earlier and fuller than their Norse counterparts (1922:116) and which state that Sigtryggr watched the fighting but took no part in it. The *Njáls saga* prose, together with verse 23 (íf 12:459–60), also agrees with these sources against 'Darraðarljóð' in seeing Clontarf as a Viking defeat.

To some degree the *Njáls saga* prose may have been brought into harmony with 'Darraðarljóð.' The poem states that an unnamed earl met his death in a volley of spears during the battle, which fits with the report in *Njáls saga* chapter 157 that Sigurðr jarl was 'skotinn spjóti í gegnum' (íf 12:451). Here, as is pointed out by Einar Ól Sveinsson (ibid n4), the Irish *Cogadh Gaedhel re Gallaibh* differs, stating that Sigurðr jarl met his death through decapitation (1867ed:194–5).

Genzmer thought 'Darraðarljóð' unlikely to be about Sigtryggr silkiskegg because, being a Christian, Sigtryggr would not have welcomed assistance from Valkyries, or a poem that contemplated it (1956:169). This argument needs modification. We now know that heathendom and Christianity coexisted in the politics and art of tenth-century York, a kingdom with which, as A.P. Smyth has shown, Dublin had close political and dynastic links. In the tenth century the Sockburn burial site was used by a secular aristocracy who could tolerate both pagan figure carving and Christian cross-heads within the one cemetery: a hogback tomb there illustrated Týr sacrificing his hand to Fenrir (Lang 1972:240 and 248). A second fragment at Sockburn, one end of a hogback, shows a man holding a shield and drinking from a horn proffered by a woman whom Lang identifies as a Valkyrie (ibid 242 and 247). Sometimes Christian and heathen are combined not merely on the one site but within the one artwork, so that on the Gosforth Cross Ragnarǫk is juxtaposed with the Crucifixion (Berg 1958:27–43). Surveying the iconography of the tenth-century Manx crosses, Sue Margeson points out the 'equal prominence' of pagan and Christian material on the Kirk Andreas cross, where 'Óðinn counterbalances a Christian figure' (1983:105). As we shall see presently, the Isle of Man may have been a temporary refuge for some of the Dublin Vikings in the early tenth century. Evidently the Vikings of the Dublin-York nexus preserved their own myths in spite of their acceptance of Christianity. What could be preserved in iconography on a stone cross could also be preserved verbally in a poem like 'Darraðarljóð.' But we might agree with Genzmer so far as to say that 1014, the date of Clontarf, would be surprisingly late for the composition of a poem wholly heathen in its sentiments.

Nora Kershaw was prompted by the disagreement over the outcome of the battle and the role of Sigtryggr, together with other less serious discrepancies, to suggest that 'Darraðarljóð' was not about Clontarf at all. She proposed that the poem actually commemorated a victory won by the Vikings almost a century before, in 919, and that in tradition the poem had been mistakenly connected with Clontarf. Confusion might have arisen because both battles were fought near Dublin and because of the similar naming of Sigtryggr caech, who fought in 919, and Sigtryggr silkiskegg, who fought in 1014 (1922:116). Since Dublin and Sigtryggr are not mentioned by name in 'Darraðarljóð,' Kershaw's theory involves the assumption that in oral tradition some kind of explanatory prose narrative accompanied the poem and made its cryptic references to people and places explicit. The two battles were also confusable because in each of them the Irish high king met his death.

In various ways 'Darraðarljóð' could be seen as an accurate reflection of Viking-Irish relations in the late ninth and early tenth centuries. The half-century from 830 to 880 was characterized by intense Viking pressure on Ireland, but in the late 870s the pressure began to ease and about forty years of comparative calm ensued. The most tangible evidence of this setback to Viking incursions was a sound defeat at the hands of a combined army from Brega and Leinster in 902. Eventually, however, the trend was reversed in 914, when a new Viking fleet put in at Waterford. Within five years Niall Glundubh, the Ui Neill overlord, was killed by the Vikings in the battle of 919. For the next sixty years the Vikings were once more on the offensive in Ireland (Hughes 1972:157). The year 919 could therefore be viewed as a turning-point in Viking-Irish relations: the great victory won in that year could well have been commemorated in a praise poem.

The severe Viking defeat in 902 may have special relevance to verse

7 of 'Darraðarljóð,' which mentions a nation, presumably the Vikings, who dwelt not in Dublin but 'on the outlying headlands.' Irish sources speak of nothing less than an expulsion of the Vikings from Dublin in 902. In the *Annals of Ulster* (entry for 901) we learn of 'the expulsion of the Gentiles from Ireland, i.e. from their shipfortress at Dublin ... They left a great part of their fleet, and escaped half dead, wounded and broken' (*Annals of Ulster* I:416–17). The Four Masters add that a section of the routed colony regrouped on Ireland's Eye, a small island north of Dublin Bay, where they were starved into submission. The remainder escaped 'half dead across the sea' (*Annals of the Four Masters* I:556–7, entry for 897). According to A.P. Smyth, whose account I am using here, the dispossessed Dublin leaders probably spent the interval from 902 to 914 either in southwest Scotland or on the Isle of Man (I 1975:60–1). 'In spite ... of the inadequate documentation relating to the Scottish Isles, Galloway, and Man, the overall picture from Icelandic records and archaeological evidence clearly suggests that these areas were firmly in the hands of the Norsemen by 900' (ibid 61). If this is right, the Norse settlements on Man and the Scottish Isles in particular would explain the statement in verse 7 of 'Darraðarljóð': the poet would be saying that the Vikings who conquered a part of Ireland in 919 had previously been living in refuge on outlying headlands, this being a reference to the islands on the other side of the Irish Sea. According to Liam de Paor, however, the Vikings were 'not perhaps wholly expelled' from Dublin, 'since they clung to the small islands off the coast' (1976:31). In the latter case, the reference in 'Darraðarljóð' could be to these islands off the Irish coast.

'Darraðarljóð' seems in verse 4 to be crediting the young king with some battles prior to his great victory. This too can be accounted for if we identify him with Sigtryggr caech and place his victory in 919. Smyth summarizes the Viking reinvasion of Ireland in the following terms (I 1975:67–70). In 916 the dynasty of Ívarr returned to Ireland with immense fleets and the obvious intention of overrunning the island. Not since the expeditions of Halfdan in 875 and 877 had the Irish Sea been visited by a Scandinavian power intent on taking control of the Viking colonies, if not the island as a whole. The arrival of Sigtryggr caech brought the invading forces to full strength in 917. He established himself at Cenn Fuait, where the Leinstermen attacked his fort with disastrous results. They lost three of their kings, including the king of Leinster and his archbishop. Sigtryggr's position was now stronger than ever, and he followed up his victory by occupying Dublin. In 918 we hear of 'war between Niall son of Aed king of Ireland and Sigtryggr grandson of Ivarr.' Thus Sigtryggr had fought two or possibly three successful battles before the culminating one of 919. His widespread campaigning would justify not merely the words 'þann er ungr konungr / átti fyrri' but also the implication of extensive conquests that lies behind the words 'þeir munu lýdir / lǫndum ráða.' If Smyth is right, extensive territorial conquest, rather than a mere retaking of Dublin, was the Viking objective from the outset.

The idea of a decisive Viking victory, which is especially evident in 'Darraðarljóð' 7 and 8, fits well with what we know of the 919 battle from the Irish side. Smyth writes that in this battle Sigtryggr confronted a hosting led by Niall and drawn from almost half the Irish kingdoms, an extraordinarily large force by the standards of the time. The high king at the head of this force could very aptly be termed a 'ríkr gramr,' as in verse 7. In the event, 'the Irish suffered their most crushing defeat since the Norwegians first appeared off their shores in 795. The high king was himself slain in the battle – the first time such a ruler was slain by Vikings in Ireland' (ibid 69–70).

The reassigning of 'Darraðarljóð' to the tenth century gives us the correct outcome to the battle and a suitably successful warrior king, while preserving the important motif that an Irish 'ríkr gramr' meets his death. The Valkyries would also fit very naturally in a tenth-century poem. Its use of the weaving motif could even be seen as inspired by an Irish poem in praise of the king who expelled the Vikings in 902 (of this more later).

One major problem, however, remains. If we keep to the Clontarf identification we can identify the 'jarlmaðr' whose death is mentioned in verse 7 as Sigurðr jarl, whereas I can find no mention in the Irish sources on the 919 battle that an earl was killed. Genzmer's identification with the archbishop slain in the 917 battle of Cenn Fuait can safely be dismissed (1956:170). Also in favour of a Clontarf identification is the statement in verse 7 that death is in store for the 'ríkr gramr,' implying that his death occurred either at the very end of the battle or else after it. Both the Norse and the Irish sources on Clontarf show Brian's death occurring as part of the aftermath of the battle.

These conflicts in the evidence rule out a firm conclusion on the date of the battle commemorated in 'Darraðarljóð.' It is in my opinion probable that 'Darraðarljóð' reflects the situation in 919 and that *Njáls saga* embodies an incorrect tradition concerning the origin of the poem, but in the present state of our knowledge this proposition cannot be proved.

The second dubious point in the *Njáls saga* prose is the name of the man who listens to the Valkyries, Dǫrruðr. Eiríkr Magnússon noted the 'obvious connection' between this name 'Dǫrruðr' and the phrase 'vef[r] darraðar' within the poem, which he takes to mean 'weaving of the spear' (1910:5).

Altogether, the word 'darraðr/dǫrruðr' presents very complex problems, both of form and of meaning. Aside from the appearance as a proper name in *Njáls saga* it is not found in prose, and even in poetry it is rare. Three of the poems in which it occurs are likely to be among the oldest in Old Norse: 'Atlakviða,' Egill's 'Hǫfuðlausn,' and Eyvindr's 'Hákonarmál.' Slightly younger, as conventionally dated, is 'Darraðarljóð' itself, but, as we have seen, this dating may be almost a century too late. Of the three remaining poems, two are types of poetic manual, bringing together older material: *Háttatal* and a *þula* (or mnemonic list) in manuscript AM 748 II 4to of the *Edda* (*Edda Snorra Sturlusonar* II 1852:494). The third poem, the 'Ævikviða' of Ǫrvar-Oddr, while of indeterminate age, is on an antiquarian subject. For a detailed discussion of 'darraðr' in these contexts see Holtsmark (1939:85–93) and Dronke (1969:49–50).

The word 'darraðr' has often been explained as a 'spear' and compared with Old English 'daroþ' / 'spear.' The Old English word is also confined to poetic diction. It occurs once in what seems to be a description of weaving, in the Exeter Book, riddle 56. The resemblances in form and incidence between 'daroþ' and 'darraðr' are therefore striking, yet, as Ursula Dronke points out, the two words cannot be identified with phonological exactness because single 'r' in one and double 'rr' in the other appear to be constants (ibid 49). The absence of 'darraðr' from the *þula* of 'spjóts heiti' / 'names for spear' (*Skj* A 665) also militates against the theory that 'darraðr' meant 'spear.' Dietrich Hofmann does not identify the two words as cognates or as borrowed in either direction in his study of linguistic contacts between Old Norse and Old English (1955:30 and 112).

Anne Holtsmark proposed the alternative meaning 'pennant' and an etymology in '*darra,' attested in Faeroese with the meaning 'hang loosely and sway' (1939:88). This sense explains all but one of the poetic examples, and is a decided improvement on 'spear' in the *Háttatal* example. *Háttatal* 52 occurs as one of a set of stanzas with fourfold parallelism. Within the stanza we find three undoubted expressions for 'banner' or 'standard' – 'gunnfana,' 'vé (stǫng),' and 'merkjum' – and parallel to them the plural noun 'skǫpt.' The word 'skǫpt' / 'shafts' is in itself rather unspecific. Since the other general word of this sort in the stanza, 'stǫng,' is particularized by the presence of 'vé' in the immediate context, I think it likely that 'darradar,' in the same couplet as 'skǫpt,' had a similar particularizing function. The phrase 'skǫpt darradar' would mean 'shafts of the pennant' – in other words 'banners.'

The two occurrences in 'Atlakviða' offer special difficulties. In the phrases 'dafar darraðr' and 'dafa darraðr' the nominative singular 'darraðr' has to be emended to fit syntactically with the context, and a genitive singular dependent on 'dafar' (accusative plural) is the safest option, the reading 'dafa' being altered in conformity (Dronke 1969:49). The phrase would then mean 'spears of the pennant,' an apt description of the type of banner where a flag or pennant was attached to a shaft fitted with a spear-head. But one of the contexts in 'Atlakviða' is a list of gifts, and Klaus von See objected that 'spear,' not 'banner,' must be intended here, because a banner or standard would not be a suitable present (1959:4n2). Presumably what he had in mind was that a banner or standard would be emblazoned with the personal emblem of its owner. This, however, must be set against *Beowulf* 2152 (and cf 1021–2), where the hero presents Hygelac, king of Geatland, with a banner or standard that he had himself received from Hroðgar, king of Denmark (cf Holtsmark 1939:91): though their syntax is difficult, the words in the *Beowulf* manuscript – 'eafor heafod segn' – imply a banner or standard with the emblem of a boar. Altogether, though, both stanzas in 'Atlakviða' where 'darraðr' occurs are so problematic that a definite conclusion is not to be won from them.

The one poetic text where real doubt attaches to Holtsmark's 'pennant' suggestion is the *þula*. Holtsmark indicated that 'darraðr' appeared there under the heading 'klæða heiti' / 'names of clothing,' as would perhaps be appropriate, figuratively at least, if the word meant 'pennant' (ibid 87 and 92–3). But as I read them the 'klæða heiti' stop some twenty-three items before 'darraðr' and the intervening words are a wild jumble, containing, among other things, *heiti* for 'woman' and 'stone.' The word 'darraðr' occurs amid a little group of *heiti* for 'nail' or 'rivet' and is followed by the abbreviation 'i.M.,' which has been interpreted as 'í merki' / 'in a banner.' Given the generally chaotic state of this list of *heiti*, the sense 'nail' or 'rivet' for 'darraðr' in this context is a possibility rather than a certainty. Such a meaning would be hard to reconcile with the other contexts in which 'darraðr' is found, but it is not uncommon for a rare *heiti* in the *þulur* to have more than one meaning, whether genuinely or through misinterpretation.

In 'Darraðarljóð' and Egill's 'Hǫfuðlausn,' 'darraðr' occurs in combination with 'vefr' / 'weaving' in the phrase 'vef[r] darraðar.' The 'Hǫfuðlausn' text is as follows:

> Vasat villr staðar
> veft darraðar
> of grams glaðar
> geirvangs raðar
>
> (íf 2:187 v 5)

The weaving of the *darraðr* was not astray from its place over the king's bright rows of shields.

Alternatively, the last two lines may read:

> fyr grams glǫðum
> geirvangs rǫðum
>
> (*Skj* A 36, B 31)

in front of the king's bright rows of shields

This verbal parallel between the two poems is highly significant. 'Hǫfuðlausn' is associated with York and 'Darraðarljóð,' as we have seen, with Dublin, two kingdoms that had very strong political and cultural connections. The interval of time between the two poems is not great, whichever dating we assign to 'Darraðarljóð.' A common poetic tradition in the two kingdoms is indicated by Gunnlaugr ormstunga's praise poem for Sigtryggr silkiskegg, which betrays influence, as to rhyme-scheme and refrain, from Egill's 'Hǫfuðlausn' (*Edda Snorra Sturlusonar* III 1880–7:323–4). Given these connections, an explanation of 'darraðr' that fits both poems will be preferable (though cf Turville-Petre 1976:xxxviii n1).

In 'Darraðarljóð' we find three phrases with 'vef[r]': 'vef[r] darraðar,' 'vefr verþjóðar,' and 'sigrvef[r].' The phrase 'vefr verþjóðar' is shown by the context to mean a weaving or interweaving formed by the bodies of the warriors as they converge and fall in battle: the specific parts of the bodies are mentioned explicitly, indeed graphically, in verse 2 (Þorkelsson 1870:29). The compound 'sigrvef[r]' has a different internal logic, where the first element in the compound is an abstract noun stating the significance of the 'weaving,' rather than its composition. The phrase 'vef[r] darraðar' would be most simply explained as parallel to one or other of these two expressions. Some explicators of 'Hǫfuðlausn' have interpreted it as a kenning for 'shield' (Wisén II 1889:40, Kock NN 80, and Mohr 1933:56 and 105). But this will not fit in 'Darraðarljóð.' Moreover, no instances are to be found of 'vefr' as a base-word for 'shield' or in other kennings elsewhere in Old Norse poetry (Meissner 1921:167).

I shall deal presently with the suggestion that 'darraðr/dǫrruðr' is an Óðinn name. But for the moment let us restrict ourselves to the proposed glosses that have some arguable basis in the poetic texts. In order of evidential strength these are 'pennant' (*Háttatal* 52) and 'nail' or 'rivet' (the *þula*): 'spear' ought also to be kept in mind as a more remote possibility. In 'Darraðarljóð' these concrete nouns are most readily explicable as parallel to 'verþjóð,' in other words as indicating the composition of the type of weaving described in the poem. Holtsmark takes 'darraðar' as genitive of definition rather than of composition, but here I believe she breaks the parallelism unnecessarily (1939:90).

On the basis of this logic 'vef[r] darraðar' is most likely to mean a 'weaving' or 'interweaving of the pennant,' in other words 'interweaving of pennants.' The genitive singular for plural here has been seen as a difficulty (for example, by Eiríkr Magnússon 1910:8, Falk 1924:6, and Mohr 1933:105). Adequate parallels are however to hand in 'Hǫfuðlausn': 'geirvangs raðar' / 'rows of the shield,' ie 'rows of shields' (Åkerblom 1899:273) and 'hræs lanar' / 'heaps of the corpse,' ie 'heaps of corpses' (von See 1959:5).

To envisage the scene of battle as an 'interweaving of pennants' may seem excessively hyperbolic. The closest analogue is the couplet of *Háttatal* 52 already mentioned where Snorri describes the shafts of standards being raised aloft in showers (*Skj* A2 66):

Sér skjǫldungs niðr skúrum
skǫpt darraðar lyptask.

More generally, the idea that 'many' banners are to be seen sometimes occurs. Þjóðólfr Arnórsson describes how 'upp fara mǫrg í morgin / merki' / 'up go many banners in the morning' (*Skj* B 348 v 7). Similarly some lines from *Sverris saga* (*Skj* B 596–7 vv 23–4):

ýtar reistu merki at móti,
margar stengr, ok bǫrðusk lengi

men raised standards against them, many shafts, and fought long

Here the 'many shafts' is in apposition with 'standards.'
It might seem easier to envisage a battle as an 'interweaving of spears' because, particularly at the onset of battle, we can imagine the air as being thick with them. Thus Arnórr in 'Magnússdrápa' 14: 'jǫrn flugu þykt sem þyrnir' / 'weapons flew as thick as thorns' (Skj B 314). The kindred idea of a forest of spears, which occurs in Middle High German poetry, is also depicted much closer to home in a tapestry from the Oseberg burial. In this battle scene, as analysed by Bjørn Hougen, we see warriors in formation, with shield-wall: above them is a 'forest of spears' (1940:115). Altogether eight rows of spears are held aloft and each row appears to touch or overlap with the next, either at tip or base. Another possible conception would be that the interweaving of spears was formed as one spear crossed another in flight (Åkerblom 1899:273). E.A. Kock explains 'vef[r] darraðar' in 'Darraðarljóð' as an 'interweaving of spears' (NN 1205 D): so too, more tentatively, Mohr (1933:56). Both scholars explain 'Hǫfuðlausn' otherwise. Conversely, Finnur Jónsson (Skj B 31), Sophie Krijn (1927:465), and Sigurður Nordal (ÍF 2:187) adopt this explanation in 'Hǫfuðlausn,' while explaining 'Darraðarljóð' otherwise. So far as I am aware, the only scholars to explain both poems in this way are Eiríkr Magnússon (1910:8) and Klaus von See (1959:4–5).

As we have seen, 'pennant,' hence the flag part of a banner, is the better supported gloss for 'darraðr': 'spear' is not an interpretation positively required by any passage, while 'nail' or 'rivet' seem impossible in the present context. The interpretation of 'vef[r] darraðar' as 'interweaving of pennants' is possible, if hyperbolic, in 'Darraðarljóð.' In 'Hǫfuðlausn' the comment that 'the interweaving of pennants was not astray from its place over / in front of the king's bright rows of shields' would mean that the standard-bearers are where they ought to be – an expression of satisfaction in a correctly marshalled army. The same gloss will therefore explain the occurrences of the phrase 'vef[r] darraðar' in both poems.

This leaves us with the one prose occurrence of 'darraðr/dǫrruðr,' the name Dǫrruðr in Njáls saga. Various scholars have regarded 'Dǫrruðr' as an Óðinn name. Finnur Jónsson thought that it was incorrectly applied to an ordinary mortal in the saga (Njála 1908ed:415). Building on this supposed Óðinn sense, Falk explained 'dafa(r) (D)arraðr' in 'Atlakviða' as a warrior kenning (1924:6) – a suggestion that has not found favour. He thought 'darraðr/dǫrruðr' also meant 'sword' and 'nail' and that these senses were derived from the Óðinn name. Jan de Vries saw 'Dǫrruðr' / 'Óðinn' as etymologically distinct from 'darraðr,' deriving from the etymon '*darr-hǫðr'; 'darraðr' he glossed as 'spear' and 'nail in a sword,' reading 'í mæki' instead of 'í merki' (1961 sv). Ursula Dronke noted the resemblance in formation between 'Dǫrruðr' and the undoubted Óðinn-*heiti* 'Geiguðr' and 'Sviðuðr,' and further the presence side by side with 'darraðr,' in the *þula*, of 'jalfaðr,' the mutated form 'Jǫlfuðr' being again a known Óðinn-*heiti*. Like Falk, she saw the 'Óðinn' sense of 'darraðr/dǫrruðr' as primary and the other common–noun sense or senses as derived from this *heiti*. Her choice here was 'pennant,' following Holtsmark. Unlike Finnur Jónsson, she saw Dǫrruðr in the saga as aptly named: his role can be regarded as Odinic, in that he learns secrets from wise women (Dronke 1969:49).

The complexity of the proposed etymologies and semantic developments and the absence of 'darraðr/dǫrruðr' from catalogues of Óðinn-*heiti* suggest that we should consider an alternative possibility: some kind of misinterpretation in *Njáls saga*. 'Dǫrruðr' in the saga has been explained as a back-formation from 'darraðar' in the poem by Eiríkr Magnússon (1910:5), Anne Holtsmark (1939:84), and Klaus von See (1959:2). The extremely limited currency of 'darraðr/dǫrruðr,' even in early poetry, obviously increases the likelihood of error. The paucity of recorded declensional forms (only nominative and genitive singular) implies that the word had become a linguistic fossil or relic. Some scholars have seen the section of *Njáls saga* that contains 'Darraðarljóð' as deriving from a hypothetical 'Brjáns saga,' which might date back as early as *ca* 1200 (Sveinsson 1933:81). But even so early a dating would not preclude error. A parallel would be the king's name 'skeiðar-Brandr' in *Ágrip*, also an early work. This notorious misinterpretation arises from a failure to recognize a synecdoche in an easy verse (*Ágrip* 1929ed:2; cf. von See 1977:64). The survival into the thirteenth century of the apparently correct use of 'darraðr,' in Snorri's *Háttatal*, would be paralleled by Sturla's correct use of 'skeiðar-brandr' in 'Hrynhenda' (*Skj* B2 117 v 14).

Njáls saga contains a number of rare or unparalleled names of the '-uðr/-aðr' type. The genitive form 'Naddaðar' in chapter 47 is evidently a blunder: Jakob Benediktsson explains it as an error for the genitive case of Nadd-Oddr, presumably via a form with single 'd,' as in *Sturlubók* (*ÍF* 1:35n3). In chapter 157, where 'Darraðarljóð' occurs, we find the names of certain Irish participants at the battle of Clontarf: they include Dungaðr, from Donnchadh, Kerþjalfaðr, from Toirdhealbhach with some distortion of the first syllable, and Margaðr, from Murchadh with a distortion that is not exclusive to *Njáls saga* (Craigie 1897:445–8). An author or compiler who had worked through this series of exotic names in '-aðr' might, in pondering 'Darraðarljóð,' mistake a rare poetic word for a Gaelic (here Scottish) proper name. There is a curious parallel between 'darraðr/dǫrruðr' in the sense of 'nail' and 'Nagli,' a very rare name borne by a Hebridean trader in *Eyrbyggja saga*. The Scottish runner in *Eiríks saga rauða* bears the name 'Haki' / 'hook.' Whether this strange pattern in the semantics of Norse names for Scotsmen is a matter of coincidence or convention I cannot tell.

Once more, a firm conclusion is not possible, but the hypothesis that the word 'darraðar' was misunderstood at some stage in the accretion of *Njáls saga* material is less complicated than the others that have been offered and in itself not unreasonable.

The third contested point in the *Njáls saga* prose is its handling of the weaving motif that pervades the earlier stanzas of the poem. In the saga, the Valkyries' weaving is shown as performed at a great distance from the battle, but with the implication that it has a magical significance of some kind. The other marvels in the immediate context have the function of instantaneously communicating news of the battle or its outcome to far-flung places, not of determining its course.

The status of the weaving motif in the poem itself has been much debated. Anne Holtsmark and Eduard Neumann gave fullest expression of the view that the weaving is to be taken literally as a magical act that is conducted by the Valkyries simultaneously with the fighting and that ensures its success. This interpretation would be in broad agreement with the saga prose. Klaus von See tried to show that the weaving had no literal status, being a metaphor for the process of fighting a battle. In his view the Valkyries are participating in the battle, and the saga prose, which has them far from the battle, is therefore a misinterpretation or extraneous embellishment.

The question is not easy to settle, because both metaphor and magic, if by that we mean sympathetic magic, are based on a perceived similarity between two disparate things. The perception of similarity between weaving and fighting a battle is evidenced very plainly in 'Darraðarljóð' verse 2. Now in an Old English example of sympathetic magic, the charm 'við færstice,' the cause of rheumatic or other bodily pain seems to be thought of literally as a 'little spear' (Storms 1948:142–6). 'Under cover of a linden shield [the magician] witnessed how the mighty women betrayed their own power of sending out spears ... '(ibid 145). This leads to the devising of a piece of sympathetic magic that will serve as a cure. 'Their secret is out and the defence is found: [the magician] will send them back another, a flying arrow from in front against them' (ibid 145–6). Nowadays we perceive the same similarity when we complain of a 'stabbing' pain, but in saying this we presumably mean only to use a metaphor.

In my discussion of the weaving motif in 'Darraðarljóð' I shall begin by analysing the description of the process that is given in the poem and then go on to enquire what the perceived similarities between weaving and battle might have been. At the start of the poem we hear that a 'warp' has been set up, this warp being, in the circumlocutory language of kennings, 'the hanging cloud of the loom beam.' The 'reiði-' element in the kenning makes clear that the warp is vertical, as in the older, vertical loom that survived in Iceland down to the late nineteenth century and in Norway virtually to the present day. For my discussion of this type of loom I am indebted to Marta Hoffmann's *The Warp-weighted Loom* (1964).

Marta Hoffmann's account of the warp-weighted loom, as used in twentieth-century Norway, is as follows (ibid 6): 'It consists of a sturdy upright on each side, set up in a sloping position, the top being supported against a wall. These uprights have a bracket at the top, in which the beam rests. The warp, sewn to this beam, is kept taut by means of weights attached to the bottom, a group of warp threads being tied to each weight. A cross bar, the shed rod, is fixed to the uprights: this divides the warp into two halves, the natural shed. The front threads lie in front of this rod; the back threads hang straight down behind. Another rod, the heddle rod, which can be moved backwards and forwards, is connected to the back threads by a number of loops – the heddles. When the weaver pulls the heddle rod forward, all the back threads move with it, and a new shed, the countershed, results.'

The setting up of the warp threads is the first stage of the weaver's work and so is mentioned logically at the beginning of the poem in the perfect tense, as of a task already complete. In verse 2 the Old Norse terminology for this process is used, constituting our only detailed medi-

'Darraðarljóð' 133

The warp-weighted loom
(after Holtsmark 1939; redrawn by Nicola Johnson)

top: front view; bottom: side view

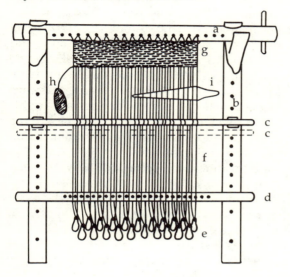

Key: English
a: beam
b: uprights
c: heddle rods
d: shed rod
e: loom weights
f: warp
g: weft
h: skein (of weft yarn)
i: sword beater

Key: Old Norse
a: rifr
b: hleinar
c: skǫpt
d: yllir
e: kljár
f: varp
g: vept
h: vinda
i: skeið

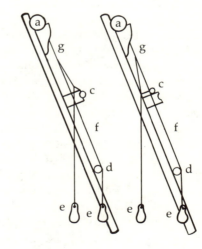

eval Scandinavian account. Taken from top to bottom of the loom, rather than as ordered in the stanza, the process has the following stages. When the warp is set up the threads must be attached to the 'rifr' / 'loom beam' (mentioned in verse 1). Then they must be passed through heddles, or loops of yarn, which are tied to the 'skapt' / 'heddle rod.' A loom can have more than one heddle rod, hence 'skǫpt,' the plural form, in our poem. Next the threads are passed alternately in front of and behind the 'yllir' / 'shed rod.' For the identification of the 'yllir' as the shed rod see Holtsmark (1939:82–3); Nora Kershaw made the same identification, but with less precision (1922:192). Finally the vertical warp threads were held taut by being attached to heavy stone or clay weights termed 'kljár,' hence '-kljáðr' / 'weighted' in the poem. These loom weights, with their distinctive hole to pass the yarn or linen thread through, are a familiar find at archaeological sites.

The poem opens, then, with this phase complete and the work ready to enter its next phase, which is the insertion of weft threads. In warp-weighted weaving the insertion of weft begins near the top of the loom, immediately below the loom beam. For a proper structure in the finished fabric the weft thread must pass over one warp thread and under the next: likewise each warp thread must pass over one weft thread and under the next. If these alternations are not painstakingly observed the strength and colour pattern of the finished fabric will be impaired. The alternation is achieved, not through a plaiting action (as some writers on this poem seem to have imagined) but by the use of the shed and heddle rods. The shed rod divides the warp into alternating backward and forward threads, creating a passage through which the weft thread can be passed. After one row of weft has been inserted along this passage the heddle rod is brought forward. This pulls the backward set of warp threads in front of the forward set, creating a second passage, along which a second row of weft thread is inserted. The second passage is termed the 'counter-shed' or 'artificial shed.' The heddle rod is then returned to its original position, so that we have the first passage or 'natural shed' again. The result is that the desired alternation of threads can be obtained without the slowness and intricacy of a plaiting motion. The use of more than one heddle rod increased the number of patterns of colour and weave that could be produced.

The insertion of weft is described in the last six lines of verse 1. The first weft threads to be inserted must be grey, to judge from the lines 'grár upp kominn / vefr verþjóðar.' Subsequently the weavers switch to a red weft, as is shown by the last two lines, 'vinur fylla / rauðum vepti.' A two-coloured fabric results.

Then, as the third step, the weavers must force the weft threads upwards towards the loom beam, compacting them so that the resulting fabric is firm and without gaps. This operation, of 'beating' the weft threads, was performed with an implement called the 'skeið' / 'sword-beater' and is referred to in the lines 'skulum slá sverðum / sigrvef þenna.'

After the second and third steps have proceeded in alternation for some time a stage is reached when the completed portion of textile stretches down almost as far as the heddle rod, forcing the weavers to bend awkwardly to insert the weft, and making the shed awkwardly narrow. To facilitate their work the weavers would then wind the completed textile up on the loom beam (Falk 1919:15, Hoffmann 1964:54). The beam was turned by a crank, raising the warp threads, with much the same action as a windlass (Old Norse 'vindáss'). The poet refers to this action with the words 'vindum vindum / vef darraðar.' Here unnecessary obfuscation has been caused by scholars who have interpreted 'vindum' as denoting the inserting of weft. The idea probably arose by association with 'vinduteinn,' the Icelandic name for the length of wood on which the weft yarn was wound. Hence Kershaw translates the above lines 'we are twisting the web' and takes that to mean 'passing the threads of the weft alternately under and over those of the warp' (1922:193). Fritzner (1954ed 'vinda'), Finnur Jónsson (*Njála* 1908ed:415n), and Klaus von See (1959:9n1) take a similar view. But, as we have seen, that was not the method by which weft was inserted. The element 'vind-' in 'vinduteinn' is better explained as referring to the winding of weft yarn on the 'teinn,' a slender curved rod that was removed when the skein or weft roll was complete (Hoffman 1964:126). The word 'vindum,' as used in 'Darraðarljóð,' finds its true counterpart in two Icelandic terms for the spoke or crank that turns the beam, 'handvinda' and 'haldvinda' (ibid 55).

Winding up the completed fabric was heavy work, because the loom weights had to be hoisted up along with the warp threads. Hoffmann observed that in twentieth-century practice more than one weaver might have to participate in this task (ibid 45). The work-song manner of 'vindum vindum' is therefore fully justified by the arduous nature of the task in real life; Vogt's strictures on the artificiality of the refrain are quite incorrect (1927:166). Several of these windings would occur during weaving before the entire fabric was woven and the loom weights removed, which may account for the repetition of 'vindum vindum / vef darraðar' through three stanzas of the poem.

The work of weaving is stated to be complete in verse 8: 'nú er vefr ofinn.' In sum, then, we hear of five phases in the weaving process. From this arises an important point about the narrative technique that I shall return to later. Phase one is described in the perfect tense ('er orpit,' 'er orpinn'), phase two in the perfect ('er kominn') and present ('fylla'), phase three in a quasi-future ('skulum slá' and 'gengr ... vefa'), phase four in the present ('vindum vindum'), and phase five in the perfect ('nú er vefr ofinn'). Since, as has been shown, these phases in real weaving are not simultaneous but successive, the action must be envisaged as progressing while the speakers are speaking. The narrative mode here is therefore what I have called running commentary.

The processes of weaving, as just outlined, and of fighting a battle may seem utterly disparate, but in fact there are surprisingly many points at which a similarity was perceived, or might reasonably have been. Just as weaving was archetypally women's work (though perhaps with exceptions, as in later centuries, in actual practice), so the guidance of battles was archetypally the work of supernatural women called Valkyries (here too with some male participation, notably from Óðinn).

The tools used in weaving and battle could also be perceived as similar. The specialist terminologies overlap with the word 'skapt' / 'shaft,' more narrowly either 'heddle rod' or 'spear shaft.' In the poem this perception of similarity is made overt in the lines 'eru dreyrrekin / dǫrr at skǫptum' / 'bloodstained spears serve as heddle rods' and is reinforced by the mention of 'skapt' in the other sense in the immediately following stanza.

The 'skeið,' or weaver's sword-beater, bears a strong visual resemblance to the sword of battle. The general shape was the same: a combination of blade and handle. In many examples of the 'skeið' the line of the blade is straight while the edges taper to a point. The resemblance to the sword of battle is even greater in Viking Age specimens, where the blade is of considerable length, from 60 to 80 cm and made of iron. Whalebone was the other common material of manufacture, and here the total length of blade and handle could be as much as 107 cm (Hoffmann 1964:279). These implements were therefore comparable in length with real swords. The action of 'skeið' and 'sverð' could also be perceived as similar, since both involve striking and penetrating: the 'skeið' penetrates the shed or passage so as to strike the weft threads in an upwards direction (cf Holtsmark 1939:93). The terminological overlap in 'sword-beater' is confined to English, but in both English and Old Norse the verb 'slá' / 'strike' and its cognates could be used to denote the action of 'skeið' and 'sverð' alike. The word 'slay' survives as a noun in modern English horizontal loom terminology, denoting the component that fulfils the function of the medieval 'skeið.' That the poet recognized the similarity of 'skeið' and 'sverð' is apparent from the lines 'skulum slá sverðum / sigrvef þenna,' which leaves the audience to intuit the equation with the weaver's implement for themselves.

Similarities might also be perceived between weaving and battle in two aspects of the visual effects that result. To produce a patterning of colours has traditionally been one of the objects of the weaver. According to Marta Hoffmann the technique of combining warp of one colour with weft of one or more colours to produce a check or other pattern in the textile has been practised since neolithic times (1964:6). Notable among Scandinavian examples is the Gerum mantle, from the Bronze Age, woven in a 'four-end twill enriched by alternating dark and light shades of woolen yarn' (Geijer 1979:242). Finds of Viking textiles at York have shown that there, as no doubt elsewhere, a rich variety of dyes was available (Hall 1984:98). Meanwhile, war poets of many nations describe the battlefield as being reddened with blood (Andersson 1972), and the skalds, displaying what Roberta Frank terms a 'vivid chromatic sense' (1978:62), sometimes elaborate on this commonplace so as to bring out patterns of colour contrast. In 'Ragnarsdrápa' 'dreyrfáar' / 'bloodstained' and 'hrafnbláir' / 'raven-dark' occur in the same stanza (Skj B 1 v 3). Each of these adjectives is placed midway through the third line in successive *helmingar*: the symmetry of placing, together with the rhyme '-fáar:bláir,' might well have led the audience to associate the two words and so to imagine the colour contrast more vividly. Some later skalds treat the contrasting colour words more boldly, in a virtual juxtaposition. In 'Útfarardrápa' 10, Haldórr has the line 'Finns rauð gjǫld – á grœnni,' where the green is of land and the red of blood-drenched arrows (Skj B 459–60). Descriptive of a sea battle are these lines from the twelfth-century 'Óláfs drápa Tryggvasonar' 22: 'skaut á grœnt með grjóti / grár ægir ná sǫrum / ... land / 'the grey sea cast up the wounded corpse, along with stones, on to the green land' (Skj B 573). Einarr Skúlason varies the application of 'grœnn,' perhaps playfully, in 'Ingadrápa' 1: 'lind varð grœn – enn grána,' where grey describes the sea but green the shield (Skj B 448). A striking display of skaldic ingenuity, built on a contrast between black and red, is to be seen in one of the Rǫgnvaldr kali *lausavísur* recounting a battle at sea (Frank 1978:151). The motif of battle producing a contrast of colours was used, then, by a succession of skalds; the poet of 'Darraðarljóð' is exceptional in associating the contrasting red of blood and grey of weapons with the colour patterns produced in weaving.

Another possible visual similarity between weaving and battle arises from the structure of a textile and of a marshalled army. In weaving, long rows of yarn are forced into contiguity, either in parallel or at right angles with one thread overlapping the other. Battle begins with an orderly formation in rows during the 'skothríð' / 'initial volley of missiles' and proceeds, with the charge, to the crush of hand-to-hand fighting. R. Allen Brown makes the following comments on the formation of the English shield-wall at the Battle of Hastings: 'We do not know how many ranks composed the line, but we do know that they stood in very close order, so close, wrote William of Poitiers, that the dead could scarcely fall and the wounded could not remove themselves from the action' (1981:11). Brown suspects 'an element of poetic licence' here, 'for clearly the shields must part for the weapons to be wielded and the great two-handed battle-axe especially required space on either side.' Again perhaps hyperbolically, some Norse poems describe the slain as lying in great heaps, one body across another: thus, in 'Krákumál' 16, 'hverr lá þverr of annan' (*Skj* B 652). These words probably echo what seems to have been a famous royal harangue incorporated by Steinn Herdísarson in 'Nizavísur' 1: 'heldr kvað hvern várn skyldu / hilmir frægr an vægja / ... of annan / ... þveran falla' / 'the famed king said that each of us should fall across the other rather than yield' (*Skj* B 376). The idea of a compacted, transverse formation approximates to the relationship between warp and weft threads in a textile, although in this case the poem contains no indication that the similarity was perceived.

In summary, similarities were perceived between weaving and battle in the type of persons who participate, the implements they use, and the appearance of the finished product. There is of course a distinction between the Valkyries, who have oversight of the fighting in some way, and the warriors, who are mere raw material.

The same association of ideas, although strange to some of us, is found elsewhere at roughly this period. The Old English riddle 56 in the Exeter Book seems to depend on a related conception, weaving seen as a series of warlike actions. The relevant part is as follows (Williamson 1977 no 54:101):

Ic wæs þær inne þær ic ane geseah
winnende wiht   wido bennegean,
holt hweorfende;   heaþoglemma feng,
deopra dolga.   Daroþas wæron
weo þære wihte,   ond se wudu searwum
fæste gebunden.

I was inside there where I saw wood, the moving timber, injure
a toiling creature; it received battle wounds, deep gashes. The
spears were a misery to that creature, and so too [was] the wood
bound fast with skill.

The riddle is generally solved as 'fabric' or 'textile': the arguments against
'flail,' Trautmann's solution, are set forth by Williamson in his edition
(ibid). The most obvious of the riddler's metaphors, or substitutions,
consists in the 'heaþoglemma' and 'deopra dolga,' which represent the
shed through which the shuttle passes. The 'daroþas' that cause misery
to the textile are not so easily identified, such is the studied vagueness
of the language. Dietrich suggested the shed rod and heddle rod
(1865:239) but Erika von Erhardt-Siebold the sword-beater (1949:15). The
twofold mention of some wooden part of the loom is also obscure; von
Erhardt-Siebold considered that the shuttle, which is 'bound to the web,'
is meant (ibid).

A second metaphorical treatment of the weaving motif occurs, as Nora
Kershaw pointed out, in an Irish praise poem composed about 909 in
memory of Cerball of Leinster and known as 'The Song of Carroll's
Sword' (Meyer 1899:9):

Mochen, a chlaidib Cherbaill! bát menic i mórenglaim,
bát menic ac cur chatha, ac dichennad ardfhlatha.

Hail, sword of Carroll! Oft hast thou been in the great woof, oft
giving battle, beheading high princes. (Meyer 1913:72)

The word 'englaim' means 'woof' or 'lining' and in spite of the translation 'woof of war,' which is sometimes cited, the metaphor is uncorrected
in the Irish. The associative basis for the metaphor lies in 'claideb' /
'sword,' which, combined with the genitives 'garmnae' or 'corthaire,'
means 'a weaver's beam' (O'Rahilly 1976:240). The metaphor is not fur-

ther elaborated in the lines that follow. Cerball, as it happens, was the king who drove the Vikings from their Dublin stronghold in 902 (Meyer 1899:8).

We see, then, that in contiguous Dark Age cultures weaving and battle were felt to have enough in common that the one could serve as a metaphor for the other. Holtsmark believed, however, that in 'Darraðarljóð' the weaving was no mere image. In her view, the Valkyries are simultaneously in two places, on the battlefield and at their loom, weaving a magical banner of the type described in Asser's Life of Alfred and in the *Encomium Emmæ*. This fits the prose of *Njáls saga*, which has the weaving and the fighting going on in two widely separated places, but not 'Darraðarljóð' itself: when, in verse 6, the speakers chant 'vindum vindum / vef darraðar, / þar er vé vaða / vígra manna' they are clearly on the battlefield, whether fighting or magically weaving. Eduard Neumann tried to meet this difficulty by arguing that in the poem those who weave are the same as those who fight; the two actions are regarded as one, occurring in the same time and space, and both literal and real (1955:152–3). This very complicated conception is of course purely a hypothetical construct and, as Klaus von See pointed out, would have no standing if an alternative, simpler way of interpreting the weaving motif could be established (1959:3).

As magical acts, weaving and spinning have often been associated with the creation or foretelling of destiny. An Irish example occurs in the *Táin Bó Cuailnge*, where a seeress is seen carrying a weaver's beam and weaving a fringe. This is a magical act that enables her to prophesy the coming battle (O'Rahilly 1976:2 and 240). O'Rahilly notes a modern instance in Scotland of two women 'a deilbh buidseacht' / 'framing witchcrafts by crossing threads of varied colours in varied manners, just as is done when threads are arranged for the loom' (1961:164). Goedheer explained Feidelm's actions in the *Táin* as connected with 'her original character as a sorceress, for weaving includes a magical power in primitive belief' (1938:82). The function of the weaving women in the *Njáls saga* prose seems to be similar – and perhaps even related, through a diffusion of folk beliefs from Scotland, as envisaged, to explain other parallels, by Bo Almqvist (1978–9:100–1). Another connection between weaving and fate, though not necessarily a magical one, is made in the Old English phrase 'wigspeda gewiofu' / 'the weaving of success in battle' (*Beowulf* 697), which God gives to the hero. These conceptions, however, do not explain 'Darraðarljóð' very well. The compound 'sigrvef[r]' in the poem could be looked on as a parallel to 'wigspeda gewiofu' in *Beowulf* because the two nouns combined with 'vefr/gewiofu' are abstract. But this leaves unexplained the other nouns combined with 'vefr' in 'Darraðarljóð': 'verþjóðar,' which is certainly concrete, and 'darraðar,' which as we saw is likely to be so. Klaus von See is therefore to my mind right in contending that 'vefr' in 'Darraðarljóð' is not a representation of fate but a reflection of the visual appearance of battle (1959:4).

I have adduced reasons for thinking that such a metaphor would have found full acceptance in the poet's own time. The view that exact visual or other correspondence is essential for metaphor has been refuted by I.A. Richards and other theorists. Richards comments that 'in general', there are very few metaphors in which disparities between tenor (subject of the metaphor) and vehicle (the specific image chosen by the author) are not as much operative as the similarities. Some similarity will commonly be the ostensive ground of the shift, but the peculiar modification of the tenor which the vehicle brings about is even more the work of their unlikenesses than of their likenesses' (1936:126). J.A. Mazzeo, discussing the conceits employed by the so-called metaphysical poets, takes the example of Homer's comparison between a huge wave breaking on a beach and an attacking army, and shows that this is not a 'fully pictorial metaphor,' though it might seem so. He comments: 'We must bear in mind that the metaphor is part identity and part difference. What Homer wants us to see is the way in which a wave under certain conditions is like an army under certain other conditions. By joining these two particular analogues, he selects those qualities of waves which can be transferred to armies' ([1952] 1962:71). There is thus no theoretical objection to a metaphor that works not when whole is matched against whole but when part is matched against part, as is necessary in my interpretation of 'Darraðarljóð.' A degree of disparity between tenor and vehicle has been seen as appropriate in the poetry of our own times, as in that of early seventeenth-century England. Richards saw the appeal of such disparities as originating in the progression from mental effort, as the audience tries to effect a connection, to gratification, when a resolution is found (1936:124–6). More recently, M.J. Apter has made a less negative assessment of the *immediate* effect of hearing metaphorical language: he suggests that the two contrasting elements, tenor and vehicle, gain an enhanced vividness in the mind of the audience, just as contrasting colour patches do when viewed simultaneously (1982:66). In metaphorical style 'a nexus of similarities and differences is created which gives the language a dynamic "living" quality' (ibid 62). These speculations on the reception of modern poetry of a self-proclaimed 'difficult' type may help us to understand how medieval audiences responded to skaldic poetry.

Meanwhile, whether we regard the weaving as metaphor or magic, we have seen that the detailed description offered in 'Darraðarljóð' does not fit with the *Njáls saga* picture of women busy in a weaver's hut hundreds of miles from the battlefield. On all scores, then, *Njáls saga* needs to be treated with scepticism in its account of 'Darraðarljóð.' The speakers are not in a weaver's hut or, in all likelihood, engaged in a literal piece of weaving; the listener, Dǫrruðr, is probably an etymological whimsy or blunder, and the subject, Clontarf, may be misplaced by almost a hundred years.

It follows that the saga prose cannot be relied on when we attempt to trace the narrative progression of 'Darraðarljóð.' We may note Einar Ól. Sveinsson's opinion that what Dǫrruðr sees in the prose description is to be understood as occurring simultaneously with the battle, not prior to it (*ÍF* 12: 454n1), but we must not argue from the prose in order to reach an understanding of the poem. The difficulties in analysing the narrative technique in 'Darraðarljóð' are formidable: I shall work through the poem stanza by stanza, noting where the problems lie and presenting some tentative solutions.

The poem opens with the statement that a warp has been set up 'fyrir valfalli.' This phrase is our first indication of the stage the battle has reached as the poem commences, but 'fyrir' is not easy to interpret. Editors and translators have most commonly explained 'fyrir valfalli' as 'presaging slaughter,' with the sense of 'fyrir' discussed by Fritzner, 'fyrir' 31. Instances known to me are Jón Þorkelsson 'það veit á mannfall' (1870:29), Guðbrandur Vigfússon 'presaging the slaughter' (1883 I:281), Finnur Jónsson 'um mörderischen kampf anzukündigen' (*Njála* 1908ed: 413n) and 'bebudende mandefald' (*Skj* B 389), Eiríkr Magnússon 'to warn of slaughter' (1910:10), Nora Kershaw 'portending slaughter' (1922:123), Andreas Heusler 'als Vorzeichen der Schlacht' (1922:375n1), and Einar Ól. Sveinsson 'sem veit á mannfall' (*ÍF* 12:455n).

Nevertheless, in spite of this substantial agreement, a sense of 'foreboding' or 'warning' for 'fyrir' seems poorly attested, other than in certain special combinations. It has this sense, for example, with the verbs 'vera' and 'verða,' as in 'opt er þat fyr oxnom, er ǫrno dreymi' / 'it often means oxen, when one dreams of eagles' ('Atlamál' 20: Neckel-Kuhn ed:250). The special nature of the verb also helps to fix a sense of 'foreboding' in such phrases as 'spá fyrir,' 'segja fyrir,' and 'dreyma draum fyrir' (Cleasby-Vigfússon 'fyrir' dative B2 and C xii). But none of these verbs is at all parallel in sense to 'verpa' ('er orpit'), where the idea is of something being made or formed, not signified.

Finnur Jónsson included under the gloss 'foran i tid (og bebudende noget)' the phrase 'fyr Eiríki glymr,' translated as 'det bulder varsler om Erik' or 'that noise is advance warning of Eiríkr' (LP 1931 'fyrir' B6). This example needs further consideration. The din of the hero's riding or arrival is a favourite theme, found in 'Eiríksmál' 3-4, 'Atlakviða' 13, 'Helgakviða Hundingsbana' I:47, 'Oddrúnargrátr' 17 and 28, and 'Baldrs draumar' 3. In the lines 'fram reið Óðinn, foldvegr dundi' / 'Óðinn rode forth, the road through the land reverberated' ('Baldrs draumar' 3: Neckel-Kuhn ed: 277), we see an implicit connection between cause (the swiftness or hardness of the riding) and effect (the din). The other examples, including 'fyr Eiríki glymr,' can be explained in the same way. There is thus no basis for supposing that 'fyrir' means 'portending' except with the two special groups of verbs already mentioned.

What other sense of 'fyrir' will fit? The range of the word is immense, as a glance at Fritzner's article will show, but the choice narrows down because of the demands of the present context. A sense 'before,' giving 'before the slaughter,' sounds plausible but must be rejected because 'fyrir' / 'before in time' governs the accusative, not the dative. In the context we find mention that something (the warp) is being formed: this can be taken as an effect or result, and then a possible function of 'fyrir valfalli' is to indicate the cause. A causal sense of 'fyrir' is discussed in section 14 of Fritzner's article: what seems to occur is a primary meaning 'in the face of' fading into a virtual causal meaning 'because of, by means of, with, through.' This is the gloss that I would give to 'fyr[ir]' in 'fyr Eiríki glymr.'

The preposition 'fyrir,' used in this sense, often governs a proper name, denoting a person whose presence causes some result. Examples are 'Haustlǫng' 15, 'knǫ́ttu ǫll ... Ullar / ... fyr mági / ... ginnunga vé brinna' / 'all the sky burned on account of Ullr's stepfather' (Skj B 17), and Sexstefja 7, 'rofizk hafa opt fyr jǫfri / ... sáttir' / 'terms of peace have often been broken by the king' (Skj B 340). Other types of noun also appear, however. An instance where the ideas of 'in the face of' and 'by means of' are about evenly balanced is 'fyr þessom eggiom / hnígr sá inn aldni iǫtunn' / 'the aged giant falls before [by means of] these edges' ('Skírnismál' 25: Neckel-Kuhn ed: 74). Cause, on the other hand, is beginning to dominate in Einarr Skúlason, 'Haraldssonakvædi': 'hjalmr springr opt fyr olmri / egghríð' / 'the helmet is often shattered in [with] the savage swordplay' (*Skj* B 426). Fritzner also cites the examples 'sjór var hvítr fyrir drifi' / 'the sea was white with foam' and 'hjǫltinn vǫru hvít fyrir silfri' / 'the hilt was white with silver.'

If my causal interpretation of 'fyrir' is correct, the forming of a warp is in some way the outcome of slaughter in battle. How that could be is not for the moment explained. Then with the words 'vefr verþjóðar' later in the stanza and more explicitly still in verse 2 the dead bodies of warriors are shown creating the warp and loom weights. The warp is formed 'with [through] the fall of the slain.' We gather from this that as the description begins the battle is already regarded as underway. The formation of the warp is described in the perfect tense ('er orpit'), as of something completed or approaching completeness.

The phrase 'fyrir geirum' in the final part of verse 1 presents further syntactic problems. Many scholars have taken it closely with 'grár,' the following word, and translated 'grey with spears,' referring to the woven fabric. The list includes Sveinbjörn Egilsson 'tela hastis leucophaea' (*LP* 1860 'grár'), Jón Þorkelsson 'grár af spjótum' (1870:29), Eiríkr Magnússon 'grey with spears' (1910:10), Finnur Jónsson 'grau von der speeren' (*Njála* 1908ed: 413n) and 'grå af spyd' (*Skj* B 389), Kershaw 'grey with spears' (1922:123), and Einar Ól. Sveinsson 'grár fyrir járnum' (*ÍF* 12:455n).

Not everybody has been satisfied with this. Guðbrandur Vigfússon took 'fyrir' as 'on' and kept it syntactically separate from 'grár' in his translation 'the gray web of the hosts is raised up on the spears' (1883 I:281): compare Heusler 'an Geren hat sich / grau erhoben / Volksgewebe' (1922:375). Konráð Gíslason argued that 'fyrir geirum / grár' is not precisely parallel with expressions like 'grár fyr hærum' / 'grey with old age' and 'grár fyr járnum' / 'grey with weapons' (II 1889: 581). He believed that 'geir-' here represented not literal spears but, analogous to 'dǫrr' in verse 2, the shafts of the loom, and commented that the grey colour of these shafts could hardly be said to confer a grey colour on the fabric. Finnur Jónsson, also obviously perplexed about these words, suggested identifying the 'spears' with the 'hleinar' / 'uprights' of the loom (*Njála* 1908ed:413n).

Further consideration seems called for. To interpret 'fyrir geirum' as 'á geirum' is strained; the equation of 'geir-' with parts of the loom is premature; the treatment of 'fyrir geirum' and 'grár' as a syntactic unit involves a reversal in word order that, while not impossible, ought to be set aside until simpler alternatives are ruled out. Parallelism with the four first lines leads us to expect that 'kominn' will group with 'fyrir geirum' just as 'orpit' groups with 'fyrir valfalli' and that 'grár' looks forward to 'vefr' just as 'vítt' (if not an adverb) looks forward to 'reidisky.' Klaus von See envisaged the 'vefr verþjódar' as 'confronting' or 'facing' the enemy spears: 'vor den Geren der Gegenpartei' (1959:7). But I see no obstacle to assuming a closer parallelism, with 'fyrir' here in the same sense as in 'fyrir valfalli.' This was Vogt's opinion, and so he translates 'bedeutend Speere,' parallel with 'bedeutend Kampftod' (1927:160). A rendering that makes better sense than Vogt's is obtained if we take both occurrences of 'fyrir' as 'in the face of / because of.' 'Because of or in the face of the spears,' warriors have fallen in overlapping rows like a woven fabric. More remote in the poem is another parallel: 'nú er fyrir oddum / jarlmadr hniginn' / 'now the earl has sunk down in the face of [or because of] the spears' (v 7). This is very close to 'Skírnismál' 25 and also to Þjódólfr Arnórsson *lv*. 1 'hauss gein fyrir steini' / 'the skull gaped open with the impact of [because of] the stone' (*ÍF* 28:52).

Another parallel between the first and second part of verse 1 is the switch from a perfect tense verb ('er orpit,' 'er kominn') to a present form ('rignir,' 'fylla'). The verb 'fylla' is most simply explained as representing an action that is in progress and continuing: thus Gudbrandur Vigfússon and Nora Kershaw 'are filling' (1883 I:281 and 1922:123), Heusler 'füllen' (1922:375), Einar Ól. Sveinsson 'fylla' (*ÍF* 12:455n), and Bayerschmidt-Hollander 'fill' (1955:358). A fairly strongly-supported alternative is to construe 'fylla' as a present-for-future: so Finnur Jónsson 'das werden die freundinnen ... füllen' (*Njála* 1908ed:413n) and 'veninder vil fylde' (*Skj* B 389), Tveiten 'fylla vil' (1966:79), and Klaus von See 'die Walküren ... "mit rotem Einschlag füllen" werden' (1959:7). These translations with the future tense presumably arise because the commentators see the Valkyries beginning their participation in verse 3: von See comments that they are not involved in the prelude to battle but appear first when the fighting has already begun (ibid 8). This is a misunderstanding that I shall deal with presently.

Meanwhile, if we take verse 1 on its own and make what sense we can of it without anticipating later stanzas, what is being recounted is evidently the first phase of battle, the *skothríd*, when spears, arrows, and other missiles were launched at the enemy from some distance. Thus spears, not swords or other thrusting weapons, are mentioned. In verse 2 we see from the gory picture of entrails and severed heads that the fight is going on in earnest (contrast von See ibid 8). But proceedings do not yet seem to have advanced beyond the *skothríd*, because again the weapons mentioned as being used in the here and now belong in the missile category: 'dǫrr' / 'spears' and 'ǫr-' / 'arrows.' The substitution of spears for heddle rods in verse 2 clarifies what is meant by the description of Valkyries inserting weft threads in verse 1: just as a weaver used the heddle rods to facilitate the insertion of weft, so the Valkyries, along with the human warriors, are using spears to 'insert weft' in their own special way, which consists in felling human bodies and staining them with blood. With hindsight the link in thought between 'fyrir geirum' and 'nú er ... / grár upp kominn / vefr verþjóðar' becomes clear as well. Although the 'yllir' / 'shed rod' is not equated with any particular weapon, it is 'ironclad' and appropriately mentioned here because it too, as we have seen, played its part in the correct insertion of the weft. The analogies depend upon a phase-by-phase collocation of the processes of weaving and war, and are only in part pictorial. The significance of this analysis for the chronology of the poem is that we are located, from verse 1, not quite classically *in medias res* but at any rate somewhat beyond the strict chronological beginning of the battle.

The first mention of a weapon suited to close fighting – the sword – comes in the final two lines of verse 2. They read as an exhortation or mutual incitation among the Valkyries to do something that as yet still belongs in the future: 'skulum slá sverðum / sigrvef þenna.' With verse 3 this new phase is beginning: 'gengr Hildr vefa / ... sverðum tognum.' The stage reached now in the battle, close fighting after the charge, is aligned with the stage in the weaving process where the workers beat the weft threads home, using the sword-beater. As I have noted, some scholars have taken the first four lines of verse 3 to mean that only now do the Valkyries begin their weaving, which conflicts with the clear statement in verse 1 that they are already at work. But the difficulty is more apparent than real, since 'sverðum tognum' can be taken not as a comitative dative with 'gengr' but as an instrumental dative with 'vefa.' 'Hildr [etc] goes to weave with unsheathed swords': previously they wove with spears. To repeat: what we see here is a new phase, not a beginning, of the Valkyries' participation in battle. This feeling for the march of events is lost by Guðbrandur Vigfússon when he translates 'are weaving' (1883 I:282); other translators and editors preserve the idea of 'going.'

In the second quatrain of verse 3 the speakers again look forward to the future course of the fighting. The auxiliary 'mun,' used emphatically three times, is clearly equivalent to future tense. But its occurrence here should not be allowed to obscure the fact that in general the poem is a 'running commentary,' interspersed with incitations and (later) prophecies by the speakers. To see the entire poem as a prophecy, as do Heusler-Ranisch (1903:11), is to read into many of the verbs, notably 'fylla' in verse 1, a futurity that is not guaranteed by the immediate context. Certainly the present indicative form can substitute for the future tense in Old Norse, there being no distinctive synthetic form; but an examination of relevant passages, including those cited by Nygaard (1905:182-3), shows that present-form verbs can be construed as future only when the context signals unambiguously that this should be done. Such signalling occurs when distinctive quasi-future analytic forms come first (in particular 'mun' and 'skal' with the infinitive), followed by the unmarked present form. Sometimes, much more rarely, distinctive analytic forms may follow the unmarked present tense, but these must then be in close proximity, for instance in the shape of a subordinate temporal clause that establishes the futurity of the main verb. These conditions are not fulfilled in verse 1. We have to wait until the end of verse 2 for the first quasi-future form ('skulum slá sverðum') and this, like the other quasi-futures, is most naturally interpreted as marking an incitation. My view of the narrative technique in 'Darraðarljóð' is in close agreement with Holtsmark (1939:93) and Neumann (1955:150), who argue that the poem keeps pace with events as they occur on the battlefield.

The next three stanzas begin with the same two lines, which therefore act as a refrain: 'vindum vindum / vef darraðar.' In interpreting these lines commentators have hesitated between the imperative and the indicative: on the one hand Guðbrandur Vigfússon has 'let us wind!' (1883 I:282) and Eiríkr Magnússon 'wind we' (1910:11); on the other hand Finnur Jónsson has 'wir winden' (*Njála* 1908ed:415n) and 'vi vinder' (*Skj* B 389–90). Kershaw seems to vacillate, though she translates with the indicative (1922:123 and 193). I should view the refrain as another mutual incitation, spoken by the Valkyries as the work of 'winding' goes on. This is the familiar work-song or sea-shanty type of incitation, accompanying the action it refers to, like 'mǫlom' in 'Grottasǫngr.'

Presumably the phase in the weaving we have now reached, when a finished section of textile is wound up onto the loom beam, is aligned, like the earlier phases, to some facet or aspect of the battle. Here, more than elsewhere, purely pictorial considerations will not help us greatly in identifying an analogue (cf von See 1959:9n1). The equation might be with that stage when 'opposing formations ... parted to draw breath,' something that Nicholas Hooper thinks was characteristic of battles in Anglo-Saxon England (1979:93). On the other hand, the cry 'vindum vindum vef darraðar,' as the refrain of the poem, is more likely to be a call to action than a signal for a tactical withdrawal. Accordingly we might prefer to connect the refrain with that phase in a battle 'when one or other force broke, and a mad rush to horse ensued, either to escape or to pursue' (ibid). This would be the moment at which the ending of the battle began, and so the stanzas with refrain would be appropriately followed by the stanzas (from verse 7) that comment on the aftermath and longer-range consequences of the fighting. Likeliest, however, if we bear in mind the detailed descriptions of fighting that follow the refrain in each stanza, is that the refrain refers not to a specific stage or manoeuvre in the battle but to the battle in general: the lines 'þann er ungr konungr / átti fyrri' point in that direction, though 'þann' may be a scribal emendation (in *Gráskinnuauki*, for unexplained 'sá' in the other manuscripts). As we have seen, these lines in their original state probably contained a reference to some past victory won by the 'ungr konungr.'

An allied problem is presented by the first quatrain in verse 5: 'vindum vindum / vef darraðar, / ok siklingi / síðan fylgjum.' Where are the Valkyries to be imagined 'following the prince?' Into the battle that is now going on? Some commentators, while not totally avoiding ambiguity, seem to think so: Guðbrandur Vigfússon translates 'and then ride to war with the young king' (1883 I:282), while Heusler-Ranisch explain these lines by referring to 6.5–6 'látum eigi / líf hans farask' (1903:xlix). Most commentators do not specify time and place: thus Finnur Jónsson 'und dem könig werden wir hernach helfen' (*Njála* 1908ed:415n) and 'og siden vil vi følge fyrsten' (*Skj* B 390) and Eiríkr Magnússon 'and faithfully the king we follow' (1910:11). Nora Kershaw hesitates between 'and we shall continue to aid the hero' (1922:123) and 'and we will afterwards aid ... ' (ibid 194). How we interpret here depends on how we interpret the refrain. If, as I think, the refrain refers to the battle as a whole, necessarily the couplet in verse 5 must signify the speakers' intention to follow the king after the present battle, that is on a subsequent campaign. We shall find similar hints as to a sequel in the final stanzas.

The verb tenses in the second *helmingr* of verse 5 are difficult but potentially significant for the poet's narrative technique. In three of the four relevant manuscripts the first verb is present, 'sjá,' but in the remaining one, *Mǫðruvallabók*, it is preterite, 'sá.' The second verb is preterite in all manuscripts, but from two different roots: *Reykjabók* has 'fylgðu' and the others 'hlífðu.' The reading 'sjá' has been adopted by a number of scholars, as having majority support in the manuscripts, across the normal lines of affiliation, and is translated as a future: thus Finnur Jónsson 'werden sehen' (*Njála* 1908ed: 415n) and 'vil se' (*Skj* B 390), Kershaw 'will look' (1922:123), and Tveiten 'vil skoda' (1966:79). Guðbrandur Vigfússon even emends to a quasi-future form: 'skolo bera' (1883 I:282). But since the Valkyries have been participating in the battle from the beginning of the poem, 'sjá,' if we adopt that reading, can be treated as a simple present tense.

If we do adopt 'sjá,' instead of 'sá,' we must account for the preterite verb ('fylgðu' or 'hlífðu') at the end of the *helmingr*. Reading 'sjá ... fylgðu,' Jón Þorkelsson suggested that this *helmingr*, unlike the previous one, was spoken not by the Valkyries but in the poet's own voice (1870:30). Other scholars who regard the second verb as past tense are Finnur Jónsson, with 'gefolgt sind' (*Njála* 1908ed:415n) and 'fulgte' (*Skj* B 390), and Kershaw, with 'have guarded' (1922:123). This preterite or perfect could be applied either to previous battles or to the foregoing phases of the current one; Heusler-Ranisch see 5.8 as an indication that the Valkyries have already served the king in earlier frays, masterminding battles and lending him their protection (1903:xlix). Konráð Gíslason, on the other hand, tried to obtain a normal sequence of tenses by rejecting 'sá' in *Mǫðruvallabók* as a scribal emendation and emending 'hlífðu' to 'hlífa,' against all the manuscripts (II 1889: 585; cf Vogt 1927:160). Of similar opinion, evidently, were Guðbrandur Vigfússon, who translated 'hlífðu' as a present ('that guard the king') without emending (1883 I:282), and Heusler in his Thule translation, which has 'wo den König Gunn / und Göndul schirmen' (1922:376).

In spite of the general preference for 'sjá,' in this instance the preterite seems the *lectio difficilior*. Following a series of present-tense verbs, a preterite would be vulnerable to alteration, orally or scribally, whereas a present form would be much less vulnerable. *Mǫðruvallabók* has some unsupported readings elsewhere that are uniformly regarded as superior, notably in verse 1: 'orpit,' '-ský,' 'fylla,' and 'bana.' If we read 'sá' and 'hlífðu,' these preterite verbs momentarily place the current battle in the past: the running commentary presentation is temporarily deserted and the audience enters into a retrospective viewpoint on events. We have seen a similar change of perspective in 'Friðgerðarflokkr' and 'Liðsmannaflokkr.'

While adopting the variant 'sá,' Eiríkr Magnússon agreed with other scholars in finding the narrative technique here unpleasing. His attempted remedy was to rearrange the *helmingar* of verses 5 and 6 in the order 6.1–4, a lacuna of four lines, 5.1–4, 6.5–8, another four-line lacuna, and finally 5.5–8 (1910:11). This, in his opinion, gave better logical and chronological sequence (ibid 13): 6.1–4 points 'to the commencement of the battle, by the banners of the opponents moving out'; 5.1–4 also belongs to the 'commencement of the fight' because that would be the most natural time for the Valkyries to 'take their side' and make their 'vow'; 6.5–8 follows immediately on 5.1–4, in the one stanza, because 'hans' in 6.6 refers back to 'siklingi' in 5.3. Finally, 5.5–8 is placed last because it 'wound up that section of the poem which dealt with the battle itself and described the sight the stricken field revealed to ... Gunnr and Gondol reviewing it; for the statement: *þærs grame hlífþo* "they who sheltered the king" shows that the battle is over and [the king] safe.'

Eiríkr's assumption of lacunae, against all the manuscript evidence, is not attractive. I believe that the *helmingar* should be left in their present order, while acknowledging that some transposition might easily have occurred because of the identical opening lines in verses 4–6. This is a choice that, like the reading 'sá,' may not represent what the poet originally said but that at least does not artificially smooth away the difficulties. If we alter a text to obtain what to one modern viewpoint seems the natural narrative sequence, we run the risk of imposing our logic and aesthetic on the poet and even of expunging the evidence as to what that poet's own logic and aesthetic actually were.

After the apparent retrospective view in the second *helmingr* of verse 5, the poet returns to the running commentary narration in verse 6. At first the speakers' concern is straightforwardly with the battle in hand, but in verses 7–8, as already in verse 5, thoughts about the longer-range future begin to obtrude. They are interlaced with a description of the battlefield in the here and now. Grammatically, the alternation is between quasi-futures ('munu ráðá,' 'kveð ek ráðinn,' 'munu bíða,' and so on) and present perfects ('er hniginn,' 'er ofinn,' and so on). This complicated sequence struck early editors as unnatural too, so that Guðbrandur Vigfússon transposes lines in verse 7 to produce the chronological order 7–8, 5–6. The 'rík[r] gram[r]' and the 'jarlmaðr' mentioned in this *helmingr* have been taken by some other scholars, notably Heusler-Ranisch, Nora Kershaw, and Klaus von See, to be one and the same person. The prophecy of his death (7.5–6) would then immediately precede an announcement that death had occurred (7–8). Kershaw translates: 'I declare that death is ordained for a mighty prince. – Even now the earl has been laid low by the spears' (1922:125). The translator appears to feel a difficulty here: the 'even now' for 'nú' and the Sternean dash seem designed to tone down the abruptness of the narrative transition. Evidently with the same purpose von See suggested an emendation to 'kvað ek' (1959:12). But really there is no obstacle to supposing, along with most commentators, that the 'gramr' and the 'jarlmaðr' are two different men: in the *helmingr* the speaker foresees an even greater loss (the king, indeed the high king) at the moment when an important leader (the earl) is felled. Whether this earl is fighting on the Irish or the Norse side is, as we have seen, uncertain: context would suggest the former, if we discarded the identification with Sigurðr.

From verse 7, and especially with the statement that the battle is over, in verse 8, the running commentary becomes more heavily interspersed with vaticination. The specific prophecies are that death is in store for the mighty king, that people hitherto confined to the coastal fringe will rule the lands, that the Irish people will feel grief, and that the news of the disaster will travel across the land. These prophecies seem to be continued in 9.5–6: 'mun lopt litat / lýða blóði.' Some scholars translate as if the text were 'er lopt litat ... ': Finnur Jónsson has 'die luft wird gefärbt' (*Njála* 1908ed:417n) and 'luften rødfarves' (*Skj* B 390), Eiríkr Magnússon 'the skies take hue' (1910:12), and Nora Kershaw 'the air is being dyed' (1922:125). Such an interpretation of 'mun' does not fit with the use of the auxiliary elsewhere in 'Darraðarljóð,' where it uniformly denotes futurity, not merely inference about the present. Guðbrandur Vigfússon has the literally correct translation: 'the air shall be dyed with the blood of men' (1883 I:283). At first glance the lines might seem to be describing the same blood-streaked sky as 9.1–4 and indeed to be recapitulating the description of the rain of blood in verse 1. I should prefer, however, to take them as looking forward to future battles, which the Valkyries believe will ensue as a consequence of this one, a belief that has already been hinted at in 5.3–4.

I therefore read verse 9 as saying that, terrible as the scene is at the field of battle today, similar terrible sights are in store for the future (perhaps the near future). Unfortunately, the text of the final two lines of the stanza is so corrupt that this and other interpretations must remain tentative. A process of oral attrition or scribal emendation seems to have gone on, and is certainly irreparable now. To survey the evidence briefly, the variant 'syngja' in 9.8 is more likely to be secondary than 'springa,' because it is an easier reading and may have entered the text through anticipation of 'syngjum' in 10.4. The word 'springa' normally means 'break, burst, fly apart'; the translation 'leap, spread' is purely speculative, from the Old English cognate 'springan' as used in *Beowulf* 18:

'blæd wide sprang' / 'his fame spread far and wide' (Þorkelsson 1870:31, Heusler-Ranisch 1903:147, and von See 1959:13). Dietrich Hofmann does not examine the possibility of Old English influence on 'springa' (1955:112–14). Though such influence, whether from Old English or another Germanic language, may be an attractive hypothesis, it is too uncertain to help with the present problem of interpretation, as also is the possibility that 'springa' here retains its common Germanic sense. In the majority of manuscripts 'spár' / 'prophecies' are somehow involved: *Reykjabók*, *Oddabók*, and *Moðruvallabók* agree here against *Gráskinnuauki*, where the compound 'sóknvarðar' / 'battle-women' (ie Valkyries) looks suspiciously like a scribal emendation or perhaps an example of simplification in oral transmission. Yet even the reading 'spár' may not represent the original text, which could well have contained a variation on the familiar motif of weapons or armour flying apart or being shattered (hence 'springa').

The opening *helmingr* of verse 10 can be divided into clauses in two different ways, and here Guðbrandur Vigfússon chooses the alternative that has not been favoured by other editors (1883 I:283, normalized by me, with Finnur Jónsson's text in *Skjaldedigtning* following for comparison):

Vel kváðu vér   Vel kváðu vér
um konung ungan,   um konung ungan
sigrhljóða fjǫld   sigrhljóða fjǫld,
sungum heilar.   syngjum heilar.

With line 3 Vigfússon associated a line in the next *helmingr*, 'geirhljóða fjǫld' in his edition – evidently as a variation in the style of Old English poetry. He translates: 'We have spoken words of might round the young king, we have sung him many a joyous lay of victory, many a lay of spears ... ' The punctuation of the first *helmingr* so that the first clause ends at 'fjǫld' (and of course without the variation structure) is found in Jón Þorkelsson (1870:32), Heusler-Ranisch (1903:60), *Njála* (1908ed: 417), Eiríkr Magnússon (1910:12), Kershaw (1922:124), and Sveinsson (ÍF 12:458). Nevertheless, Vigfússon's division of the *helmingr* into two couplets gives excellent sense and deserves to be revived. The first couplet, 'vel kváðu vér / um konung ungan,' refers back to the poem we have just been hearing and in which the Valkyries 'spoke well of the young king' by celebrating his success in battle. The preterite, applied to a poetic recitation or composition that has just been completed, is used in the same way and at the same point in Egill's 'Hǫfuđlausn.' In the second couplet Vigfússon emended 'syngjum' to the preterite 'sungum,' so obtaining a parallel with the first couplet. But this kind of editorial tidying up is undesirable, as masking the fluid movement in tense and time that characterizes 'Darrađarljóđ' as well as other poems of its genre. Left unemended, 'sigrljóđa fjǫld / syngjum heilar' expresses a wish for the future. We have already noted that the Valkyries are pledged to follow their king to further battles, which are to be expected as an aftermath of this one, such will be the rancour of the losing side. Now the Valkyries voice their expectations of a succession of victories, to be commemorated in further poems of praise.

In the second *helmingr* of verse 10 the Valkyries address their human listener for the first time. This man ('hinn') could be any warrior with ears to hear. In the *Mǫđruvallabók* and *Gráskinnuauki* texts he is enjoined to 'say' ('segi') whereas in *Reykjabók* and *Oddabók* he is to 'entertain' ('skemti'). Konráđ Gíslason found 'skemti' too cheery for such a macabre context (II 1889:594); similarly Eiríkr Magnússon (1910:20). The reading 'segi' was also adopted by Finnur Jónsson (*Njála* 1908ed:417 and *Skj* B 391), Nora Kershaw (1922:124), and Einar Ól. Sveinsson (*ÍF* 12:458). While not adopting 'skemti' into their text, Heusler-Ranisch defended this variant as metrically superior (1903:60), and they were followed in this by E.A. Kock (NN 2043). Klaus von See argued that 'skemta' / 'to entertain' was the appropriate word to use of a skald reciting a praise poem (1959:13). The reading 'skemti' could also be defended as more difficult and specific than 'segi,' which looks like an example of the loss of particularity consequent on oral tradition. Certainly to reject the notion that a praise poem like 'Darrađarljóđ' can 'entertain' or 'amuse' is to import alien cultural assumptions. A related idea is Egill's delivery of 'Hǫfuđlausn' 'ór hlátra ham' / 'from the skin of laughter' (ie the breast): the reference in the kenning is to the laugh of jubilation that attends a victory or the discomfiture of an opponent – appropriately, since 'Hǫfuđlausn' is concerned with Eiríkr blóđøx's triumphs in battle. This kind of laughter, along with the theme of entertainment in the hall, is discussed as it appears in Anglo-Saxon literature by S.I. Tucker (1959:222–4). Klaus von See compares 'Darrađarljóđ,' where a listening poet is implied, to 'Haraldskvædi,' where the poet reports a conversation between a Valkyrie and a raven (1959:13). In 'Darrađarljóđ' this 'frame' is more sketchily established, and not until the end of the poem. A somewhat similar postponement of references to the listener has been seen in 'Liđsmannaflokkr.'

The poem concludes with a final brief incitation to ride off (á braut') and out ('út'). From the previous verses it is clear that 'út' means 'out from the battlefield,' not (as in the *Njáls saga* prose interpretation) 'out from the weaver's hut.' The command to carry unsheathed swords may be a further indication that fresh battles lie in store for the Valkyries (but cf von See ibid 14). This final stanza contains only four lines, but since the first two stanzas also deviate from the regular eight lines there is no reason to speculate with Vogt (1927:161) and others that four lines have been lost at the end of the poem.

To summarize on the narrative technique in 'Darraðarljóð': A process or progressive action is being described. In weaving terms, in verse 1 we see the Valkyries 'fylla' their warp with a 'rauðum vepti,' in verse 2 they are about to 'slá' it, in verses 4-6 they 'vinda' their weaving up, and in verse 8 the process is complete: 'nú er vefr ofinn.' In military terms, verse 1 is appropriate to the *skothríð*, or initial phase; in verse 3 the piercing and smashing of armour by the sword still lie in the future, but by verse 5 the bloodying of shields lies in the past (if we read 'sá' with *Mǫðruvallabók*), otherwise in the present; in verses 7-8 the fighting appears to be over, the death of the 'ríkr gramr' being the one foreseen but as yet unfulfilled event. A fully retrospective view of the action asserts itself only in verses 10-11, together, I think, with 5.5-8. Elsewhere we have the illusion that the action is unfolding before the speakers' eyes.

Nearly all scholars have seen 'Darraðarljóð' as a unity. Exceptional were Lehmann-von Carolsfeld, who went so far as to argue that the poem in its extant form represents a conflation of two separate works: in one we have ten-line stanzas where the supernatural women are described as Norns, in the other eight-line stanzas where they are described as Valkyries. Awkward for this theory was the presence of the word 'vefa' in the supposed Valkyrie stanzas, since weaving is presumed to be an exclusively Norn pursuit. The authors speculated, however, that originally some more suitable verb, such as 'vega' or 'kjósa,' stood here (1883:142).

If we avoid speculation and scrutinize the text as it stands we find a familiar kind of structure, given what else we know of skaldic aesthetic, namely a general tripartite symmetry. At the approximate centre is a three-stanza block containing the brief work-song-like refrain (vv 4-6). Preceding that we have verses 1-3 (a total of twenty-eight lines) and after it verses 7-11 (thirty-six lines). Sticklers for exact symmetry might speculate that an eight-line stanza has dropped out before or after verse 3, but there is no evidence that the skalds planned their compositions with the numerological exactitude of a Dante or a Spenser. In 'Liðsmannaflokkr' too the refrain is placed 'off-centre' in verses 3 and 9 of a ten-stanza poem. The linking of the first section of the poem with the last through repetition of vocabulary is also a feature of other works. The words 'ský' and 'blóði' occur in both verses 1 and 9, 'geir' in verses 1 and 10, 'dreyr' and 'sigr' in verses 2 and 10, and 'sverðum' in verses 2, 3, and 11; of these words only 'blóð' (in 'blóðgar' 5.6) appears elsewhere in the poem. The first three and the last three verses are all included in the pattern.

The praise poetry of the Vikings and medieval Scandinavians is preserved in so fragmentary a state that for the most part we cannot now tell what, if anything, conferred a distinctive character upon individual poems. Indeed, the impression used to be that they possessed no special character but were merely a monotonous tally of carnage, plunder, and victory. Yet the very familiarity of the themes must on occasion have stimulated the poet's invention. The choice not simply of a Valkyrie as speaker but of weaving terminology as a vehicle for much of the description was a bold stroke of poetic individuation, one that outdoes all other extant praise poems.

For poets of the Middle Ages to display their knowledge of non-poetic crafts is of course not strange. The technicalities of milling, blacksmithing, and even medicine were, with other trades and professions, the object of poetic virtuosity among various poets in various countries. Unlike Chaucer's Host, they knew how to 'speke in terme.' But that which in the beginning gave the poem its individual life comes, by an irony, to sound its death-knell. As traditional crafts died out the poems that played dazzling games with specialist terminologies declined into obscurity.

Though especially difficult in its central conceit (or 'controlling metaphor'), 'Darraðarljóð' is notably simple and unpretentious in its metre and stanza-form. The combination of vividness and simplicity may have been what ensured this poem the most lasting life of all in oral tradition. In his novel *The Pirate* Sir Walter Scott tells, at third hand, the curious report of an Orkney clergyman who 'remembered well when some remnants of the Norse were still spoken in the island called North Ronaldshaw. When Gray's Ode, entitled the "Fatal Sisters," was first published, or at least first reached that remote island, the reverend gentleman had the well-judged curiosity to read it to some of the old persons of the isle, as a poem which regarded the history of their own country. They listened with great attention to the preliminary stanzas: –

> Now the storm begins to lour,
> Haste the loom of hell prepare,
> Iron sleet of arrowy shower
> Hurtles in the darken'd air.

But when they had heard a verse or two more, they interrupted the reader, telling him they knew the song well in the Norse language, and had often sung it to him when he asked them for an old song. They called it the Magicians, or the Enchantresses. It would have been singular news to the elegant translator, when executing his version from the text of Bartholine, to have learned that the Norse original was still preserved by tradition in a remote corner of the British dominions' (Scott 1901ed: 566; cf Sophus Bugge 1901:74).

THREE RECONSTRUCTED POEMS

So far each of the poems presented here has been preserved as an entity in the medieval prose compilations. Although these poems have offered obstacles to scholarly interpretation and although their prose environment has on occasion created obscurities, there has been little or nothing to obscure their status as unitary works, except on occasion the zeal of modern interpreters. With the verses to which I shall move in ensuing chapters the picture is different, because their prose environment establishes them as *lausavísur* and not as the constituent stanzas of unitary poems. As in chapter 1, I shall be arguing that this compositional isolation is not intrinsic to the verses in question but a result of fragmenting tendencies in the prose. I shall show that it is possible to reassemble these purported *lausavísur* into poems that possess a structure and narrative technique closely similar to those of the four poems analysed in the previous chapters.

'Torf-Einarr's Revenge'

In *Orkneyinga saga* a group of five stanzas is attributed to a very early figure in those islands' history, Torf-Einarr (ÍF 34:12–16 vv 2–6). Some of the stanzas also appear in *Fagrskinna* and *Heimskringla*. In *Orkneyinga saga* and *Heimskringla* they are presented as improvisations, composed over a period of some months during and after Einarr's revenge of his father Rǫgnvaldr. Klaus von See has contended that in this matter the sagas give a false impression and that originally Einarr's verses constituted a single poem; at some point, perhaps with the writer of *Orkneyinga saga* in its extant form, this poem was broken up and the constituent stanzas inserted at various points in a prose narration of Einarr's revenge and its aftermath (1960).

1 Sékat Hrólfs ór hendi
  né Hrollaugi fljúga
  dǫrr á dólga mengi;
  dugir oss fǫður hefna!
  En í kveld, meðan knýjum,
  of kerstraumi, rómu,
  þegjandi sitr þetta
  Þórir jarl á Mœri.
         (*Skj* A 31 v 1; von See 1960:34)

I do not see spears fly from Hrólfr's hand or from Hrollaugr at the throng of our foes: it is right for us to avenge our father! Yet in the evening, while we press our attack, Þórir jarl sits this out silently over the mead at Mœrr.

2 Margr verðr sénn at sauðum
  seggr með breiðu skeggi,
  en ek at ungs í Eyjum
  allvalds sonar falli.
  Hætt segja mér hǫlðar
  við hugfullan stilli:
  Haralds hefk skarð í skildi
  – skalat ugga þat – hǫggvit.

                                        (Skj A 32 v 5; von See 1960:34)

Many a full-bearded man is noted for [the slaughter of] sheep, but
I myself for the killing of the king's young son on the islands.
Men say that I am in danger from the valiant king: I have no cause
to fear that. I have hewed a notch in Haraldr's shield.

3 Ey munk glaðr, síz geirar
  – gótt's vinna þrek manni –
  bǫðfíkinna bragna
  bitu þengils son ungan;
  þeygi dylk, nema þykki
  – þar fló grár at sárum
  hræva nagr of holma –
  holunda val sem gœlak.

                                        (Skj A 32 v 3; von See 1960:34)

I shall always be happy since the spears of men keen for battle
pierced the king's young son: it befits a man to do a heroic deed.
Neither will I conceal that it seems as if I appease the raven; the
grey eagle flew over the islands towards the carnage.

4 Rekit telk Rǫgnvalds dauða
  – rétt skiptu því nornir:
  nú's folkstuðill fallinn –
  at fjórðungi mínum.
  Verpið, snarpir sveinar,
  þvít sigri vér ráðum
  – skatt velk hánum harðan –
  at Háfœtu grjóti!

                                        (Skj A 32 v 2; von See 1960:35)

I make known that Rǫgnvaldr's death is avenged, for my part (as
one of four brothers): the Norns shared the task out rightly; now
the pillar of the people has fallen. Cast stones at Hálfdan háfœta,
brave men, for the victory is ours: I select hard tribute-money
for him.

5 Eru til míns fjǫrs margir
   menn um sannar deildir
   ór ýmissum áttum
   ósmábornir gjarnir.
   En þó vitu þeygi
   þeir, áðr mik hafi feldan,
   hverr ilþorna arnar
   undir hlýtr at standa.
        (*Skj* A 32 v 4; von See 1960:35)

Many highborn men, of various families, are eager for my life,
on account of genuine conflicts. And yet they cannot tell who is
destined to stand beneath the eagle's claws, before they have
killed me.

The stanza order above is that of *Orkneyinga saga*. *Fagrskinna* has the
order 1, 4, and 3 (1902–3ed:296–8) and *Heimskringla* 1, 4, 5, and 2 (*ÍF*
26:131–3 vv 53–6). The order in Finnur Jónsson's skaldic edition, 1, 4, 3,
5, and 2, is a combination of *Fagrskinna* and *Heimskringla* and has no
independent authority (*Skj* A 31–2; B 27–8). In what follows I shall refer
to the five stanzas as 'Einarsflokkr.'

Snorri used *Orkneyinga saga* as a source for the part of *Heimskringla*
that concerns us here (*ÍF* 26:lx), and so the two texts can be considered
together. The story they tell is that Rǫgnvaldr jarl was surprised at Mœrr
and killed by Hálfdan and Guðrøðr, two sons of Haraldr hárfagri. Þórir,
Rǫgnvaldr's son, was pusillanimously reconciled with Haraldr, through
whose good graces he succeeded to the earldom. Haraldr's son Hálfdan
then raided in the Orkneys, styling himself king there after Torf-Einarr
had fled to Scotland. But the same year Torf-Einarr returned and
defeated Hálfdan in a great battle, from which Hálfdan himself eventu-
ally escaped under cover of darkness. At this point in the two sagas
Torf-Einarr recites verse 1. We then hear how Hálfdan was captured the
next morning and put to death, with the 'blood-eagle' cut in his back.

164 Viking Poems on War and Peace

Orkneyinga saga now brings in verses 2 and 3, and then, as Hálfdan's simple interment is arranged, verse 4. *Heimskringla* differs, having only verse 4 at this point. Both sources then deal with the lengthy period during which Einarr established himself anew in the Orkneys. Meanwhile news of Hálfdan's death travelled to Norway, causing anger in Haraldr's other sons, warnings of which travelled back to the Orkneys. In both sagas Torf-Einarr recites verse 5 as a defiant reply to these warnings. In the event, though, Haraldr himself launched an expedition against his Orkney foe, and Torf-Einarr sought refuge in Scotland once more. In *Heimskringla* he recites verse 2 while still in exile there; as we have seen, *Orkneyinga saga* has that verse in a different context.

There are obviously some major differences between these two sources in their handling of the verses. Snorri transposes verse 2 and omits verse 3. While in *Heimskringla* the verses are spread over a long period, in *Orkneyinga saga* they are grouped much more compactly (except for verse 5). In chapter 1 we noted discrepancies of the same kind in the prose treatments of the prophetic verses concerning Haraldr harðráði's invasion of England.

The treatment in *Fagrskinna*, though brief, contains further significant differences (1902–3ed:296). Indrebø considered that where these verses were concerned *Fagrskinna* was probably dependent not on *Orkneyinga saga* but on an unknown source (1917:107; cf Ellehøj 1965:165–6 and Fidjestøl 1982:28, 33, and 38). They are cited out of their chronological place, in the course of a genealogy of William the Conqueror, William being a descendant of Torf-Einarr's brother Gǫngu-Hrólfr, the same Hrólfr who is abused in verse 1:

Gǫngu-Hrólfr jarl var sonr Rǫgnvalds Mœrajarls, bróðir Þóris jarls þegjanda ok Torf-Einars í Orkneyjum, ok Hrollaugr hét einn, svá sem Einarr segir þá er hann hafði drepit Hálfdan hálegg son Haralds ins hárfagra, er áðr hafði drepit fǫður hans.

The earl Gǫngu-Hrólfr was the son of Rǫgnvaldr, earl of Mœrr, and the brother of earl Þórir þegjandi and of Torf-Einarr, in the Orkneys, and one was called Hrollaugr, as Einarr says when he had killed Hálfdan háleggr, the son of Haraldr hárfagri, who had previously killed his father.

Following on this, verses 1, 4, and 3 are quoted without further prose passages and the chapter comes to an end. It seems from *Fagrskinna*, then, as if verse 1 and the others were not separated in recitation by the escape, recapture, and death of Hálfdan; instead, they were all recited at the same time, after Hálfdan's death. This is in spite of the fact that verse 1 reads as if the fight is still in progress.

The comparison with *Fagrskinna* in itself casts doubt upon the reliability of the presentation of the verses in *Orkneyinga saga* and *Heimskringla*. In his article Klaus von See further queries this reliability by pointing out a series of inconsistencies between verse and prose, some of which go back to *Orkneyinga saga*, while others seem to originate with Snorri. I shall take the former points first.

From verse 3 we learn that Hálfdan dies in a volley of spears ('síz geirar / ... bitu þengils son ungan'). In verse 1 the same idea is hinted at, with the negative information on how Einarr's brothers are *not* killing Hálfdan ('sékat Hrólfs ór hendi / né Hrollaugi fljúga / dǫrr á dólga mengi'). In contrast, the *Orkneyinga saga* prose, followed by *Heimskringla*, states that Hálfdan was killed by the sword. This comes as part of the elaborate story according to which Hálfdan dies not during the fight but the next day and not through a normal death in battle but through the cutting of the blood-eagle: 'lét Einarr rísta ǫrn á baki honum með sverði' / 'Einarr had an eagle cut in his back with the sword' (ÍF 34:13). The motif of the blood-eagle, suspect wherever it occurs, here looks very like a late romanticizing addition, borrowed directly or indirectly from a more famous revenge story, the 'Reginsmál' version of Sigurðr's vengeance of his father Sigmundr (von See 1960:36–7): there too the motif is an accretion (Frank 1984:341).

> Nú er blóðugr ǫrn   bitrom hjǫrvi
> bana Sigmundar   á baki ristinn.
>   (Neckel-Kuhn ed:179 v 26)

Now the blood-eagle has been cut with the cruel sword in the back of Sigmundr's killer.

Another of von See's suggestions was that the role of Haraldr hárfagri had been altered in the prose (1960:37). In the verses Hálfdan is repeatedly called Haraldr's son and in particular the lines 'Haralds hefk skarð í skildi / ... hǫggvit' (v 2) imply that in killing Hálfdan Einarr's object is to harm the king. That would in turn suggest that Haraldr himself had been implicated in the death of Rǫgnvaldr. In the prose narrative, however, Haraldr and Rǫgnvaldr are allies; when Haraldr's sons kill

Rǫgnvaldr it is on their own initiative: Haraldr's anger on hearing of the deed is so great that Hálfdan flees the country (ÍF 34:12). Again, von See thinks that verse 4 shows Hálfdan acting as Haraldr's agent, collecting tribute on behalf of the Norwegian crown, whereas the prose sends him out as a Viking raider.

Thus as early as *Orkneyinga saga* the prose accompanying these verses already contained some misleading statements. When Snorri adapted it in *Heimskringla* he introduced further distortions. His omission of verse 3 can be explained as an attempt to camouflage the disagreement between verse and prose on the manner of Hálfdan's death. The residual inconsistency between the prose and verse 1 presumably escaped his notice (von See 1960:39). A parallel instance, involving the loss in *Flateyjarbók* of a *helmingr* from Arnórr's 'Magnússdrápa,' is discussed by Fidjestøl (1982:41-2).

According to von See, Snorri kept verse 2 but altered its significance in two ways (1960:39). Taking the first two lines of verse 2 ('margr verðr sénn at sauðum / seggr með breiðu skeggi') to refer to Gǫngu-Hrólfr and connecting them with the story of Hrólfr's banishment from Norway, he either originated or lent his authority to the variant 'sekr' / 'exiled' for 'sénn.' This variant appears only in *Heimskringla* and is clearly secondary. The phrase 'sekr of' / 'exiled for' is standard, whereas 'sénn at,' comparable with 'kendr at' / 'known for,' is quite unusual. A telltale sign that 'sekr of' is not original is that in 2.3 the preposition with 'sekr' understood is 'at,' not 'of': the resulting 'sekr at' does not make sense in context, because it should mean 'condemned to,' not 'condemned for.'

This change brought another one in its wake. In order to give the mention of exile relevance Snorri moved verse 2. *Orkneyinga saga* contained the following account of Torf-Einarr's escape from royal vengeance (ÍF 34:16):

> En nǫkkuru síðarr fór Haraldr konungr vestr um haf ok kom í Eyjar. Einarr stǫkk ór Eyjum ok yfir á Katanes.

> Some time later king Haraldr sailed west across the sea and came to the Orkneys. Einarr fled from the islands and across to Caithness.

Snorri evidently chose to interpret this flight as a sort of banishment and added verse 2 to the account of it, along with other little touches that improve the marriage between verse and prose (ÍF 26:133):

Haraldr konungr bauð lið út ok dró saman her mikinn ok fór
síðan vestr til Orkneyja. En er Einarr jarl spurði, at konungr
var austan kominn, þá ferr hann yfir á Nes. Þá kvað hann
vísu [v 2].

King Haraldr called out his retinue, assembled a large army, and
then sailed west to the Orkneys. But when Einarr learnt that
the king had arrived from the east he sailed over to Caithness.
Then he said a verse [v 2].

This looks like a simple adjustment of the *Orkneyinga saga* material, rather than an importation from some independent source. The mention of a large army would be an easy embellishment, and when Snorri adds the detail that Torf-Einarr heard of ('spurði') the king's expedition he is no doubt drawing on verse 2 itself ('hætt segja mér holdar / við hugfullan stilli').

My only doubt about von See's reconstruction of Snorri's procedure is whether he was responsible for the transposition of verse 2. The *Fagrskinna* text, which antedates Snorri's, agrees with him, against *Orkneyinga saga*, in beginning with verses 1 and 4. Moreover, Snorri used *Fagrskinna* in the compilation of *Heimskringla*, as has been demonstrated by Bjarni Aðalbjarnarson (1937:173–236). This opens up the possibility that he was familiar with both stanza orders and rejected the *Orkneyinga saga* order in favour of the other.

Finally, Snorri seems to have modified the prose to make it fit better with verse 5 (von See 1960:42). Before the citation of verse 5 in *Orkneyinga saga* there is a statement that Hálfdan's brothers wanted vengeance. The verse itself states that 'many' men from 'various' families, all of them 'highborn,' are eager to kill him. In other words, this is only the most recent in a series of conflicts involving Torf-Einarr. Snorri therefore appended a few words to the effect that Hálfdan's brothers soon found support outside the family for their mission of vengeance (ÍF 26:132):

> En er tíðendi þessi spyrjask í Nóreg, þá kunnu þessu stórilla
> brœðr Hálfdanar ok tolðu hefnda fyrir vert, ok margir sonnuðu
> þat aðrir.

> And when these events became known in Norway Hálfdan's
> brothers took the news very badly and said vengeance was
> called for, and many others confirmed that.

Here 'margir' and 'sǫnnuðu' neatly replicate the wording of the verse.

On the basis of this evidence von See argued that Torf-Einarr's verses originally formed a separate and self-contained poetic narrative that did not easily lend itself to incorporation in saga prose. He was also able to show that the verses were self-sufficient as a narrative unit (1960:42). All the essential names, except Torf-Einarr's own, are given once and once only. Thus the brothers Hrólfr, Hrollaugr, and Þórir are named in verse 1, Haraldr (hárfagri) and the Orkneys in verse 2, and Rǫgnvaldr and Hálfdan in verse 4. Other references to them are through common nouns and periphrases: Rǫgnvaldr is 'fǫður' in verse 1, Hálfdan 'ungs allvalds sonar' in verse 2, 'þengils son ungan' in verse 3, and 'folkstuðill' in verse 4, and Haraldr 'allvalds' and 'hugfullan stilli' in verse 2 and 'þengils' in verse 3. Even 'Eyjum' in verse 2 is varied, so that we find 'holma' in verse 3. Such consistency and aesthetic rigour would be pointless unless the verses were to be heard and appreciated as a unit.

In Dietrich Hofmann's detailed critique (1978–9) of von See's conclusions, he noted that verse 1 describes an earlier state of affairs (during the battle) than the other stanzas (after the battle): this suggested to him that they could not have been recited in uninterrupted succession. Doubting, however, that the poet could have made up, in the confusion of battle, a verse that fitted so well with the rest of the group, he agreed with von See that verse 1 must actually have been composed in retrospect, after the battle, like the others. (This, as we have seen, is the arrangement in *Fagrskinna*.)

In Hofmann's view, the Torf-Einarr verses must always have formed an integral part of a prosimetrum narrative. He argues that if verse 1 was composed retrospectively it would have needed some kind of prose introduction; correspondingly, he thinks, some kind of prose statement to clarify that Hálfdan's death had occurred must have preceded verses 2–5. From these small beginnings Hofmann envisages a rapidly increasing prose ingredient in the prosimetrum. Two different detailed scenarios are suggested. In one Torf-Einarr tells the entire story (with verses included) himself. In the other the narrative is a collective effort, the leader's contribution being restricted to the verses while the prose was recited by a member of the retinue. A first performance at Torf-Einarr's house, after the burial of Hálfdan, would rapidly have been followed by other performances, introducing variations and embellishments and leading ultimately to the sort of distortions we have seen in *Orkneyinga saga*.

Hofmann recognizes that on this reconstruction of events there must always have been something fictive about the verses, since those who had aided Torf-Einarr during the fight would know that in fact he had not made up a verse there and then. He suggests, however, that it might have been a convention for eye-witnesses to embellish their narration with verses that in reality were composed after the event but that represented their true feelings at the time better than sober prose could. The audience would recognize this as the convention it was, and not take exception to it as a distortion of the truth.

In my opinion, there is more hypothesis here than the evidence will bear. But Hofmann's recognition that an element of fiction is built into these verses leads, as I shall show, to a third and simpler way of accounting for all the available evidence.

Torf-Einarr is not otherwise heard of as a composer of poetry, but the *flokkr* about his revenge must have achieved some fame because a special metre, the *Torf-Einarsháttr*, is named after him in the commentary to *Háttatal* (*Snorra Edda* 1931ed:238–9 v 55). This is a version of a metre called *munnvǫrp*, with a tightening up of the rules so that the odd lines never contain any kind of *hending*, the even lines always contain *skothending*, and the first rhyming syllable occupies the third place in a D-type line (Sievers' classification), augmented by the usual dissyllabic cadence (ibid 239). The result is four couplets of the following type:

> Hverr séi jǫfra œgi
> jarl fjǫlvitrum betra,
> eða gjarnara at gœða
> glym harðsveldan skjalda?
> stendr af stála skúrar
> styrr ólítill Gauti,
> þá's folks jaðarr foldir
> ferr sig-Njǫrðum varða.
>   (*Skj* II B 76)

The even lines in this demonstration stanza seem to be a generalization of 'ósmábornir gjarnir' (5.4).

Clearly Snorri regarded Torf-Einarr as the author of the four stanzas that he quoted in *Heimskringla* and that were no doubt the model for his stanza in *Háttatal*. Immediately before Einarr's verses in *Orkneyinga saga* and *Heimskringla*, however, stands a couplet *about* Einarr (ÍF 34:11

and 26:129). The author is not mentioned, but the metre is exactly the same as in the Torf-Einarr attributions and quite distinct from Snorri's artificially tidied-up version:

> Hann gaf Tréskegg trollum,
> Torf-Einarr drap Skurfu.
>
> (ÍF 34:11)

> He gave [Þórir] tréskegg to the trolls; Torf-Einarr slew [Kálfr] skurfa.

Here the first line corresponds in metre to 2.1, 'margr verðr sénn at sauðum,' and the second to 1.7, 'þegjandi sitr þetta.' Rhyme and alliteration are patterned just as in the *flokkr*. Also in common is the use of nicknames, conspicuous in the couplet because we find two of them in as many lines, and in the *flokkr* because of the sex-shifting pun between 'háfœta' and 'háleggr'; 'skurfa' is also apparently feminine gender, suggesting perhaps that Torf-Einarr's opponents were consistently portrayed as effeminate, according to the methods of poetic *níð*. The exception here is Þórir tréskegg, whom von See tentatively identifies with the 'seggr með breiðu skeggi' in the *flokkr* (1960:39).

A natural conclusion from these shared characteristics would be that the author of the couplet and the author of the *flokkr* were one and the same person. The couplet and the *flokkr* would represent two fragments from an early poem (or perhaps a cycle of poems) about Torf-Einarr, the *flokkr* being the hero's direct speech at the time of his probably most celebrated deed and the couplet a piece of third-person narrative. The possibility of a confusion between the author of a poem and the character who speaks within it has already been noted: a close parallel would be the handling of 'Snjófríðardrápa' in *Flateyjarbók* (Halldórsson 1969, Poole 1982).

Any attempt to comment on the narrative technique of 'Einarsflokkr' is bound to be hampered by our uncertainty regarding the original order of the verses. One might argue that the *Orkneyinga saga* order is preferable, as the more difficult, since the audience has to wait until verse 4 to find out who is being killed and who is being avenged, or at least what their names are. Such postponement of identification, associated with *ofljóst*, is also found in 'Liðsmannaflokkr.' But it is safer to discuss the handling of the story only so far as can be done without committing oneself to a particular stanza order.

An introductory stanza, with present-tense verbs, describes the fight in progress. For the speaker, in other words, the battle is in the here and now. If we take verse 2 next we find that the speaker's perspective has shifted: what was present in verse 1 ('meðan knýjum / ... rómu') is now mentioned in the perfect ('Haralds hefk skarð í skildi / ... hǫggvit'). If, alternatively, we read verse 4 as the second stanza, the narrative pattern is much the same: there is a statement in the perfect tense that Hálfdan is dead ('nú's folkstuðill fallinn'). In verse 2 the present reality is that Torf-Einarr is being warned about retaliation from Haraldr ('hætt segja mér hǫldar / við hugfullan stilli'). In verse 4 it is the possession of victory ('sigri vér ráðum') and the command to build Hálfdan a burial mound ('verpið, snarpir sveinar / ... / at Háfœtu grjóti' and 'skatt velk hánum harðan'). In verse 4 a single instance of the preterite also occurs ('rétt skiptu því nornir'); whether this refers to the time of the battle or to a time immediately preceding it would be hard to determine. In verse 3, which probably came as the third stanza originally, regardless of the relative position of verses 2 and 4, the events of the battle are clearly referred to in the preterite ('síz geirar / ... / bitu þengils son ungan' and 'þar fló grár at sárum / hræva nagr of holma'). The present reality is the joy of both hero and raven. In verse 5 the concern is exclusively with the present and future.

The result is a poem of the running commentary type, a dramatic monologue where events unfold around the hero as he speaks. There is therefore no need to assume, with Hofmann, an interval of time between the recitation of verse 1 and the following verses. Nor is there any need for a prose explanation that Hálfdan's death has occurred, because verses 2 and 4 contain precisely this information, couched in the perfect tense, as befitting an action performed in the speaker's very recent past.

The relationship between the earlier verses (along with verse 2) and verse 5 depends on a choice between variant readings. If, with two manuscripts of *Orkneyinga saga*, we read 'sannar fréttir' / 'true reports,' the recitation of the verse should logically follow the arrival in Norway of reports that Hálfdan has been killed and so must occur a good time after the other verses. The other reading, however, is 'sannar deildir' / 'genuine conflicts,' and this, being much the less obvious combination, is preferable. Torf-Einarr is then not saying that news has reached Norway but that various prior conflicts ensure that many men are after his blood: the couplet already quoted is fair proof of that. In this we have another example of the continuity between the couplet and the *flokkr*. The conclusion is that verse 5 can follow immediately upon the other verses in recitation and thus that all five stanzas can be read consecutively without prose explanations or links.

The 'Einarsflokkr,' as a dramatic monologue, has a 'voice' characterized by irony and indirection. As in 'Liðsmannaflokkr,' actions may be communicated by means of a contrast with the inaction of others rather than by a direct description. In verse 1 the emphasis falls on those brothers who shirk revenge: Einarr's performance of his duty emerges only parenthetically and generally ('meðan knýjum / ... rómu'), leaving us to infer other details from the negative description applied to Hrólfr and Hrollaugr. It is not Einarr the brave avenger but Þórir the silent drinker who commands virtually the whole second *helmingr*. An unusually complex interweaving of clauses (at least by the standards of this poem) brings the opposites of their conduct into juxtaposition, so that the speaker alternates between the praiseworthy and the blameworthy: 'meðan knýjum / – of kerstraumi – rómu / – þegjandi sitr.' In verse 2 another comparison, with the broad-bearded man whose acts of daring are confined to sheep, precedes an explicit statement of what the hero has done. In the second *helmingr* of verse 3 the martial boasting has to be approached through the litotes and convoluted syntax of 'þeygi dylk nema þykki.' In verse 4 the supremely triumphant 'skatt velk hánum harðan' reminds us ironically of what the victim came expecting and did not receive: a servile payment of tribute. These glancing allusions, combined with the interweaving of past, present, and future, create the illusion of a thinking mind, moving rapidly between the deed itself and its various implications.

'Egill's Duel with Ljótr'

About midway through *Egils saga* the hero engages in single combat with Ljótr, a berserk from Sweden. While depriving the luckless Swede of his leg and life, Egill also makes up five verses:

1 Esa Friðgeiri fœri –
   fǫrum holms á vit, sǫrvar;
   skulum banna mjǫk manni
   mey – ørlygi at heyja
   við þann's bítr ok blótar
   bǫnd élhvǫtuð Gǫndlar –
   alfeigum skýtr œgir
   augum – skjǫld at baugi.
   (*Skj* A 56 v 28; ÍF 2:202–3 v 37)

   Friðgeirr is not capable of fighting a battle with a man who bites his shield at the rim and makes sacrifices to the gods. The berserk flashes forth the glare of a doomed man. Off we go, comrades, to the duelling ground; we must forbid the maiden to that man.

2 Esat lítillar Ljóti –
   leik ek við hal bleikan
   við bifteini – bœnar –
   brynju – rétt at synja;
   búumk til vígs, en vægðar
   vón lætka ek hónum;

skapa verðum vit skjaldi
skœru, drengr, á Mœri.

(Skj A 56 v 29; ÍF 2:203 v 38, except last two lines)

It is not right to refuse Ljótr his little request – with my sword I toy with the pale man. We prepare for combat and I give him no expectation of mercy; the two of us are going to make trouble for the shield at Mœrr.

3 Hǫggum hjaltvǫnd skyggðan,
 hœfum rǫnd með brandi,
 reynum randar mána,
 rjóðum sverð í blóði;
 stýfum Ljót af lífi,
 leikum sárt við bleikan,
 kyrrum kappa errinn –
 komi ǫrn á hræ – jǫrnum.

(Skj A 56 v 30; ÍF 2:204 v 39)

May I strike his burnished sword, raise my shield to meet his blade, put my sword to the test, dye the weapon red with blood, sever Ljótr from life, play cruelly with the pale man, subdue the maddened champion with my weapons! May the eagle light on his corpse!

4 Fyrir þykki mér, fúra
 fleins støkkvandi, nøkkvat –
 hrædisk hodda beiðir
 happlauss – fara kappi;
 stendrat fast, sá's frestar,
 fleindǫggvar stafr, hǫggum;
 vábeiða ferr víðan
 vǫll fyr rotnum skalla.

(Skj A 56 v 31; ÍF 2:204–5 v 40)

Comrade, I fancy that the champion departs somewhat in front; the luckless fellow takes fright; he wavers and holds back from striking; the wretch flees across the broad field before his bald assailant.

5 Fell sá's flest et illa –
fót hjó skald af Ljóti –
ulfgrennir hefr unnit;
eir veittak Friðgeiri:
séka lóns til launa
logbrjótanda í móti;
jafn vas mér í gný geira
gamanleikr við hal bleikan.

(Skj A 56–7; ÍF 2:205–6 v 41)

The warrior who has done much evil fell; the poet cut his leg off: I gave Friðgeirr peace. I do not look for any reward in return from the breaker of gold rings; it was sheer play for me in combat with the pale man.

These verses occur in chapter 64 of the saga (ÍF 2:199–206). Returning south from a disappointing meeting with King Hákon, Egill lodges with the nephew of his staunch friend Arinbjǫrn. Friðgeirr, the nephew, seems downcast and the sister (she is not named) distraught. After three days, when he is about to resume his journey, Egill learns that the cause is a berserk named Ljótr, who has been demanding a marriage settlement with the sister. On being refused he has challenged Friðgeirr to single combat. Next day Egill and his host go together to Vǫrl, the island where the *holmganga* is to take place. Ljótr immediately goes berserk, but Egill triumphantly dispatches him in two rounds.

In general, scholars have been sceptical about this episode. André Bley, who regarded most of the saga as fiction, thought Ljótr strikingly reminiscent of the giants in the medieval romances. He distinguished two different berserk stereotypes in the sagas, one genuine – the warrior who enters a special state of consciousness during battle – and one fictive – a typical medieval 'wild man' of extraordinary size and strength, who abducts or rapes beautiful women (1909:156). He suggested that since the French chivalric epics that contain these giants were actually translated into Norwegian in the thirteenth century, the Ljótr episode might represent an imitation that was composed later than the rest of *Egils saga* and interpolated into its text (ibid 158). There is a sequel to the episode later in the saga, when Egill lays claim to Ljótr's property (ch 68), but Bley regarded this too as an interpolation. In his view the motifs and details of characterization it contained might have been borrowed from elsewhere in the saga; moreover, some of them were used incongruously in their new context (ibid 161–4).

E. Sattler attempted a precise identification of the source for Ljótr, namely the giant Harpin in Chrétien's *Yvain* (1911:669). This adventure begins with the hero receiving hospitality at a castle but marvelling to find his hosts in a state of sorrow and lamentation. The cause is Harpin, who has demanded the daughter of the lord of the castle in marriage. Upon being refused, he has captured and killed some of the sons and plans to continue in this way if the daughter is not handed over the next morning. The lady of the castle is Gauvain's sister, so, in the name of his friendship with Gauvain, Yvain agrees to help. With the aid of a lion Yvain wins a very fierce fight. Sattler ends inconclusively, acknowledging that *Yvain* could not have directly influenced *Egils saga* but without discussing the possibility of an interpolation (ibid 670–1).

Like Bley, Gwyn Jones thought in terms of a general influence from the romances: 'In Friðgeirr's weeping sister I felt I recognized an old acquaintance: the tearful ... virgin ... whom Owein and Percival and Gawain rescue from a monstrous suitor in various corners of the romances. If this is no delusion, then Egill has here been cast by his author for the role of knight-errant, and one must admire the skilful references to Arinbjǫrn which lend the episode such little credibility as it has' (1946–53:301 n11).

Liestøl preferred to look closer to home for analogues, pointing out the similarities between the Ljótr *holmganga* and *fornaldarsaga* combats with berserks (1929:154). Bjarni Einarsson, who regards chapter 64 as quite unhistorical, notes the resemblances to another adventure within *Egils saga*, the Värmland episode (chs 70–6), and comments on the general tendency for motifs and stock adventures to be reworked and repeated within this and other sagas (1975:15, 102, and 259). The need to assume foreign influence, especially when to do so poses literary-historical problems, has further been queried by Benjamin Blaney, who notes that both the Ljótr and the Harpin episodes involve a very common type, the unwelcome suitor, and that the only unusual shared motif is the kinship between the lady of the house and the hero's best friend (1982:291–2).

I would explain the sequel in chapter 68 not (with Bley) as an interporation but on the same lines adopted by Bjarni Einarsson in dealing with chapter 64, in other words as a duplication in oral tradition of material elsewhere in the saga. Egill's moody silence at the beginning of the chapter, along with Arinbjǫrn's friendly concern and the hero's request for help, is reminiscent of chapter 56. So too is the cause of his gloom, the difficulty in claiming what he regards as rightfully his property. His specific worry, that King Hákon has taken possession of the property, is precisely the same as besets Arinbjǫrn's nephew Þorsteinn in chapter 62, when he tries to claim his inheritance. Arinbjǫrn's undertaking to help, in a full awareness that he will be hampered by Egill's poor relations with the king, is paralleled in chapter 56 and (more distantly) in the famous 'hǫfuðlausn' episode (ch 59). Another episode with broad similarities is Arinbjǫrn's assistance to Þorsteinn in gaining the attention of Aðalsteinn (ch 62). Hákon's doubts about Arinbjǫrn's true loyalties are reminiscent of chapter 56 and chapter 60, two occasions where Arinbjǫrn is interceding with Eiríkr on Egill's behalf. When this ever-generous friend personally compensates Egill for his losses we are reminded of chapter 56, where he made good the destruction of Egill's ship by Eiríkr's men. The hero's dramatic return to cheerfulness is an idea also found in chapters 55 and 56. In short, chapter 68 contains nothing that could not have been taken over and reused from the episodes where Egill is feuding with Eiríkr and Berg-Ǫnundr. These are episodes that are likelier to have a genuine basis in tradition and that precede chapter 68 in the saga's chronology of events. The claimed family connection between Arinbjǫrn and Friðgeirr has its counterpart in the equally suspect assertion that Eyvindr skreyja had a brother called Álfr askmaðr and that Gunnhildr, the wife of Eiríkr, was their sister (Einarsson 1975:101, ÍF 2:123n4, and ÍF 26:185n2).

So far as I am aware, the only sustained attempt to prise a kernel of historical truth out of the Ljótr episode comes from Johan Hovstad. Drawing on analogues in *Landnámabók* he argued that the extant version of the incident is a romanticization of an actual combat undertaken by Egill in order to gain property of some kind. Even he accepts, however, that a *holmganga* undertaken to rescue a woman from a berserk is a prevalent motif in the *fornaldarsögur*, so that the Ljótr verses, which state that the hero's object was to rescue such a woman, are probably not genuine (1946:88 and 92).

The general consensus that the Ljótr episode, along with its verses, is an unhistorical accretion fits well with the fairly meagre evidence for dating offered by the language and diction of the verses. The verb 'blótar' in verse 1 is a weak reformation of older 'blœtr' (Jónsson 1901:99). The latter form is the more likely one to have been used by the historical, tenth-century Egill, since we find it still competing with 'blótar' in manuscripts of the late twelfth and early thirteenth century (Larsson 1891 'blóta'). The weak form is here guaranteed by metre, occupying the final dissyllabic cadence in the line.

Noreen thought the word suspect for an additional reason: being himself a heathen, Egill could scarcely have ridiculed his opponent for making sacrifices (1922:33). Caution is needed with such an argument, given our less than full knowledge of pagan-Christian polemics in the tenth century, but probably the Ljótr verses are influenced here by the flyting in *Hallfreðar saga*, where the hero inveighs against the heathen practices of his rival.

In verse 1 the use of 'œgir' as a simple agent noun, without a defining noun to convert it into a kenning, is hard to parallel. Meissner notes that such agent nouns were hardly ever used in poetry without the equivalent of a grammatical object (1921:285). He cites one possible skaldic parallel, but this – 'sættir' in 'Glælognskviða' 4 (*Skj* A 325) – depends on one manuscript's doubtfully authentic completion of a fragmentary stanza (Magerøy 1948:11). Eddaic poetry offers 'stýrir' in 'Helgakviða Hundingsbana' I:26 and, conjecturally, 'œgir' as an emendation in verse 55 of the same poem. The dating of this poem is quite uncertain but, according to Einar Ól. Sveinsson, it is not likely to be much earlier than 1050 (1962:483). Finnur Jónsson emended to 'bauga œgir' / 'frightener (ie breaker) of rings,' which in itself would be good but brings another emendation in its wake (1884:152–3; cf Reichardt 1928:166). If we accept the manuscript readings, as Kock (*NN* 145) and Nordal do, we have in undefined 'œgir' a usage that cannot be shown to antedate 1030, the approximate date of 'Glælognskviða,' at the very earliest.

The external and internal evidence, taken together, makes it implausible that the historical Egill composed these verses about an encounter with Ljótr. Most obviously spurious, from a linguistic and stylistic standpoint, is verse 1, with 'œgir' and 'blótar,' but the five stanzas, as we shall see, hang closely together, so that if one is spurious they are all likely to be so (cf *íF* 2:x).

If Egill is not the author, there is always the possibility that these verses were made up by the same person who gave us the saga in its extant form. Some have thought that Snorri wrote *Egils saga*: in that case the presence in the Ljótr verses of an older type of *aðalhending* – 'rǫnd:brandi' and 'vǫll:skalla' – that does not occur in firm Snorri attributions would require explanation. The same difficulty applies even if Snorri is not the author of the saga, because it is usually regarded as a product of the thirteenth century, perhaps not later than 1230 (Björn Sigfússon *KLNM* 'Egils saga').

If the Ljótr stanzas were removed from their present context they would in themselves tell a coherent story. In verse 1 we learn what the object of the combat is ('skulum banna mjǫk manni / mey') and why the speaker is having to undertake it ('esa Friðgeiri fœri / ... ørlygi at heyja'). A stage direction in the text ('fǫrum holms á vit, sǫrvar') covers the journey to the duelling ground. The berserk is graphically described in the second *helmingr*, and in verse 2 we learn his name. Except for 'leik ek við hal bleikan,' which seems to be an anticipation of future action, the preparations for combat and gloating over the likely outcome are the themes of this stanza. It is incidentally made clear that Ljótr has demanded the *holmganga* ('esat lítillar Ljóti / ... bœnar / ... rétt at synja'). In verse 3 the speaker utters exhortations to himself as the fight begins and in verse 4 he describes the opponent's defeat, beginning with hesitation and ending with outright flight. Here the speaker adds a little self-description ('fyr rotnum skalla'), which for some in the audience might be distinctive enough to identify Egill as the hero. The final stanza covers the death of Ljótr, noting the nature of the blow: it is the cutting off of a leg, part of the stereotypical fate for berserks in the sagas. Also noted are the other consequences, a return of peace for Friðgeirr and a noble refusal of any reward on the part of the speaker (who now calls himself a skald, somewhat reinforcing the hints of an identification in verse 4).

The handling of other verses in *Egils saga* has from time to time aroused scepticism. In particular, it has long been recognized that the *níðvísur* against Eiríkr and Gunnhildr, whether authentic or not, are misleadingly separated in the prose and in fact do not make sense unless read in uninterrupted succession (Almqvist 1965:108–14, and references there given). In the Ljótr episode too the prose wears the air of an intrusive element, interfering with a straightforward poetic narrative.

When the speaker says 'esat lítillar Ljóti / ... bœnar / ... rétt at synja,' these words, read without reference to the prose, mean that the speaker would not like to see Ljótr denied his fight simply because Friðgeirr is no match for him (a point explained in the previous stanza). Instead, the prose between verses 1 and 2 motivates the words by showing Ljótr issuing a second challenge, not now to Friðgeirr but to Egill himself: 'Gakk þú hingat, inn mikli maðr, á hólminn ok bersk við mik' (ÍF 2:203) / 'Come here to the duelling ground, big man, and fight with me.'

Another reduplication of a motif can be detected in the prose accompanying verse 1. I have mentioned that this stanza can very straightforwardly be read as covering the journey to the duelling ground ('fǫrum holms á vit, sǫrvar'). In the prose, however, the journey is made (from

Blindheim, Friðgeirr's home, to the island of Vǫrl) *before* Egill speaks the verse. The line just quoted is applied in the prose to Egill's last few strides to join Ljótr within the confines of the *holmganga* (ÍF 2:202).

Moreover, the presence of the prose spoils the intrinsic drama of verse 4. The stanza consists of a rapid rise to a climax: Ljótr is drawing back, he is scared, he is wavering, he holds back his stroke, and (yes!) he is running away. Shorn of the prose the stanza reads as a running commentary. We might explain the presence of this prose passage as an attempt at verismilitude: Egill's poetic utterance is placed not in the heat of combat but in a lull after it, as if to anticipate Jan de Vries's scepticism about verse making in times of crisis.

Viewed as a unitary poem these five stanzas show all the technical integration that we have come to expect from examples in earlier chapters. The most prominent linking device is the *aðalhending* 'leik-:bleik-,' which occurs three times, once near the beginning (2.2), once near the middle (3.6), and once at the very end (5.8). Repeated similarly is the name Ljótr (2.1, 3.5, and 5.2). The other significant name, Friðgeirr, appears at the very beginning (1.1) and near the end (5.4). The neat symmetry of these arrangements is striking. On each occasion the speaker seems to allude to the 'frið-' element in the name in a punning way, which the prose reinforces: 'hafði hann ok ekki staðit í barðǫgum' / 'nor had he taken part in battles' (ÍF 2:202).

Links between successive stanzas are also apparent. Thus verses 1 and 2 begin with 'esa' and both contain the word 'skjǫld/skjaldi.' The latter is a by-form of the dative case found also in verses ascribed to Kormakr, Þormóðr, and Þórarinn svarti. With the phrase 'skapa skjaldi skœru' / 'create strife for the shield,' compare *Háttatal* 19 'skapar flaustum deilu' / 'creates strife for the ships' (*Skj* II B 66); the personifying idea of speaking of an object's 'peace' being disturbed is sometimes found in kennings. In the ensuing stanzas, verses 2 and 3 are linked by repetitions already pointed out, verses 3 and 4 both contain the word 'kappi' and the cognates 'hǫggum' / 'we strike' and 'hǫggum' / 'blows' (dative plural); a further cognate, 'hjó,' appears in verse 5.

These verses about the fight with Ljótr, viewed as an uninterrupted sequence, display a narrative technique that is broadly similar to that of the 'Einarsflokkr': the present tense is used for the main march of events. In the Ljótr verses the final stanza sums up the entire action, whereas in 'Einarsflokkr' this kind of recapitulation and summation is interspersed with the main narrative. Both sets of verses are therefore of the running-commentary type. They are also both dramatic monologues, with a fictive speaker. The monologue includes commands to the speaker's comrades and incitements addressed to himself.

The Ljótr verses have aesthetic as well as narrative unity. The design is pleasingly symmetrical, with preparations and explanations in the first two stanzas, the 'incitation' at the centre, and the result and aftermath in the last two. The prose passages that come between these carefully linked stanzas, although brief, are evident accretions that detract from the unity. Possibly the *flokkr* was composed for recitation *en bloc* during an oral performance of *Egils saga*. Its subsequent dispersal through the prose narrative would then be paralleled by the dismemberment of the *ævikviða* in *Ǫrvar-Odds saga*, where, similarly, each stanza is made to follow the action to which it refers.

Within the genre of 'running-commentary' battle poems, the Ljótr poem represents an adaptation of the themes and formulas to humorous ends, just as 'Friðgerðarflokkr' confounds genre expectations by being an adaptation to peaceful ends. Here we witness not an *ǫrleikr* in earnest but a *gamanleikr*. The stereotypical situation is ironically reversed: a raging berserk is worsted at his own profession by a poet – and a bald-headed one at that. The incitation in verse 3, in its detail and rapid-fire ferocity, far outdoes those uttered by the genuine warriors in other poems of the genre, approaching the comic exaggeration that characterizes Touchstone's threats in *As You Like It* 5.1. If Egill was from the first the subject of the poem, the noble rejection of any reward ('séka lóns til launa / logbrjótanda í móti') might well have struck the audience as ironically discordant with his normal disposition in the saga, where he is portrayed as among the most grasping and property-conscious of men.

Eiríkr Viðsjá: A Battle on the Heath

In 1014 a battle was fought on a heath in the west of Iceland between factions from Borgarfjǫrðr and Breiðafjǫrðr (Þórðarson 1937–9:98; ÍF 3:cxv). The latter part of *Heiðarvíga saga* describes this event, focusing on the figure of Barði Guðmundsson, a man from the north of Iceland, not far from the Breiðafjǫrðr district, who seeks vengeance for the death of his brother. With five men, he descends on his prospective victims, the Gíslungar, while they are mowing hay; two of them escape, but the third, Gísli, is killed. Feeling that this is an inadequate revenge, Barði's men disregard his command to retreat immediately. The result is a close pursuit on the part of Barði's enemies from the south, so that when the battle on the heath ensues it is not on a site of Barði's choosing. Barði and his northern allies sustain fewer casualties than the southerners, but as reinforcements are constantly arriving from the south they eventually retreat, bringing the battle to an end. The subsequent manoeuvres are legal rather than military and ultimately lead to a settlement. According to the saga, Eiríkr viðsjá, a man of Barði's faction, made up verses in the course of these events. There are seven verses in all. Although a part of the saga narrative, chapters 34–7, is very poorly preserved, there seems to be no likelihood that it originally contained further verses by Eiríkr (cf Helgason 1950–1).

1 Blóðs – hǫfum hlynr of heiði
hræborðs farit norðan –
vér hyggjum nag nœra –
nítján saman, rítar:
þó getum hins, at, hríðar
hlunntams, munim sunnan,

ǫrr – hyggr skald til skœru –
skæs, nǫkkuru færi.
>   (Skj A 209; ÍF 3:287 v 4)

Nineteen of us have come from the north over the heath together, warrior; we intend to feed the raven: though I dare say somewhat fewer of us will return from the south, seafarer; the poet has his mind on battle.

2 Flykkjask frægir rekkar;
fúss es herr til snerru;
þjóð tekr hart á heiði
herkunn dragask sunnan:
fara biðr hvergi herja
harðráðr fyrir Barði
geira hreggs frá glyggvi
gunnnǫrunga sunnan.
>   (Skj A 209; ÍF 3:299 v 10)

Renowned warriors assemble; the army is eager for battle; well-known men from the south are massing together fast on the heath. Resolutely, Barði commands the forces not to draw back anywhere from the warriors' northward assault.

3 Fast hǫldu vér foldu;
fram þoki herr at snerru;
lǫtum randa vǫl reyndan
ryðjendr í ben snyðja:
skalk, þótt sagt sé sunnan
sverðél taki at herða –
rjóðum hart á heiði
hjalmríð – ór stað bíða.
>   (Skj A 209; ÍF 3:300 v 11)

Let us hold the field tenaciously; let the army move forth to battle; make the trusty sword dart into the wound, as we clear the way. I shall stand my ground though it is said that the attack grows fiercer from the south; let us redden the sword ruthlessly on the heath.

4 Hlotit hǫfum, rjóðr, af reiði
randir, þuðra branda –

beruma vægð at vígi,
Veggbergr – saman leggja:
mjǫk hefk heyrt at hjarta
hug þínum við brugðit;
nú skulum, foldar fjǫtra
fúrleynir, þat reyna.
     (*Skj* A 210; ÍF 3:304 v 12)

It is our lot to clash shields together in anger, reddener of thin blades; we shall not flinch in the fight, Veggbergr. I have heard your character greatly praised for courage; now we shall put that to the test, miserly man.

5 Lǫgu lýðar frægir
lǫgðis skeiðs á heiði –
lind sprakk í rym randa
rauð – ellifu dauðir:
hitt vas áðr, es auðar
ógnar gims í rimmu –
jókum sókn við sœki
sárþíslar – fekk Gísli.
     (*Skj* A 210; ÍF 3:322 v 15)

Eleven renowned warriors lay dead on the heath; the red shield was shattered in the fight: it was beforehand that Gísli met his destiny in battle; we increased the onslaught against him.

6 Þrír hafa alls af ǫru
ítrstalls liði fallit –
vér ruðum sverð í sǫrum –
sigrborðs viðir norðan:
en fúrþollar fellu
Fjǫlnis seiðs á heiði –
gerðisk grimmt með fyrðum
gunnél – níu sunnan.
     (*Skj* A 210; ÍF 3:322–3 v 16)

Altogether three men of our brave force from the north have fallen; we reddened the sword in wounds: but nine warriors from the south fell on the heath; a savage battle was waged amongst men.

7 Styrr lét snarr ok Snorri
sverðþing háit verða,
þars geirviðir gørðu
Gíslunga hlut þungan:
enn varð eigi in minna
ættskarð, þats hjó Barði –
fell geysla lið Gísla –
gunnnǫrunga sunnan.

(Skj A 210; ÍF 3:323 v 17)

Valiant Styrr and Snorri caused a battle to be fought, where the warriors ensured a sad fate for Gísli's following; no smaller, though, was the depletion brought about by Barði in the family of warriors from the south; Gísli's force fell in copious numbers.

Selected variants:

v 7 1 'snart' *Fourth Grammatical Treatise* (FGT); 3 'gnyuerdir' *Heiðarvíga saga* (Hs); 4 'Gíslungum' FGT; 5 'var' FGT; 6 'eitt' (for ætt-') Hs

The author of *Heiðarvíga saga* has been regarded as 'one of the pioneers among the authors of family sagas' (Björn Sigfússon KLNM '*Heiðarvíga saga*'). The saga seems to have greatly influenced such successors as *Eyrbyggja saga*, *Grettis saga* (cf B.M. Ólsen 1937–9:201–2), and *Njáls saga* (ÍF 3:xcviii; cf Heinrichs 1976:130). Nordal believed that *Heiðarvíga saga* was the oldest of the sagas of Icelanders (ÍF 3:cxxxvi) and located its writing down and (to some degree) composition at the monastery of Þingeyrar, which he saw as the principal centre for the writing of sagas in Iceland from about 1170 into the thirteenth century (ibid cxxxvi). The material in the saga would, he pointed out, have been of local interest at Þingeyrar, two of whose abbots at this period had family connections with Illugi svarti, a member of the Borgarfjǫrðr faction. To some extent the author may have relied on his own invention, as in the conversation between Barði Guðmundsson and Óláfr helgi, but Nordal saw him as having a great fund of oral traditions, some more reliable than others, to draw on (ibid cxxx–cxxxi). This included informants in both the Breiðafjǫrðr and the more distant Borgarfjǫrðr districts. Nordal speculated that a brief written account of Barði's following and the deaths in the *heiðarvíg* might also have been available to him (ibid cxv).

An obvious further possibility is that verses like those ascribed to Eiríkr viðsjá were among the author's sources. In the saga Eiríkr is said to have been a skald 'ok eigi lítill fyrir sér' / 'and not a paltry one either' (ibid 265), but the only verses with which he is credited in this or other sources are the present seven. Finnur Jónsson considered that their archaic form and tone guaranteed their authenticity as work from the beginning of the eleventh century (I 1920:517). He noted also two examples of conflict between these verses and the saga narrative that suggested that the same person was unlikely to have composed both (1912:19). Jan de Vries seems to have been in agreement with Finnur on these points (I 1964:261).

While not impugning the authenticity of these particular verses, Nordal was sceptical concerning many of the other *lausavísur* in the saga. He noted that of the five persons who are ascribed verses in the surviving part of the text, only Tindr Hallkelsson appears as a skald in other unrelated sources. Styrr's berserks, who were assigned one or perhaps two stanzas in the original version of the saga, have always been regarded with suspicion, both as poets and as workers (Sveinsson 1968:4–6, Harris 1976:77). A lost *lausavísa* purportedly spoken by Styrr himself after his death would also, in Nordal's opinion, have been a later embellishment (íF 3:cxl). Gísli's single stanza is open to the same suspicion, because the saga story requires us to believe that Þormóðr, the only brother of Gísli to survive the *heiðarvíg*, committed the verse to memory in the thick of the action (ibid cxli).

Adding to these causes of disquiet, Nordal thought certain verses in *Heiðarvíga saga* betrayed the influence of a set of poems that would have been known to members of the community at Þingeyrar. In the Eiríkr viðsjá verses the line 'beruma vægð at vígi' (4.3) resembles Halldórr ókristni's 'hykkat vægð at vígi' ('Eiríksflokkr' 5), while 'lǫtum randa vǫl reyndan / ryðjendr' (3.3–4) resembles 'lǫtum randhœing reyndan / ríða' in a *lausavísa* assigned to one Nefari in *Sverris saga* (Skj B 518). Oddr, a Þingeyrar monk, had access to the 'Eiríksflokkr' when he wrote his *Óláfs saga Tryggvasonar* around the year 1190. Karl Jónsson, an abbot of Þingeyrar, composed a portion of *Sverris saga*, according to the prologue, though whether this portion included the Nefari verse is uncertain. The implied date of the verse is 1186: Karl is known to have been in Norway between 1185 and 1188 and so in an excellent position to have collected it himself (íF 3:cxlii n1; Ludvig Holm-Olsen KLNM '*Sverris saga*').

On the basis of these and other observations Nordal divided the verses of *Heiðarvíga saga* into two categories. Certain of them he saw as a fabrication on the part of the Þingeyrar author or perhaps his closest informants. Other verses were in Nordal's opinion considerably older than the writing down of the saga, perhaps even correctly attributed, and used as a source by the author of the prose. Among these were the Tindr Hallkelsson, Eiríkr viðsjá, and Gestr ascriptions. To explain the apparent influence of 'Eiríksflokkr,' the Nefari *lausavísa*, and other poetry, Nordal speculated that the work of Eiríkr, Tindr, and Gestr was poorly preserved and had to be retouched, in which process the Þingeyrar monk incorporated snatches from the *Óláfs saga Tryggvasonar* and *Sverris saga* verses, which he knew well (ÍF 3:cxliii).

The apparent importations from 'Eiríksflokkr' and the Nefari *lausavísa* do not greatly affect the integrity of the Eiríkr viðsjá text. The main result is that 3.3-4 becomes suspect as possibly a spurious restoration of a lost original text. Even so, I find Nordal's theory of importations unconvincing. He himself noted that 'beruma vægð at vígi' has another analogue in 'barkak vægð at vígi': the latter line comes from a verse attributed to Þórarinn máhlíðingr (*Skj* B 105 v 1). In turn the 'Máhlíðingavísur' (vv 1, 6, and 9) can be linked with Tindr Hallkelsson's 'Hákonardrápa' 9, via the elements in the clause 'Hroptr of náði / hjaldrskýja val nýjum' (normalized from *Skj* A 147). This suggests that the influences might be more complex and, in some cases at least, earlier than Nordal allowed for. In particular, a thorough scrutiny of the work of the Hákon jarl circle of poets on the one hand, and the verses cited in *Heiðarvíga saga* and the closely related *Eyrbyggja saga*, on the other hand, might be fruitful.

Nordal's reasons for thinking that the saga author did not compose the verses ascribed to Eiríkr seem to have been twofold. He pointed out, without elaboration, that the verses given to him in chapter 40 were inserted in the narrative in a place that was unlikely to have been chosen for verses if the author himself had composed them (ÍF 3:cxli). He also considered that the author had used Eiríkr's verses 5 and 6 as a source for the number of dead in the *heiðarvíg*. Eiríkr states that twelve men died altogether, if we count Gísli, nine of them from the Borgarfjǫrðr faction. Gísli's place in this tallying up is not entirely clear, but the general count of Borgarfjǫrðr dead agrees with the Tindr *lausavísa*, which mentions nine casualties (ibid 308 v 13). The prose contradicts itself on this matter: the account of the reconciliation agrees with Eiríkr and Tindr that the Borgarfjǫrðr faction sustained nine deaths, whereas in the actual narrative of the battle a total of eleven men from that side is reached (ibid 307n2).

Further to these arguments, we may note that Eiríkr viðsjá would be an odd person, of the various available characters in the saga, to invent verses for. As we have seen, he is not mentioned as a skald elsewhere and his part in the present saga is not of great significance. Aside from his verse making he appears in only three contexts: Þórarinn inn spaki names him as one of the men whom Barði should summon (ibid 265); going to collect him, Barði discovers that he has already ridden out to fetch Þorljótr Gjallandafóstri (ibid 274); Þórarinn inn spaki names him again as he advises Barði on the tactics to be followed (ibid 285). The next mention of Eiríkr, along with the first of his verses, comes as Barði's expedition gets under way. Barði asks him how he thinks the journey is likely to go, and the reply is verse 1 (ibid 287). Then, when the southern pursuit is sighted, Barði counsels a further tactical withdrawal, following Þórarinn's instructions. This seemingly prompts Eiríkr to recite verse 2, which contradicts the foregoing by stating that Barði is commanding his following not to withdraw. Barði retorts: 'Eigi segir þú nú satt' / 'Now you are not telling the truth' (ibid 299–300). But Barði's men have no appetite for further retreat, even though it will place them in a superior position for the ensuing battle, and Barði is obliged to yield to the consensus. As they dismount from their horses and entrust them to the protection of Koll-Gríss, Eiríkr recites verse 3 (ibid 300). Then the southern faction overtakes the northerners, and battle is joined. After a lengthy description a new character is introduced (ibid 303–4):

Ok þat er sagt, at maðr hét Þorljótr, kappi mikill; hann átti heima á Veggjum; sumir segja hann frá Sleggjulœk; hann barðisk við Eirík viðsjá, ok áðr þeir berðisk, kvað Eiríkr vísu [v 4].

And it is said that a man was called Þorljótr, a great warrior; his home was at Veggir; some say he was from Sleggjulœkr; he fought with Eiríkr viðsjá, and before they fought Eiríkr said a verse. [v 4].

The fight between the two men ends in Þorljótr's death, and a lull in the general hostilities now ensues. Noteworthy here is that Þorljótr is introduced specifically for the encounter with Eiríkr: he has no other part in the story. The fight between them, along with the verse, appears to be 'tacked on' at the end of the battle description, immediately after its natural climax, the victory of Barði over the southerners. In *Landnámabók* we hear of a 'Ljótr á Veggjum Þorbjarnarson Ísröðarsonar landnámsmans' who fell in the *heiðarvíg*, and this man has generally been identified with Þorljótr (B.M. Ólsen 1937–9:201). Björn M. Ólsen thinks it evident that here *Heiðarvíga saga* was drawing on oral traditions that were independent of those used in *Landnámabók* and that the author of *Heiðarvíga saga* did not know *Landnámabók*. Independent or not, an oral tradition concerning Ljótr/Þorljótr clearly existed, perhaps with Eiríkr's verse already attached to it, and we can see the saga author incorporating it, not altogether felicitously, into his narrative. This narrative then continues with a long description of the *þing*, the settlement, and the outlawry of Barði and others. Eiríkr viðsjá is first mentioned again in chapter 40, when an unnamed man asks him about the battle and the number of dead. This inquiry is not attached to any particular scene or place, beyond the vague 'þat var um vetrinn' / 'it was during the winter.' Eiríkr answers with verse 5. Another example of an inquiry from an unnamed person concerning the number of dead immediately follows, this too without attachment to a particular time or scene. Eiríkr answers with verse 6. Finally, there is general discussion of the heavy losses sustained by the southerners, and Eiríkr says verse 7. There the chapter ends: the new chapter deals with Barði's comrades' departure from Iceland, while Eiríkr, for his part, is henceforth 'out of the saga.'

This evidence suggests that the seven stanzas attributed to Eiríkr viðsjá predate the compilation of *Heiðarvíga saga* and had to be worked into a narrative that originally had no prominent role for him. A plausible way of explaining this would be to suppose that the seven stanzas were originally a unitary composition, handed down in tradition somewhat separate from the other material used in the compilation of the saga. We might, for instance, have here a *flokkr* composed to follow the prose narrative of the battle. The integration of its individual stanzas into the prose narrative would represent the activity of a later redactor.

Read separately from the saga prose, this reconstructed poem falls very naturally into the pattern we have observed in the other poems. Of the three reconstructed poems, two – those ascribed to Torf-Einarr and Egill – can be viewed as dramatic monologues where speaker and author are distinct – just as they are in the death-songs of Ǫrvar-Oddr and Ragnarr loðbrók. In these dramatic monologues, as in Donne's 'The Flea' and Browning's 'Fra Lippo Lippi,' the speaker uses the present tense because he is describing what he sees happening in the here and now: for him it is not present historic but a true progressive present. The perfect or preterite are used only of events that antedate the actions currently being described by the speaker. Within the monologue, again as in Donne or Browning, the speakers' words imply the actions or speeches of others at the scene: the heaping of stones over Hálfdan, the defiance displayed by Veggbergr, Egill's being accompanied by his comrades to the duelling ground. In 'Grottasǫngr' the speech of Fenja and Menja, king Fróði's unwilling slaves, is similarly organized, beginning with an incitation in work-song style,

> Auð mǫlom Fróða ...   (Neckel-Kuhn ed:297 v 5)

> Let us grind Fróði's wealth ...

The action progresses as the speech (or work-song) progresses. The workers start feeling weary: 'aurr etr iliar' / 'the dirt eats at our soles' (v 16). But they incite each other to redoubled effort: 'tǫcom á mǫndli, mær, scarpara' / 'turn the handle harder, maiden' (v 20). Then in verse 21 comes an abrupt switch to the preterite, when the speaker looks back on the action so far as complete:

> Mól míns fǫður   mær ramliga ...;
> stucco stórar   støðr frá lúðri,
> iárni varðar ... (v 21)

> My father's daughter ground mightily; the massive, ironclad supports collapsed beneath the bin ...

As the stanza ends the action begins again and with it the present tense: 'mǫlom enn frammar' / 'let us grind still more' (vv 21 and 22).

The Eiríkr viðsjá *flokkr* differs from these poems in that the attribution may be genuine: in other words, poet and speaker may be identical. If so, the skald narrates with hindsight, after the battle, but uses the present historic to create the illusion that action and description are simultaneous. Four of the seven stanzas are taken up with the prelude to battle, incitation being combined with a commentary on the advance of the opposing forces. Then in the final three stanzas running commentary is abruptly abandoned in favour of a retrospective view that stresses not the detail of the fighting but the death-toll; possibly one or two stanzas describing the battle have been lost here, but I think it likelier that the *flokkr* is complete as it stands. If that is right, it resembles the Egill *flokkr* in being built symmetrically around the fight, though not lavishing so much graphic detail on it. Symmetry of that kind is lacking in the Torf-Einarr *flokkr*, which, at least as now preserved, has no prelude section but launches immediately into a combination of incitation and battle-description; this section, itself brief, is followed by a relatively prolonged contemplation of the aftermath. In these respects 'Einarsflokkr' corresponds most closely to 'Darraðarljóð,' where the narration also begins *in medias res* and gives prominence to the aftermath, whereas the Egill and Eiríkr viðsjá *flokkar*, with their symmetry and even apportionment of the narrative space, resemble 'Friðgerðarflokkr.'

In the deployment of concatenation and other types of patterning this *flokkr* shows the same richness as the Nissa section of *Sexstefja*, 'Friðgerðarflokkr,' and 'Liðsmannaflokkr.' The lexical links between verses 1 and 2 are prominent because placed at the end of their respective lines: 'heiði' (1.1 and 2.3) and 'sunnan' (1.6, 2.4, and 2.8). The pattern with 'sunnan' is further reinforced by the occurrence of 'norðan,' also at line end (1.2), and by the use of the first syllable in *aðalhending* each time it occurs ('hlunn-,' '-kunn,' 'gunn-'). A carry-over of 'h' alliteration (1.1–2, 5–6, 2.3–4, 5–6) acts as another type of link, and we also find a pattern of complementarity in the distribution of the *hendingar*:

1.3 vér hyggjum nag nœra
2.7 geira hreggs frá glyggvi

In these symmetrically placed lines (third in respectively the first and last *helmingar* of the pair of stanzas) an unrhymed syllable in the one is rhymed in the other. An elaboration of this pattern is seen in 1.7 (again symmetrically placed):

ǫrr – hyggr skald til skœru

Similarly, the unrhymed syllable in 1.8 –

skæs, nǫkkuru færi

– finds its rhyme in 2.1:

flykkjask frægir rekkar

Links of a kindred sort exist between verses 2 and 3. There is a double carry-over of alliteration: 'f' in 2.1–2 and 3.1–2, 'h' in 2.3–4, 5–6, and 3.7–8. The wording of the second lines is very similar:

2.2 fúss es herr til snerru
3.2 fram þoki herr at snerru

A chiastic linking of lines in the stanza pair can also be detected:

    2.3 þjóð tekr hart á heiði
    3.7 rjóðum hart á heiði

Line-end repetitions continue with 'heiði' (as just cited) and 'sunnan' (2.4, 2.8, and 3.5). Forms and cognates of 'harðr' / 'hard' enter into the lexical patterning as well: 'hart' as just cited, 'harðráðr' in 2.6, and 'herða' in 3.6.

In verses 3 and 4 alliteration is carried over triply: 'f' in 3.1–2 and 4.7–8 (an example of chiasmus), 'h' in 3.7–8 and 4.5–6, and 'r' in 3.3–4 and 4.1–2. As usual this is reinforced by verbal repetition, which also contributes to a chiastic pattern: 'foldu/foldar' in 3.1 and 4.7, 'reyndan/reyna' in 3.3 and 4.8, and 'rjóðum/rjóðr' in 3.7 and 4.1. In the latter instance the rhyme scheme contributes as well:

    3.7 rjóðum hart á heiði
    4.1 hlotit hǫfum, rjóðr, af reiði

A non-chiastic type of symmetry can be seen in 'randa/randir' (3.3 and 4.2).

Less heavily linked are verses 4 and 5, where the devices are restricted to carry-over of alliteration ('r' in 4.1–2 and 5.3–4) and the associated repetition of 'randa' (4.2 and 5.3).

In verses 5 and 6 the customary rich abundance of linking devices is once more evident. Alliteration is doubly carried over: vowels in 5.5–6 and 6.1–2 and 's' in 5.7–8 and 6.3–4, producing a chiasmus in combination with the other devices. Unrhymed 'grimmt' in 6.7 echoes the symmetrically placed and also unrhymed 'rym' in 5.3, and the emphasis on these not very common types is furthered by 'gims:rimmu' in 5.6. Verbal links are present as well: 'á heiði' in 5.2 and 6.6, both times in *aðalhending* and in the now expected position at line end, and, adding to the chiasmus, 'sár/sǫrum' in 5.8 and 6.3. The resemblance between 5.2 and 6.6 increases if we accept Konráð Gíslason's emendation 'seiðs' for 'skeiðs' in 5.2 (*Skj* A 210).

In verses 6 and 7 alliteration is triply carried over, as in verses 3 and 4: 's' in 6.3–4 and 7.1–2, vowels in 6.1–2 and 7.5–6, and 'g' in 6.7–8 and 7.3–4 and 7–8. The only two lines to fall outside the pattern are 6.5–6, and they have the 'f' alliteration that was prominent in verses 2, 3, and 4. The last lines are strikingly similar:

6.8 gunnél – níu sunnan
7.8 gunnnǫrunga sunnan

This is extended by the repetition of 'fallit/fellu/fell' in 6.2, 6.5, and 7.7 and of 'sverð' in 6.3 and 7.2. If we read 'geirviðir' in 7.3, from the quotation in the *Fourth Grammatical Treatise*, instead of 'gnýverðir,' with the saga manuscript, the result is a repetition of 'viðir' in 6.4. In Nordal's opinion the saga manuscript at this point is a late fourteenth-century replacement of material that had become illegible in the original copy, and so not of great authority (*íF* 3:ci). Chiasmus, a familiar feature elsewhere in the verses, is created by the distribution of 'g' and vowel alliteration and by the verbal link between the second and the second-last lines of the pair of stanzas:

6.2 ítrstalls liði fallit
7.7 fell geysla lið Gísla

The mention, just previously, of sustained 'f' alliteration is a reminder that sometimes not merely two but several stanzas are linked by a particular type of repetition. In all but two of the verses the phrases 'of heiði / á heiði' occur, always at line end. Particularly marked and probably of structural significance are the links between beginning and end. The first three verses, like the last two, are characterized by a fondness for the words 'sunnan' and 'norðan,' these too always at line end. In verses 2, 6, and 7 'sunnan' combines in *aðalhending* with 'gunn-,' and indeed the last line in verses 2 and 7 is identical: 'gunnnǫrunga sunnan.' Nordal noticed this verbatim repetition but thought it due to corruption in oral transmission, since in his view Eiríkr was unlikely to have repeated himself in such a fashion (ibid cxli). However, the same use of repetition, evidently so as to link the end of a poem back to its beginning, has been seen in the Ljótr *flokkr*, where the name Friðgeirr appears in the first and last stanzas, and in other poems. The complementary adverb 'norðan,' in *aðalhending* with '-borðs,' creates a complementary pattern:

1.2 hræborðs farit norðan
6.4 sigrborðs viðir norðan

Thus the first verse is linked with the second-last verse, and the second verse with the last verse. As in the Ljótr verses, a conspicuous reinforcement of this pattern comes with a proper name, Barði (at the end of 2.6 and 7.6, both times in *aðalhending*). The word 'geir' in 2.7 and 7.3, if the text of the *Fourth Grammatical Treatise* is right, is a less obvious element in the symmetry.

Conclusions

The poems discussed in the previous seven chapters constitute, in my opinion, a special genre, where the mode of narration is running commentary. The main march of events is indicated by the present tense, while normally the preterite or perfect are reserved for actions that precede the stage currently reached in the narrative. This genre can be divided into two subtypes. In one, unvarying use is made of the present tense to denote the progression of events: in this group belong the three poems attributed respectively to Torf-Einarr, Egill, and Eiríkr viðsjá. In the other, running-commentary narration is to some degree blended with conventional retrospective narration. The present tense of the running commentary, used alongside the preterite of the retrospective survey, takes on the feel of a present historic, an idiom that was evidently also current in other types of early Norse-Icelandic poetry. Clearly of the second (mixed) subtype are 'Friðgerðarflokkr,' *Háttatal*, *Sexstefja*, and 'Liðsmannaflokkr.' Here present and preterite are used interchangeably of actions within a single succession of events. The 'Merlínússpá,' describing the battle of the dragons, in part follows the same pattern. Finally, 'Darraðarljóð' may belong to the group, but the evidence (a single verb in a single manuscript) is slight and a position in the other group possible.

In this genre the narrative normally falls into three phases, prelude, action, and aftermath. Although truncation or virtual omission of one of these stages occurs in the Torf-Einarr and Eiríkr viðsjá *flokkar* and in 'Darraðarljóð,' each is at least implied. Typically the opposing forces are shown converging, the progress of the battle is sketched, and the result and repercussions are indicated. Except in 'Liðsmannaflokkr' there is a compact 'unity of action,' in Aristotle's sense. The brisk forward impetus is never compromised by richness of detail or prolixity of speeches, such as is characteristic of the Old English 'Battle of Maldon.' The frequent use of incitations admits an element of futurity into the narration: we view the events of the poem as they happen, as they begin to happen, or just before they happen. Three of the poems are 'open-ended,' in that the ending hints at future events that cannot yet be recounted, at least within the knowledge of the speaker. By contrast, a strong feeling of closure is found in 'Liðsmannaflokkr' and the Egill and Eiríkr viðsjá flokkar.

The incitations and the associated use of vocatives establish the presence of the speaker and other personages within the poems. In all the poems, except arguably 'Friðgerðarflokkr,' the speaker's presence is felt sufficiently to justify use of the term 'dramatic monologue.' The voice in 'Friðgerðarflokkr' is detached and critical, but elsewhere the speaker is located at the heart of the action; if not the protagonist, he is at least a participant and no mere observer. He knows what is right, both tactically and morally, and he is shown acting on these inner certainties. He is sometimes further characterized by his scorn for the opponent – seen as effeminate by Torf-Einarr, as feeble and perhaps also mercenary (a 'hodda beiðir' / 'requester of treasures') by Egill, and a miser ('foldar fjǫtra fúrleynir' / 'concealer of gold') by Eiríkr viðsjá. The speaker may also reflect ironically or critically on his own comrades, although a suggestion of *esprit de corps* is naturally more usual. An element of self-directed irony, as with Egill and perhaps too the 'Liðsmannaflokkr' speaker, can sometimes be detected.

Typically, unity is created in poems of this genre through intricate interstanzaic linking, large-scale vocabulary repetition, and the linking of the beginning of the poem with the end. Devices of the same sort can be seen in other extant poems, for example 'Víkingarvísur,' Egill's 'Hǫfuðlausn,' and 'Geisli.' Exceptional for the virtual absence of such devices is the Torf-Einarr *flokkr*.

In the prose works, poems of this genre are preserved in two different forms. Sometimes, as with 'Friðgerðarflokkr,' 'Darraðarljóð,' the Torf-Einarr *flokkr* (in *Fagrskinna*), the *Sexstefja* excerpt (except v 1), and 'Liðsmannaflokkr' (in 'Oldest Saga'), the constituent stanzas are treated as parts of a single poem. In other cases, as with the Egill and Eiríkr viðsjá *flokkar*, the Torf-Einarr *flokkr* (in *Orkneyinga saga* and *Heimskringla*), and perhaps the 'Liðsmannaflokkr' (in *Knýtlinga saga*), the constituent stanzas are treated as *lausavísur*. The illusion that the speaker is speaking in the midst of the action, a convention in dramatic monologue, becomes converted into literal reality. A similar thing has happened in the prose that accompanies 'Darraðarljóð' in *Njáls saga* and 'Krákumál' in *Ragnars saga* (AM 147, 4to version), except that these poems have not been broken up into *lausavísur*.' 'Darraðarljóð' becomes a song of triumph delivered by Valkyries as the battle progresses and 'Krákumál' the warrior's dying speech. In the prosimetrum narrative into which these poems have entered, the identity of the skald who composed the verses is immaterial and therefore eclipsed. The same is probably true of the *flokkar* spoken by Egill and Torf-Einarr, and the *Knýtlinga saga* attribution of 'Liðsmannaflokkr' to a collective of *liðsmenn* may likewise be an inference from verse 1 or other stanzas where a plurality of speakers might seem to be present.

Two interrelated tendencies are therefore evident in the prose. One is to dramatize the circumstances in which a poem was composed, relying on data inferred from the poem. The other is to dismember the poem into *lausavísur*. The second tendency is related to the first because it takes the dramatizing process to an extreme where each stanza of the poem is referred to a specific occasion. These tendencies, together or separately, may be found in prose works as early as the twelfth century. The *Ágrip* account of 'Bersǫglisvísur' 12 seems to go back to oral tradition. *Heiðarvíga saga*, too, may preserve oral tradition in its handling of at least one of the Eiríkr viðsjá verses. 'Oral tradition' here does not equate with 'authentic tradition': it merely means that the aetiological story that explains the verse was fabricated at an early stage. Other early examples are *Morkinskinna*, in its use of the verses prophesying Haraldr harðráði's death, *Orkneyinga saga*, with its very similar handling of the Torf-Einarr verses, and the prose commentary to 'Darraðarljóð,' if derived from *Brjáns saga. We can see from the treatment of the Torf-Einarr *flokkr* and of the satirical verses by Eyvindr skáldaspillir in *Heimskringla* that Snorri shared with his predecessors the interest in inventing or perpetuating these aetiological stories. The same tendencies continue in such subsequent works as *Egils saga* (the Ljótr sequence and the *níðvísur*), *Gunnlaugs saga ormstungu* (Poole 1981), *Hávarðar saga Ísfirðings* (Holtsmark 1927 and 1928, Poole 1975:152–91), and *Hulda/ Hrokkinskinna* (the Oddr Kíkinaskáld verses). Probably a late example is the treatment of 'Snjófríðardrápa' in *Flateyjarbók* (Halldórsson 1969, Poole 1982). The *fornaldarsögur*, where we have seen examples in *Hálfs saga* and *Ǫrvar-Odds saga*, are as given to these tendencies as the kings' sagas and the sagas of Icelanders.

All seven poems discussed in this book are ostensibly products of the

Viking Age. Occasionally, however, it turns out not to be the poet who flourished at that period but merely the speaker. In such instances the poet may be seen as the imaginative recreator of the speech and actions of an illustrious, already half-romanticized Viking past.

Bibliography

Aðalbjarnarson 1937   Aðalbjarnarson, Bjarni *Om de norske kongers sagaer.* Skrifter utgitt av Det Norske Videnskaps-Akademi i Oslo. II. Historisk-Filosofisk Klasse 1936 no 4. Oslo 1937
Ágrip 1929ed   *Ágrip af Nóregs konunga sögum* ed Finnur Jónsson. ASB 18. Halle 1929
Åkerblom 1899   Åkerblom, Axel 'Bidrag til tolkningen af skaldekvad' ANF 15 (1899) 269–74
Åkerblom 1917   Åkerblom, Axel 'Bruket av historiskt presens i den tidigare isländska skaldediktningen (till omkr 1100)' ANF 33 (1917) 293–314
Albeck 1946   Albeck, Gustav *Knytlinga. Sagaerne om Danmarks Konger.* Copenhagen 1946
Almqvist 1965   Almqvist, Bo *Norrön niddiktning ...I: Nid mod furstar.* Nordiska texter och undersökningar 21. Uppsala 1965
Almqvist 1978–9   Almqvist, Bo 'Scandinavian and Celtic Folklore Contacts in the Earldom of Orkney' SBVS 20 (1978–9) 80–105
Amory 1978–9   Amory, Frederick 'Saga Style in Some Kings' Sagas' APS 32 (1978–9) 53–86
Andersson 1972   Andersson, Theodore 'Blood on the Battlefield. A Note on the *Ludwigslied* v 49' Neophil 56 (1972) 12–17
Anglo-Saxon Chronicle   *Two of the Anglo-Saxon Chronicles Parallel ...* ed Charles Plummer. 2 vols. Oxford 1892 and 1899
The Anglo-Saxons   ed James Campbell. Oxford 1982
Annals of the Four Masters   *Annala Rioghachta Eireann: Annals of the Kingdom of Ireland by the Four Masters ...* ed and tr J. O'Donovan. 5 vols. Dublin 1848–51
Annals of Ulster   *Annala Uladh: Annals of Ulster ...* ed and tr W.M. Hennessy and B. MacCarthy. 4 vols. Dublin 1887–1901

Apter 1982   Apter, M.J. 'Metaphor as Synergy.' In *Metaphor: Problems and Perspectives* ed D.S. Miall. Brighton 1982. 55–70

Ashdown 1930   Ashdown, Margaret *English and Norse Documents Relating to the Reign of Ethelred the Unready.* Cambridge 1930

Axelson 1959–60   Axelson, Sven 'Om Knytlingasagas datering samt dens författare' *(N)HT* 39 (1959–60) 140–4

Bayerschmidt-Hollander 1955   *Njáls saga* tr C.F. Bayerschmidt and Lee M. Hollander. New York 1955

Berg 1958   Berg, Knut 'The Gosforth Cross' *Journal of the Warburg and Courtauld Institutes* 21 (1958) 27–43

Beyschlag 1950   Beyschlag, Siegfried *Konungasögur: Untersuchungen zur Königssaga bis Snorri. Die älteren Übersichtswerke samt Ynglingasaga.* BiblAM 8. Copenhagen 1950

Blaney 1982   Blaney, Benjamin 'The Berserk Suitor: The Literary Application of a Stereotyped Theme' *SS* 54 (1982) 279–94

Bley 1909   Bley, André *Eigla-Studien.* Recueil de travaux publiés par la Faculté de Philosophie et Lettres de l'Université de Gand fascicule 39. Ghent 1909

Boer 1892   Boer, R.C. 'Über die Ǫrvar-Odds saga' *ANF* 8 (1892) 97–139

de Boor [1930] 1964   de Boor, Helmut 'Die religiöse Sprache der Vǫluspá und verwandte Denkmäler.' 1930. Reprinted in Helmut de Boor *Kleine Schriften* I. Berlin 1964. 209–83

de Boor [1951] 1966   de Boor, Helmut 'Die nordische Svanhilddichtung.' 1951. Reprinted in Helmut de Boor *Kleine Schriften II.* Berlin 1966. 184–95

Brooks 1978   Brooks, N.P. 'Arms, Status, and Warfare in Late-Saxon England.' In *Ethelred the Unready* 81–103. See *Ethelred* 1978.

Brown 1981   Brown, R. Allen 'The Battle of Hastings' *Proc Battle* 3 (1980) 1–21. Woodbridge 1981

Bugge 1867   Bugge, Sophus, ed ... *Sæmundar Edda hins fróða.* Christiania 1867

Bugge 1901   Bugge, Sophus *Norsk Sagaskrivning og Sagafortælling i Irland.* Kristiania 1901–8

A. Campbell 1946–53   Campbell, Alistair 'Knúts saga' *SBVS* 13 (1946–53) 238–48

A. Campbell 1949   See *Encomium Emmæ.*

M.W. Campbell 1971   Campbell, M.W. 'Queen Emma and Ælfgifu of Northampton: Canute the Great's Women' *Med Scan* 4 (1971) 66–79

Chase 1985   Chase, Martin '*Concatenatio* as a Structural Element in the Christian *Drápur*.' Unpublished paper given at the Sixth International Saga Conference, Helsingør 1985

Child 1882–98   Child, Francis, ed *The English and Scottish Popular Ballads.* 5 vols in 10. New York and London 1882–98

Christensen 1969   Christensen, A.E. *Vikingetidens Danmark.* Copenhagen 1969

Cleasby-Vigfússon 1874   Cleasby, Richard, and Guðbrandur Vigfússon *An Icelandic-English Dictionary* ... Oxford 1874

Cogadh Gaedhel re Gallaibh 1867ed   *Cogadh Gaedhel re Gallaibh* ... ed and tr J.H. Todd. Rolls Series. London 1867

Craigie 1897   Craigie, William 'Gaelic Words and Names in the Icelandic Sagas' *Zeitschrift für celtische Philologie* 1 (1897) 439–54

Dietrich 1865   Dietrich, F. 'Die Räthsel des Exeterbuchs: Verfasser, Weitere Lösungen' *ZDA* 12 (1865) 232–52

Dolley 1978   Dolley, Michael 'An Introduction to the Coinage of Æthelræd II.' In *Ethelred the Unready* 115–33. See Ethelred 1978.

Dronke 1969   Dronke, Ursula *The Poetic Edda* vol. 1 *Heroic Poems.* Oxford 1969

Edda Snorra Sturlusonar I 1848; II 1852; III 1880–7   *Edda Snorra Sturlusonar* ed Sveinbjörn Egilsson, Jón Sigurðsson, and Finnur Jónsson. 3 vols. Copenhagen 1848–87

Eddica minora 1903ed   *Eddica minora* ... ed Andreas Heusler and Wilhelm Ranisch. Dortmund 1903

Egils saga   See ÍF 2.

Egilsson 1860   Egilsson, Sveinbjörn *Lexicon Poëticum antiquæ linguæ septentrionalis.* Copenhagen 1860

Einarsson 1961   Einarsson, Bjarni *Skáldasögur.* Reykjavík 1961

Einarsson 1975   Einarsson, Bjarni *Litterære forudsætninger for Egils saga* Reykjavík 1975

Elder Edda Neckel-Kuhn ed   *Die Lieder des Codex Regius nebst verwandten Denkmälern* ed Gustav Neckel, rev Hans Kuhn. 2 vols. Heidelberg 1962–8

Ellehøj 1965   Ellehøj, Svend *Studier over den ældste norrøne historieskrivning. BiblAM* 26. Copenhagen 1965

Encomium Emmæ 1949ed   *Encomium Emmæ Reginæ* ed Alistair Campbell. Camden 3rd series 72. London 1949

English Historical Documents c. 500–1042 ed Dorothy Whitelock. Rev ed. London 1979

von Erhardt-Siebold 1949   von Erhardt-Siebold, Erika 'The Old English Loom Riddles.' In *Philologica: The Malone Anniversary Studies* ed T.A. Kirby and H.B. Woolf. Baltimore 1949. 9–17

Ethelred 1978   *Ethelred the Unready* ed David Hill. British Archaeological Reports, British Series 59. Oxford 1978

Eysteinsson 1953–7   Eysteinsson, J. Sölvi, 'The Relationship of *Merlínússpá* and Geoffrey of Monmouth's *Historia*' *SBVS* 14 (1953–7) 95–112

Fagrskinna 1902–3ed   *Fagrskinna. Nóregs konunga tal* ed Finnur Jónsson. *SUGNL* 30. Copenhagen 1902–3

Falk 1919   Falk, Hjalmar *Altwestnordische Kleiderkunde. Vid Skr.* Kristiania 1919
Falk 1924   Falk, Hjalmar *Odensheite. Vid Skr.* Kristiania 1924
Fell 1982–3   Fell, Christine 'Unfriđ: An Approach to a Definition' SBVS 21 (1982–3) 85–100
Fidjestøl 1982   Fidjestøl, Bjarne *Det norrøne fyrstediktet.* Øvre Ervik 1982
Flateyjarbók I 1860; II 1862; III 1868   *Flateyjarbók* ed C.R. Unger and Guđbrandur Vigfússon. 3 vols. Christiania 1860–8
Fms 6   *Fornmanna sögur* ... vol 6 *Sögur Magnúsar konúngs góđa. Haralds konúngs harđráđa ok sona hans* [ed Þorgeir Guđmundsson and Rasmus Rask]. Copenhagen 1831
Frank 1978   Frank, Roberta *Old Norse Court Poetry. The Dróttkvætt Stanza. Islandica* 42. Ithaca NY 1978
Frank 1984   Frank, Roberta 'Viking Atrocity and Skaldic Verse: The Rite of the Blood-Eagle' *English Historical Review* 99 (1984) 332–43
Freeman 1877   Freeman, E.A. *The History of the Norman Conquest of England, Its Causes and its Results.* 5 vols [3rd ed of vol 1 pub 1877]. Oxford 1875–9.
von Friesen 1909   von Friesen, Otto 'Historiska runinskrifter' *Fornvännen* 4 (1909) 57–85
Fritzner 1954ed   Fritzner, Johan *Ordbog over det gamle norsk Sprog.* 2nd ed. Christiania 1883–96 rpt Oslo 1954
Gaimar 1960ed   Gaimar, Geffrei *L'Estoire des Engleis* ed Alexander Bell. Oxford 1960
Geijer 1979   Geijer, Agnes *A History of Textile Art.* London and Stockholm 1979
Genzmer 1956   Genzmer, Felix 'Das Walkürenlied' ANF 71 (1956) 168–71
Geoffrey 1911–29ed   Geoffrey of Monmouth *Historia Regum Britanniæ* ... ed Edmond Faral. In Edmond Faral *La Légende Arthurienne.* Paris 1911–29
Geoffrey 1929ed   Geoffrey of Monmouth *The Historia Regum Britanniæ* ... ed Acton Griscom. London 1929
Gering 1886   Gering, Hugo *Kvæđa-brot Braga ens gamla Boddasonar* ... Halle 1886
Gíslason I 1875; II 1889   Gíslason, Konráđ ed *Njála.* 2 vols. Copenhagen 1875–89
Goedheer 1938   Goedheer, A.J. *Irish and Norse Traditions about the Battle of Clontarf.* Haarlem 1938
Gordon 1961   Gordon, Ida L. 'Oral Tradition and the Sagas of Poets.' In *Studia centenalia in honorem memoriæ Benedikt S. Þórarinsson* ... ed B.S. Benedikz. Reykjavík 1961. 69–76
Grágás 1852ed   *Grágás* ... ed Vilhjálmur Finsen. 4 vols. Ia and Ib 1852; II 1879; III 1883. Copenhagen 1852–83

Gransden 1974   Gransden, Antonia *Historical Writing in England c. 550– c. 1307*. London 1974

'Grettisrímur'   See *Rímnasafn*.

Gutenbrunner 1937   Gutenbrunner, Siegfried 'Zu den Strophen des "Holzmannes" in der Ragnars saga ... ' *ZDA* 74 (1937) 139–43

Hákonar saga 1952ed   *Hákonar saga Ívarssonar* ed Jón Helgason and Jakob Benediktsson. *SUGNL* 62. Copenhagen 1952

Hálfs saga 1909ed   *Hálfs saga ok Hálfsrekka* ed A. Le Roy Andrews. *ASB* 14. Halle 1909

Hall 1984   Hall, Richard *The Viking Dig*. London 1984

Hallberg 1978–9   Hallberg, Peter 'Eyrbyggja sagas ålder – än en gång' *APS* 32 (1978–9) 196–219

Halldórsson 1969   Halldórsson, Ólafur 'Snjófríðar drápa.' In *Afmælisrit Jóns Helgasonar* ... ed Jakob Benediktsson, Jón Samsonarson, Jónas Kristjánsson, Ólafur Halldórsson, and Stefán Karlsson. Reykjavík 1969. 147–59

Harris 1976   Harris, Joseph 'The Masterbuilder Tale in Snorri's *Edda* and Two Sagas' *ANF* (1976) 66–101

Háttatal 1879–81ed   *Háttatal Snorra Sturlusonar* ed Th. Möbius. 2 vols. Halle 1879–81

Heimskringla 1893–1901ed   *Heimskringla* ... ed Finnur Jónsson. 4 vols. *SUGNL* 23. Copenhagen 1893–1901

Heinrichs 1976   Heinrichs, Anne ' "Intertexture" and Its Functions in Early Written Sagas ...' *SS* 48 (1976) 127–45

Helgason 1950–1   Helgason, Jón 'Blað Landsbókasafns úr Heiðarvíga sögu' *Landsbókasafn Íslands. Árbók* 7–8 (1950–1) 127–35

Hemings þáttr 1962ed   *Hemings þáttr Áslákssonar* ed Gillian Fellows Jensen. Vol 3. *EdAM* ser B. Copenhagen 1962

Heusler 1922   Heusler, Andreas *Die Geschichte vom weisen Njal* (with trans of 'Darraðarljóð' by Felix Genzmer). Jena 1914 and 1922

Heusler-Ranisch 1903   See *Eddica minora*.

Hoffmann 1964   Hoffmann, Marta *The Warp-weighted Loom*. Oslo 1964

Hofmann 1955   Hofmann, Dietrich *Nordisch-englische Lehnbeziehungen der Wikingerzeit*. *BiblAM* 14. Copenhagen 1955

Hofmann 1978–9   Hofmann, Dietrich 'Sagaprosa als Partner von Skaldenstrophen' *Med Scan* 11 (1978–9) 68–81

Hollister 1962   Hollister, C.W. *Anglo-Saxon Military Institutions*. Oxford 1962

Holtsmark 1927   Holtsmark, Anne 'Om visene i Hávarðar saga.' In *Festskrift til Hjalmar Falk* ... Oslo 1927. 279–88

Holtsmark 1928   Holtsmark, Anne 'Litt om overleveringen i Håvards saga.'

In *Festskrift til Finnur Jónsson* ... ed Johs Brøndum-Nielsen, Elof Hellquist, O.F. Hultman, Sigurður Nordal, and Magnus Olsen. Copenhagen 1928. 67-83

Holtsmark 1939 Holtsmark, Anne ' "Vefr Darraðar" ' *MM* 1939. 74-96

Holtsmark 1950 Holtsmark, Anne 'Myten om Idun og Tjatse i Tjodolfs Haustlǫng' *ANF* 64 (1950) 1-73

Holtsmark 1954 Holtsmark, Anne 'Olav den Hellige og "Seierskjorten" ' *MM* 1954. 104-8

Holtsmark 1956 Holtsmark, Anne *Studier i norrøn diktning* Oslo 1956

Hooper 1979 Hooper, Nicholas 'Anglo-Saxon Warfare on the Eve of the Conquest: A Brief Survey' *Proc Battle* 1 (1978) 84-93. Ipswich 1979

Hougen 1940 Hougen, Bjørn 'Osebergfunnets billedvev' *Viking* 4 (1940) 85-124

Hovstad 1946 Hovstad, J. 'Tradisjon og diktning i Egils saga' *Syn og Segn* 52 (1946) 83-96

Hughes 1972 Hughes, Kathleen *Early Christian Ireland: Introduction to the Sources*. Ithaca NY 1972

ÍF 1 *Íslendingabók. Landnámabók* ed Jakob Benediktsson. Reykjavík 1968

ÍF 2 *Egils saga Skalla-Grímssonar* ed Sigurður Nordal. Reykjavík 1933

ÍF 3 *Borgfirðinga sǫgur* ed Sigurður Nordal and Guðni Jónsson. Reykjavík 1938 rpt with additional material 1956

ÍF 6 *Vestfirðinga sǫgur* ed Björn K. Þórólfsson and Guðni Jónsson. Reykjavík 1943

ÍF 7 *Grettis saga Ásmundarsonar* ed Guðni Jónsson. Reykjavík 1936

ÍF 8 *Vatnsdœla saga* ed Einar Ól. Sveinsson. Reykjavík 1939

ÍF 12 *Brennu-Njáls saga* ed Einar Ól. Sveinsson. Reykjavík 1954

ÍF 26-8 *Heimskringla* .... ed Bjarni Aðalbjarnarson. Reykjavík 1941, 1945, 1951

ÍF 34 *Orkneyinga saga* ed Finnbogi Guðmundsson. Reykjavík 1965

ÍF 35 *Sǫgur Danakonunga* ed Bjarni Guðnason. Reykjavík 1982

Indrebø 1917 Indrebø, Gustav *Fagrskinna*. Kristiania 1917

Indrebø 1922 Indrebø, Gustav 'Aagrip' *Edda* 17 (1922) 18-65

Jameson 1981 Jameson, Fredric *The Political Unconscious: Narrative as a Socially Symbolic Act*. Ithaca NY 1981

John 1977 John, Eric 'War and Society in the Tenth Century: The Maldon Campaign' *Transactions of the Royal Historical Society* 5th ser 27 (1977) 173-95

Johnsen 1916 Johnsen, O.A. *Olav Haraldssons ungdom indtil slaget ved Nesjar* ... Skrifter utgitt av Videnskapsselskapet i Kristiania Historisk-Filosofisk Klasse 1916 no 2. Kristiania 1916

Jones 1946-53 Jones, Gwyn 'History and Fiction in the Sagas of the Icelanders' *SBVS* 13 (1946-53) 285-306

Jones 1960   Jones, Gwyn tr *Egil's Saga.* Syracuse 1960
Jónsson 1884   Jónsson, Finnur *Kritiske Studier over en Del af de ældste norske og islandske Skjaldekvad.* Copenhagen 1884
Jónsson 1901   Jónsson, Finnur *Det norsk-islandske Skjaldesprog omtrent 800–1300.* SUGNL 28. Copenhagen 1901
Jónsson 1904   Jónsson, Finnur 'Om Njála' *ÅNOH* 1904. 89–166
Jónsson 1912   Jónsson, Finnur 'Sagaernes lausavísur' *ÅNOH* 1912. 1–57
Jónsson I 1920; II 1923; III 1924   Jónsson, Finnur *Den oldnorske og oldislandske litteraturshistorie.* 2nd ed. 3 vols. Copenhagen 1920–4
Jónsson 1926–8   Jónsson, Finnur *Ordbog til de af SUGNL udgivne rímur* ... SUGNL 51. Copenhagen 1926–8
Jónsson 1931   Jónsson, Finnur *Lexicon Poeticum antiquæ linguæ septentrionalis* ... Rev ed. Copenhagen 1931
Kershaw 1922   Kershaw, Nora *Anglo-Saxon and Norse Poems.* Cambridge 1922
Keynes 1978   Keynes, Simon 'The Declining Reputation of King Æthelred the Unready.' In *Ethelred the Unready* 227–53. See Ethelred 1978.
Keynes 1980   Keynes, Simon *The Diplomas of King Æthelred 'The Unready' 978–1016* ... Cambridge 1980
Knýtlinga saga 1919–25ed   See *Sǫgur Danakonunga.*
Knýtlinga saga 1982ed   See ÍF 35.
Kock NN   Kock, E.A. *Notationes Norrœnæ* ... Lunds Universitets Årsskrift NF Avdelning 1. Lund 1923–44
Kock I 1946; II 1949   Kock, E.A. *Den norsk-isländska skaldediktningen.* 2 vols. Lund 1946–9
Krause 1925   Krause, Wolfgang 'Erklärungen zur ältesten Skaldendichtung.' Nachrichten von der Gesellschaft der Wissenschaften zu Göttingen. Philosophisch-historische Klasse 1925. 134–40
Krijn 1927   Krijn, Sophie 'Nogle bemærkninger om Egils stil' *Edda* 27 (1927) 462–85
Kristjánsson 1972   Kristjánsson, Jónas *Um Fóstbrædrasögu.* Stofnun Árna Magnússonar á Íslandi. Rit I. Reykjavík 1972
Kristjánsson 1981   Kristjánsson, Jónas 'Learned Style or Saga Style?' In *Speculum norrœnum* 260–92. See *Speculum norrœnum.*
Kuhn 1937   Kuhn, Hans 'Zum Vers- und Satzbau der Skalden' *ZDA* 74 (1937) 49–63
Kuhn 1952   Kuhn, Hans 'Heldensage vor und ausserhalb der Dichtung.' In *Edda, Skalden, Saga: Festschrift zum 70. Geburtstag von Felix Genzmer* ed Hermann Schneider. Heidelberg 1952. 262–80
Lang 1972   Lang, J.T. 'Illustrative Carving of the Viking Period at Sockburn-on-Tees' *Archaeologia Aeliana* 4th ser 50 (1972) 235–48

Larson 1909–10   Larson, L.M. 'The Political Policies of Cnut as King of England' *American Historical Review* 15 (1909–10) 720–43

Larsson 1891   Larsson, Ludvig *Ordförrådet i de äldsta isländska handskrifterna* Lund 1891

Legendary Saga 1922ed   *Óláfs saga hins helga. Efter ... Delagardieske samling nr. 8 II* ed O.A. Johnsen. Kristiania 1922

Legendary Saga 1982ed   *Óláfs saga hins helga. Die 'Legendarische Saga' über Olaf den Heiligen ...* ed and tr Anne Heinrichs, Doris Janshen, Elke Radicke, and Hartmut Röhn. Heidelberg 1982

Lehmann-von Carolsfeld 1883   Lehmann, K., and H. Schnorr von Carolsfeld *Die Njalssage, insbesondere in ihren juristischen Bestandtheilen.* Berlin 1883

Lexicon Poeticum antiquæ linguæ septentrionalis ... ed Finnur Jónsson. 2nd ed. Copenhagen 1931

Liestøl 1929   Liestøl, Knut *Upphavet til den islandske ættesaga.* Oslo 1929

Lloyd 1939   Lloyd, J.E. *A History of Wales from the Earliest Times to the Edwardian Conquest.* 3rd ed. 2 vols. London 1939

Louis-Jensen 1977   Louis-Jensen, Jonna *Kongesagastudier: Kompilationen Hulda-Hrokkinskinna. BiblAM* 32. Copenhagen 1977

LP 1860   See Egilsson 1860.

LP 1931   See *Lexicon Poeticum.*

McKenzie 1981   McKenzie, Bridget Gordon 'On the Relation of Norse Skaldic Verse to Irish Syllabic Poetry.' In *Speculum norrœnum* 337–56. See *Speculum norrœnum.*

Magerøy 1948   Magerøy, Hallvard *Glælognskviða av Toraren Lovtunge.* Bidrag til nordisk filologi 12. Oslo 1948.

Magnússon 1910   Magnússon, Eiríkr, ed *Darraðarljóð.* Coventry 1910. Also published as '*Darraðarljóð*': *Old Lore Miscellany of Orkney* 3 (1910) 78–94

Margeson 1983   Margeson, Sue 'On the Iconography of the Manx Crosses.' In *The Viking Age in the Isle of Man* ... ed Christine Fell, Peter Foote, James Graham-Campbell, and Robert Thompson. London 1983. 94–106

Marold 1983   Marold, Edith *Kenningkunst. Ein Beitrag zu einer Poetik der Skaldendichtung.* Quellen und Forschungen zur Sprach- und Kulturgeschichte der germanischen Völker NF 80. Berlin 1983

Mazzeo [1952] 1962   Mazzeo, J.A. 'A Critique of Some Modern Theories of Metaphysical Poetry.' In *Seventeenth-Century English Poetry* ed W.R. Keast. New York 1962. 63–74

Meissner 1921   Meissner, Rudolf *Die Kenningar der Skalden* ... Rheinische Beiträge und Hülfsbücher zur germanischen Philologie und Volkskunde I. Bonn and Leipzig 1921

Meyer 1899   Meyer, Kuno 'The Song of Carroll's Sword' *Revue Celtique* 20 (1899) 7–12

Meyer 1913   Meyer, Kuno *Selections from Ancient Irish Poetry.* London 1913
Mitchell 1981   Mitchell, W.J.T., ed *On Narrative.* Chicago 1981
Moberg 1941   Moberg, Ove *Olav Haraldsson, Knut den store och Sverige.* Lund (for Copenhagen) 1941
Moberg 1945   Moberg, Ove 'Två historiografiska undersökningar' *ÅNOH* 1945. 5-45
Mohr 1933   Mohr, Wolfgang *Kenningstudien. Beiträge zur Stilgeschichte der altgermanischen Dichtung.* Stuttgart 1933
Morkinskinna 1932ed   *Morkinskinna* ed Finnur Jónsson SUGNL 53. Copenhagen 1932
Mundal 1984   Mundal, Else 'Heilagmann som sa sex' *Norskrift* 42 (1984) 36-57
Neckel-Kuhn ed   See *Elder Edda.*
Neumann 1955   Neumann, Eduard *Der Schicksalsbegriff in der Edda.* Giessen 1955
Njála 1908ed   *Brennu-Njálssaga* ... ed Finnur Jónsson ASB 13. Halle 1908
NN   See Kock NN
Nordal 1914   Nordal, Sigurður *Om Olav den helliges Saga* ... Copenhagen 1914
Noreen 1922   Noreen, Erik *Studier i fornvästnordisk diktning 2. samlingen.* Uppsala Universitets Årsskrift 1922. 4
Nygaard 1896   Nygaard, Marius 'Den lærde stil i den norrøne prosa.' In *Sproglig-historiske Studier tilegnede Professor C.R. Unger.* Kristiania 1896. 153-70
Nygaard 1905   Nygaard, Marius *Norrøn syntax.* Kristiania 1905
Nygaard 1916   Nygaard, Marius 'Bemerkninger, rettelser og supplementer til min Norrøn syntax ...' *Vid Skr* 1916 no 5. Kristiania 1971
'Óláfs ríma Haraldssonar'   See *Rímnasafn.*
Ólason 1983   Ólason, Vésteinn 'Kveðið um Ólaf helga' *Skírnir* 157 (1983) 48-63
Olrik I 1903; II 1910   Olrik, Axel *Danmarks heltedigtning. En Oldtidsstudie.* 2 vols. Copenhagen 1903-10
B.M. Ólsen 1937-9   Ólsen, Björn M. *Um Íslendingasögur.* SSÍ 6:3. Reykjavík 1937-9
M. Olsen [1933] 1938   Olsen, Magnus 'Fra Hávamál til Krákumál.' Rpt in Magnus Olsen *Norrøne Studier.* Oslo 1938. 234-44
M. Olsen 1945   Olsen, Magnus 'Skaldevers om nøds-år nordenfjells.' In *Studia septentrionalia* II: *Festskrift til Konrad Nielsen* ... Oslo 1945. 176-92
O'Rahilly 1961   O'Rahilly, Cecile *The Stowe Version of the Táin Bó Cuailnge.* Dublin 1961
O'Rahilly 1976   O'Rahilly, Cecile *Táin Bó Cuailnge: Recension I.* Dublin 1976
Qrvar-Odds saga 1892ed   *Qrvar-Odds saga* ed R.C. Boer. ASB 2. Halle 1892

de Paor 1976   de Paor, Liam 'The Viking Towns of Ireland.' *Proceedings of the Seventh Viking Congress Dublin 15–21 August 1973* ed B. Almqvist and D. Greene. Dublin 1976. 29–37

Perkins 1969   Perkins, Richard 'A Medieval Icelandic Rowing Chant' *Med Scan* 2 (1969) 92–101

Plummer 1892–9   See *Anglo-Saxon Chronicle*.

Poole 1975   Poole, Russell 'Skaldic Poetry in the Sagas ... ' Ph D diss Toronto 1975

Poole 1980   Poole, Russell 'In Search of the Partar' *SS* 52 (1980) 264–77

Poole 1981   Poole, Russell 'Compositional Technique in Some Verses from *Gunnlaugs saga*' *JEGP* 80 (1981) 469–85

Poole 1982   Poole, Russell 'Ormr Steinþórsson and the *Snjófriðardrápa*' *ANF* 97 (1982) 122–37

Poole 1985A   Poole, Russell '*Darraðarljóð* 2: ǫrum hræladr' *MM* 1985. 87–94

Poole 1985B   Poole, Russell 'The Origins of the '*Máhlíðingavísur*' *SS* 57 (1985) 244–85

Poole 1985C   Poole, Russell 'Some Royal Love-verses' *MM* 1985. 115–31

Poole 1987   Poole, Russell 'Skaldic Verse and Anglo-Saxon History: Some Aspects of the Period 1009–1016' *Speculum* 62 (1987) 265–98

Ragnars saga 1906–8ed   *Ragnars saga: Vǫlsunga saga ok Ragnars saga loðbrókar* ed Magnus Olsen. SUGNL 36. Copenhagen 1906–8

Reichardt 1928   Reichardt, Konstantin *Studien zu den skalden des 9. und 10. jahrhunderts*. Palaestra 159. Leipzig 1928

Richards 1936   Richards, I.A. *The Philosophy of Rhetoric*. London 1936

Rímnasafn 1905–22ed   *Rímnasafn: samling af de ældste islandske rimer* ed Finnur Jónsson. 2 vols. SUGNL 25. Copenhagen 1905–22

Saga Óláfs konungs hins helga 1941ed   *Den store saga om Olav den hellige ...* ed O.A. Johnsen and Jón Helgason. 2 vols. Oslo 1941

Sattler 1911   Sattler, E. 'Das Märchen von "Retter in der Not" in Chrestiens Yvain und in der Egilssaga' *Germanisch-romanische Monatsschrift* 3 (1911) 669–71

Schier 1976A   Schier, Kurt 'Die Húsdrápa von Úlfr Uggason und die bildliche Überlieferung altnordischer Mythen.' In *Minjar og Menntir. Afmælisrit helgað Kristjáni Eldjárn ...* ed Guðni Kolbeinsson, Bjarni Vilhjálmsson, Jónas Kristjánsson, Þór Magnússon. Reykjavík 1976. 425–43

Schier 1976B   Schier, Kurt 'Húsdrápa 2: Heimdall, Loki und die Meerniere.' In *Festgabe für Otto Höfler zum 75. Geburtstag*. ed Helmut Birkhan. Philologica Germanica 3. Vienna 1976. 577–88

Scott 1901ed   Scott, Walter *The Pirate*. London 1901

von See 1959   von See, Klaus 'Das Walkürenlied' *Beiträge zur Geschichte der deutschen Sprache und Literatur* 81 (1959) 1–15

von See 1960   von See, Klaus 'Der Skalde Torf-Einar Jarl' *Beiträge zur Geschichte der deutschen Sprache und Literatur* 82 (1960) 31–43

von See 1977   von See, Klaus 'Skaldenstrophe und Sagaprosa ... ' *Med Scan* 10 (1977) 58–82

Sijmons-Gering 1903–6   I *Die Lieder der Edda* ed B. Sijmons. Halle 1906 II Gering, Hugo *Vollständiges Wörterbuch zu den Liedern der Edda*. 2 vols. Halle 1903

Skáldatal   See *Edda Snorra Sturlusonar* III 1880–7.

Skáldskaparmál   See *Snorra Edda* 1931 ed

Skj A and B   *Den norsk-islandske skjaldedigtning ...* ed Finnur Jónsson. Copenhagen 1912–15

Smyth I 1975; II 1979   Smyth, A.P. *Scandinavian York and Dublin*. 2 vols. Dublin 1975–9

Snorra Edda 1931 ed   *Edda Snorra Sturlusonar ...* ed Finnur Jónsson. Copenhagen 1931

Sǫgur Danakonunga   ed Carl af Petersens and Emil Olson. SUGNL 46. Copenhagen 1919–25

Speculum norrœnum   *Speculum norrœnum. Norse Studies in Memory of Gabriel Turville-Petre* ed Ursula Dronke, Guðrún P. Helgadóttir, Gerd Wolfgang Weber, and Hans Bekker-Nielsen. Odense 1981

Sprenger 1951   Sprenger, Ulrike *Præsens historicum und Præteritum in der altisländischen Saga*. Basel 1951

Storms 1948   Storms, Godfrid *Anglo-Saxon Magic*. The Hague 1948

Sturlunga saga 1946 ed   *Sturlunga saga* ed Jón Jóhannesson, Magnús Finnbogason, and Kristján Eldjárn. 2 vols. Reykjavík 1946

Sveinsson 1933   Sveinsson, Einar Ól. *Um Njálu*. Reykjavík 1933

Sveinsson 1962   Sveinsson, Einar Ól. *Íslenzkar Bókmenntir í Fornöld* Reykjavík 1962

Sveinsson 1968   Sveinsson, Einar Ól. 'Eyrbyggja sagas kilder' *Scripta Islandica* 19 (1968 pub 1969) 3–18

Thietmar 1889 ed   *Thietmari Merseburgensis Episcopi Chronicon* ed J.M. Lappenbergh and F. Kurze. Hanover 1889

Þórðarson 1937–9   Þórðarson, Matthías 'Vígin á Tvídægru' *Árbók hins íslenzka Fornleifafélags* (1937–9) 98–107

Þorgils saga ok Hafliða 1952 ed   *Þorgils saga ok Hafliða* ed Ursula Brown. Oxford 1952

Þorkelsson 1870   Þorkelsson, Jón *Skýringar á vísum í Njáls sögu* Reykjavík 1870

Þórólfsson 1950   Þórólfsson, Björn K. 'Dróttkvæði og rímur' *Skírnir* 124 (1950) 175–209
Tucker 1959   Tucker, S.I. 'Laughter in Old English Literature' *Neophil* 43 (1959) 222–6
Turville-Petre 1968   Turville-Petre, E.O.G. *Haraldr the Hard-Ruler and his Poets*. Dorothea Coke Memorial Lecture ... at University College London ... London 1968
Turville-Petre 1976   Turville-Petre, E.O.G. *Scaldic Poetry*. Oxford 1976
Tveiten 1966   Tveiten, H. *Norrøne Skaldekvad*. Oslo 1943 rpt 1966
Vestlund 1929   Vestlund, Alfred 'Om strofernas ursprungliga ordning i Sigvat Tordarsons Bersǫglisvísur' *ANF* 46 [tillægsbind] (1929) 281–93
Vigfússon 1883   Vigfússon, Gudbrandur, and F. York Powell *Corpus Poeticum Boreale* ... 2 vols. Oxford 1883
Vogt 1927   Vogt, W.H. *Stilgeschichte der eddischen Wissensdichtung I. Der Kultredner (þulr)*. Breslau 1927
de Vries 1955   de Vries, Jan, 'Der Mythos von Balders Tod' *ANF* 70 (1955) 41–60
de Vries 1961   de Vries, Jan *Altnordisches etymologisches Wörterbuch*. Leiden 1961
de Vries I 1964; II 1967   de Vries, Jan *Altnordische Literaturgeschichte*. 2nd ed. 2 vols. Berlin 1964–7
Whitelock 1937–45   Whitelock, Dorothy 'Scandinavian Personal Names in the Liber Vitæ of Thorney Abbey' *SBVS* 12 (1937–45) 127–53
Williamson 1977   Williamson, Craig ed *The Old English Riddles of the 'Exeter Book'*. Chapel Hill NC 1977
Wisén I 1886; II 1889   Wisén, Theodor ed *Carmina norrœna: ex reliquiis vetustioris norrœnæ poësis selecta* ... 2 vols. Lund 1886–9
Wood 1959   Wood, Cecil 'Kormak's Stanzas Called the "Sigurðardrápa"' *Neophil* 43 (1959) 305–19

Index

Adam of Bremen: on Knútr 98; on Óláfr helgi 92
Ágrip: date 10; handling of skaldic verses in 7, 8–10, 130, 197; information on Óláfr helgi 92
Åkerblom, Axel: views on present historic tense 24, 44, 46–7, 49, 51, 54, 77–9, 82
Anglo-Saxon Chronicle: compared with Scandinavian sources 93, 95, 101–6, 115
Annals of the Four Masters 123
Annals of Ulster 123
Arnórr: 'Magnússdrápa' (*dróttkvætt*) 7, 65, 129, 166
'Atlakviða': use of 'darraðr' in 125–6, 130
attributions, variant 53, 91, 94–5, 99
audience: references to in poetry 108, 153; using second and third person in alternation 77

Bæjarbók: handling of skaldic verses in 7
ballads 29–30
Battle of Clontarf 119, 120–2, 125, 131
Beowulf 45, 126, 140–1, 151
berserks 175–7
Bragi: his 'Ragnarsdrápa' 137; incidence of present historic tense in 'Ragnarsdrápa' 44–7, 49; mention of Bragi in *Háttatal* 19; variant attribution 53

carry-over of alliteration. *See* concatenation, phonological
chiasmus 83–4, 109, 192–3
Cogadh Gaedhel re Gallaibh 121
collective composition of poetry 99–100
colour words in skaldic poetry 137–8
concatenation 196; definition 69; lexical concatenation 69–70, 83–4, 109–10, 180, 191–3; phonological concatenation 12, 69, 70, 83–4, 111, 191–3

'Darraðarljóð': discussion of 116–56; historical data in 120–5; influence on 'Merlínússpá' 37; narrative technique in 142–54; relation to *Njáls saga* prose 119–42; structure

of 154–5; text of 116–19; weaving motif in 131–42
'darraðr' 125–31
Dǫrruðr 119, 125, 129–31
dramatic monologue 171, 180–1, 189, 196
Dublin: connections with York 121–2, 127; Viking settlement in 120, 122–4

Edda, Snorra 6
Egill: 'Hǫfuðlausn' 125, 127–9, 153; lausavísa on Lund 3–4, mention in Háttatal 19; verses on his duel with Ljótr 173–81
Egils saga: date 178; handling of verses in 179–80, 197; incidence of present historic tense 25; lausavísur 3–4, 10; origins of Ljótr episode 175–7. See also Egill
Einar Gilsson: attribution of 'Selkolluvísur' 30–1; 'Óláfs ríma Haraldssonar' 26–7; skaldic poems 30
Einarr skálaglamm: 'Vellekla' 5
Einarr Skúlason: 'Geisli' 196; 'Ingadrápa' 137
'Einarsflokkr': discussion 161–72; narrative technique 168–72; speaker's voice 172; structure 168; text 161–3. See also Torf–Einarr
Eiríkr viðsjá: his verses on the heiðarvíg 182–94; role in Heiðarvíga saga 187–9
Encomium Emmæ: on Knútr 98; on Knútr and Þorkell 101–5, 107, 140
excerpted verses: definition and illustrations 3, 5–6; prefatory formulas 5–6, 64, 76
Exeter Book riddles 125, 138–9
exhortation. See incitation

Eyrbyggja saga: connection with Heiðarvíga saga 187; incidence of present historic tense 25
Eyvindr skáldaspillir: 'Hákonarmál' 125; 'Háleygjatal' 5; verses on the Norwegian famine 12–16

'Fáfnismál': influence on 'Merlínússpá' 37
Fagrskinna: handling of Sexstefja in 67, 69; handling of skaldic verses in 13, 17; indebted to Knúts saga 97–8; use of 'Einarsflokkr' 161, 164–5, 167, 168
Fidjestøl, Bjarne: review of evidence for longer skaldic poems 6, 64, 96–7
Flateyjarbók: handling of skaldic verses in 7, 8, 11–12, 166, 170, 197
flokkr: form 7, 9, 76
Florence of Worcester 102, 106
'Friðgerðarflokkr': attributions 75–6; discussion 73–85; incidence of present historic tense 77–80, 83; name 75; position in Heimskringla 66; text 73–5
'friðr': concept of 71
future tense with 'mun' 146–7, 151
'fyrir': semantic range of 142–5

Gaimar, L'Estoire des Engleis 103–4
Geoffrey of Monmouth: Historia Regum Britanniae 36
Gerum mantle 137
Gísla saga: functional use of lausavísa in 4; incidence of present historic tense 25
Gosforth Cross 121
Grágás 22
'Grettisrímur': date 27; use of Grettis saga in 27–8

Index 213

Grettis saga: adaptation in 'Grettis-rímur' 27–9; incidence of present historic tense 25
'Grípisspá': incidence of present historic tense 32; influence on 'Merlínússpá' 37
'Grottasǫngr' 147, 190
Gunnlaugr Leifsson: incidence of present historic tense in 'Merlínússpá' 36–44
Gunnlaugr ormstunga: praise poem for Sigtryggr silkiskegg 127
Gunnlaugs saga ormstungu 197

Hákon jarl, skalds associated with 187
Hákonar saga Ívarssonar: date 66; handling of *Sexstefja* in 66–8; Latin summary of 67; relation to *Morkinskinna* 67–8
Haldórr: 'Útfarardrápa' 137
Hálfs saga: handling of verses in 19–22
Halldórr ókristni: 'Eiríksflokkr' 81, 186–7
Hallfredar saga 80–1, 178
Hallfredr: 'Hákonardrápa' 80
'Haraldskvæði': use of raven motif 80, 153
harangue. See incitation
Háttatal: incidence of present historic tense 34–6; stanza form ascribed to Ragnarr loðbrók 19; use of 'darraðr' in 125–6, 128, 130; use of term *hjástælt* 50
'Hávamál' 22
Hávardar saga Ísfirðings 197
heddle rod 132–5, 136, 139, 146
Heiðarvíga saga: connection with *Eyrbyggja saga* 185, 187; connections with Þingeyrar 185–7; date 25,

185; incidence of present historic tense 25
'Heilagra Manna Drápa': incidence of present historic tense 32
Heimskringla: as a source for Einar Gilsson 26–7; citation of 'Sigurðardrápa' 49, 51; 'Friðgerðarflokkr' in 73, 75–7, 78; indebtedness to *Fagrskinna* 167; omission of skaldic verses 65, 97, 98, 164, 166; *Sexstefja* in 64–6, 68, 69; skaldic verses in 7, 8–9, 11, 14–15, 17–18, 166, 197; use of *Hákonar saga Ívarssonar* 66–7; use of 'Einarsflokkr' 161, 163–70
'Helgakviða Hjǫrvarðssonar': incidence of present historic tense 3
'Helgakviða Hundingsbana' I: incidence of present historic tense 32
Hemings þáttr: skaldic verses in 17
Henry of Huntingdon: on Knútr 98
Historia Norwegiae: on Óláfr helgi 92
Hœnsa-Þóris saga: incidence of present historic tense 25
Hulda/Hrokkinskinna: handling of 'Friðgerðarflokkr' in 76–7, 79; handling of *Sexstefja* in 64–6; misunderstandings of skaldic verse in 79; skaldic verses in 7–8, 12, 18, 197

improvisations. See *lausavísur*
incitation 19, 107, 138, 146–7, 154, 179, 181, 190, 196

'Jómsvíkingadrápa': refrain in 110–1
Jómsvíkinga saga: on Knútr and Þorkell 101, 104
Jónsson, Finnur: editorial decisions in *Den norsk–islandske skjaldedigtning* 3, 6, 12, 55, 64, 76, 79, 120, 186;

on 'Liðsmannaflokkr' 93–4, 96, 100, 108, 111; views on present tense 24
Jórunn skáldmær: *Sendibítr* 7

Kálfr 31
kennings 180; in 'Darraðarljóð' 128, 130, 132; in Eyvindr 15–16; in 'Friðgerðarflokkr' 83; in 'Liðsmannaflokkr' 110, 112–15; in Ljótr verses 178; in 'Merlínússpá' 37; in 'Ragnarsdrápa' 45, 46; in *rímur* 26, 30; in *trémaðr* verses 22
Knútr: career in England 91–3, 100–7, 113
Knúts saga 91, 92, 94, 97–8
Knýtlinga saga: abridgment in 97–8; indebtedness to *Knúts saga* 91–2; 'Liðsmannaflokkr' in 90–9; sources 91; Þorkell inn hávi in 98, 104
Kock, E.A.: 'revised' skaldic edition 6
Kormakr: 'Sigurðardrápa' 49–51
'Krákumál': attribution to Ragnarr loðbrók 18–19; battle description 138; use in *Ragnars saga* 20

lausavísur: attributed to Óláfr helgi 95–6; creation in the sagas 8–23, 196–7; definition and illustrations 3–5; difficulty of distinguishing from excerpted verses 6–8; evidence outside the sagas 22; functional use in the sagas 4; identified by Åkerblom 77–8; identified by Finnur Jónsson 93; prefatory formulas 5, 6, 15, 20, 64, 69; problem of authenticity 177–8, 186; purported *lausavísa* in *Sexstefja* 64, 69

Laxdœla saga: incidence of present historic tense 25; on 'Húsdrápa' 51–2, 54
'learned style' 43; present historic as a mark of 44
legal constraints on verse-making 22
Legendary Saga: indebtedness to *Knúts saga* 92; 'Liðsmannaflokkr' in 90–9; on Þorkell inn hávi 104
'Liðsmannaflokkr' 86–115; attribution of 91–100, 112; date 91, 94, 108–9; linking devices in 109–11; narrative technique in 107–9; as praise of both Knútr and Þorkell inn hávi 100–7; refrain 110–11; the speaker in 111–15; text of 86–90; textual history of 90–9
linguistic dating of skaldic verse 177–8
linking of beginning of poem with end 196; in 'Darraðarljóð' 155; in Eiríkr viðsjá verses 193–4; in 'Friðgerðarflokkr' 84–5; in 'Liðsmannaflokkr' 109; in Ljótr verses 180; in *Sexstefja* 71
loom beam 132–6
loom weights 132–5, 144

Man, Isle of 122, 123
'Máríuvísur': incidence of present historic tense 32
memorization of poems 20, 186
metaphor 131–2, 139–42
misinterpretations of verse: in *Ágrip* 130; in *Háttatal* 34; in *Heimskringla* 18, 166; in *Njáls saga* 130–1, 154
Morkinskinna: relation to *Hákonar saga Ívarssonar* 67–8; *Sexstefja* in 65; skaldic verses in 7, 8, 11–12, 17, 197

names, Gaelic, in *Njáls saga* 131
narrative technique: in 'Darraðarljóð' 136, 142, 146–7, 148, 154; in 'Einarsflokkr' 170–2; in Eiríkr viðsjá verses 189–91; in 'Liðsmannaflokkr' 107–9, 115; in longer skaldic poems 3, 195; in *Sexstefja* 68; in visual media 49. *See also* running commentary
níð 170
Njáls saga: Gaelic names in 131; incidence of present historic tense 25; indebtedness to hypothetical 'Brjáns saga' 130, 197; as source for 'Darraðarljóð' 119–21. *See also* 'Darraðarljóð'

occasional verses. *See lausavísur*
Oddr, *Óláfs saga Tryggvasonar* 186–7
Oddr Kíkinaskáld 11
ofljóst 95, 113, 170
Óláfr helgi: attribution of *lausavísa* to 95–6; attribution of 'Liðsmannaflokkr' to 91–9; campaigns in England 92–3, 95–6, 101
'Óláfs drápa Tryggvasonar' 137
Óláfs saga helga (Snorri version): skaldic verses in 8; as source for the name *Sexstefja* 68
Old English metrical charm, 'við færstice' 132
'Oldest Saga of St Óláfr' 91, 94, 95
omission of skaldic verses in prose works 65, 97, 98, 164, 166
oral tradition 197; in *Ágrip* 10; 'Darraðarljóð' in 122, 153, 155–6; 'Liðsmannaflokkr' in 96–7, 110; oral stage of saga composition 23, 25, 68, 185, 188–9
Orkneyinga saga: date 66; traditions on Sigtryggr silkiskegg 121; use of 'Einarsflokkr' 161, 163–71, 197
Ǫrvar–Odds saga: handling of verses in 19–20; use of 'darraðr' in 125
Oseberg burial 129
Óttarr svarti: 'Hǫfuðlausn' 93

parallelism. *See* concatenation
'Pétrsdrápa': incidence of present historic tense 32
present historic tense: distinguished from the progressive present 189, 195; in ballads 29–30; in eddaic poetry 32–4; in Eiríkr viðsjá verses 190; in fourteenth-century skaldic poetry 32; in 'Friðgerðarflokkr' 77–80, 83; in *Háttatal* 34–6; in 'Haustlǫng' 47–9; in 'Húsdrápa' 52–5; in 'Kátrínardrápa' 31; in Latin 43; in 'Liðsmannaflokkr' 107–9; in 'Merlínússpá' 36–44, 78; in prose 24–5; in 'Ragnarsdrápa' 44–7; in *rímur* 26–31; in 'Selkolluvísur' 30–1; in *Sexstefja* 68, 78; in 'Sigurðardrápa' 49–51; in Sigvatr's 'Knútsdrápa' 82; in 'Vǫlsungsrímur fornu' 31
present substituting for future 52, 145, 147
prosimetrum 23, 168, 197

'Ragnarsdrápa'. *See* Bragi
Ragnars saga: use of 'Krákumál' 20; use of *trémaðr* verses 20–2
refrain: in 'Darraðarljóð' 135–6, 147–8, 154; in 'Húsdrápa' 55; in 'Liðsmannaflokkr' 110–11, 155
rhyming: non–structural 70, 83, 84, 137, 191–2
'Rígsþula': incidence of present historic tense 33

rímur: definition 26; incidence of present historic tense 26–30
Rǫgnvaldr kali: *lausavísa* 137–8
running commentary narration 55, 195; in 'Darraðarljóð' 136, 146–7, 149–51; in 'Einarsflokkr' 171; in Eiríkr viðsjá verses 190; in 'Friðgerðarflokkr' 78, 79; in 'Liðsmannaflokkr' 108; in Ljótr verses 180; in 'Merlínússpá' 44

Saga Óláfs konungs hins helga: skaldic verses in 7
Saxo Grammaticus, *Gesta Danorum*: on Óláfr helgi 92; Starkaðr and Hjalti in 19
Scott, Sir Walter: version of 'Sir Patrick Spens' 29–30; *The Pirate* 155–6
'Selkolluvísur' 30–1
Sexstefja. See Þjóðólfr Arnórsson
shed rod 132–5, 139, 146
shield poems 44–9, 51
Sigtryggr caech 122–4
Sigtryggr silkiskegg 120–1, 127
'Sigurðarkviða in skamma': incidence of present historic tense 32
Sigvatr: 'Austrfararvísur' 7; 'Bersǫglisvísur' 8–10; 'Knútsdrápa' 82, 98; 'Nesjavísur' 7; 'Víkingarvísur' 93, 95
Skáldatal: on Kormakr 51; on Ragnarr loðbrók 19
'Skáldskaparmál': on Kormakr's 'Sigurðardrápa' 50
'skemta' 153
skothríð 138, 145–6, 154
Snorri Sturluson: as author of *Egils saga* 178. See also *Háttatal* and 'Skáldskaparmál'

Sockburn burial site 121
'Song of Carroll's Sword, The' 139–40
speaker 19, 23, 44, 68, 79, 170–1, 179, 181, 189–90, 196, 198; in 'Darraðarljóð' 142, 146–7, 149–51, 154–5; in 'Liðsmannaflokkr' 95, 107–9, 111–15
'springa' 151–2
stál 49–50
Starkaðr 19
stef. See refrain
Steinn Herdísarson: 'Nizarvísur' 65, 67, 138
structure 195–6; of 'Darraðarljóð,' 'Einarsflokkr,' Eiríkr viðsjá verses, and Ljótr verses 190–1. See also 'Darraðarljóð' and 'Einarsflokkr'
Sturla Þórðarson: *Hákonar saga* 25; *Íslendinga saga* 25
Sturlunga saga: verses on the Sauðafellsfǫr 99
Styrmir fróði Kárason: version of *Óláfs saga helga* 90–9
Sverris saga 128–9, 186–7
sword-beater 135, 136–7, 139, 146
sympathetic magic 131–2

Táin Bó Cuailnge 140
Theodoricus: *Historia de antiquitate regum norvagiensium* 10
Þjóðólfr: incidence of present historic tense in 'Haustlǫng' 47–9
Þjóðólfr Arnórsson: Nissa episode from *Sexstefja* 59–72; text of poem 59–64
Þórarinn loftunga: 'Tøgdrápa' 81
Þórarinn máhlíðingr: 'Máhlíðingavísur' 187

Index 217

Þórbjǫrn hornklofi: 'Glymdrápa' 114
Þorgils saga ok Hafliða 20
Þorkell inn hávi: career in England 93, 96, 98, 100–7, 113
Þormóðr Kolbrúnarskáld 5
Thorney *Liber Vitæ*: as witness on Þorkell inn hávi 105
Þorsteins saga: on Sigtryggr silkiskegg 121
'Þrymskviða': incidence of present historic tense 33–4
þula 125–7, 128
Tindr Hallkelsson 186, 187
tmesis 114
Torf–Einarr: mention in *Háttatal* 19, 169; poems about 169–70. See also 'Einarsflokkr'

Ulfcetel 93, 104, 113, 115
Ulfr Uggason: 'Húsdrápa' 51–5; influence of 'Sigurðardrápa' on 51–2; use of present historic tense 52–5

'Vellekla' 81
'Vitnisvísur': incidence of present historic tense 32
'Vǫlsungsrímur fornu': incidence of present historic tense 31
'Vǫlundarkviða': incidence of present historic tense 33
'Vǫluspá': influence on 'Merlínússpá' 37

warp–weighted loom 132–6; *diagram* 133
weaving 131–41, 155
William of Jumièges: traditions on Óláfr helgi 92
work-song 135, 147

York: textiles at 137. See also Dublin

TORONTO MEDIEVAL TEXTS AND TRANSLATIONS

General Editor: Brian Merrilees

1 *The Argentaye Tract* edited by Alan Manning
2 *The Court of Sapience* edited by E. Ruth Harvey
3 *Le Turpin français, dit le Turpin I* edité par Ronald N. Walpole
4 *Icon and Logos: Sources in Eighth-Century Iconoclasm* translated by Daniel J. Sahas.
5 Marie de France *Fables* edited and translated by Harriet Spiegel
6 Hetoum *A Lytell Cronycle* edited by Glenn Burger
7 *The de Brailes Hours: Shaping the Book of Hours in Thirteenth-Century Oxford* by Claire Donovan
8 *Viking Poems on War and Peace: A Study in Skaldic Narrative* by R.G. Poole